MW00830241

ISBN 978-0-979933-77-6

Produced by
JaDon Management Inc.
1405 4th Ave. N. W. #109
Ardmore, Ok. 73401

Original Cover Art by:
James Kessler

James Kessler and *Because of Him* Art Ministries
James Kessler received a degree in advertising art in 1979 and worked in the health care system with mentally and physically challenged adults for many years. He now travels and shares God's message through the use of artwork. Along with Christian art and portrait commissions, he also designs logos for other ministries.

Because of Him Art Ministries
P.O. Box 52
Everson, Pa 15631
e-mail: becauseofhim@zoominternet.net
(724) 887-0804

SEVENTY WEEKS ARE DETERMINED...

FOR THE RESURRECTION

By Don K. Preston D. Div.

Foreword

Daniel 9:24-27 is one of the most pivotal and interesting prophecies in the Bible. Students of the Scriptures have always been fascinated and intrigued by the enigmatic "Seventy Weeks" prophecy.

This critical set of verses serves as the source for the wildly popular doctrine of dispensational premillennialism, and the infamous "gap theory" that posits a now two thousand year gap between the sixty ninth and the seventieth week. Without that interregnum, dispensationalism crumbles to the ground. In my book *Seal Up Vision and Prophecy*, referred to later in this work, I demonstrate that there is no gap in the countdown. In this work however, I have a different focus.

The amillennial eschatology of my youth does not know what to do with Daniel 9:24f, except to tell the dispensationalists that they are wrong about it. It has been my experience that while amillennialists will stridently condemn the millennial view, when pressed to offer a positive exegesis of the text they are hard pressed to do so. This has been borne out in numerous formal public debates.

The postmillennial paradigm tries harder to understand this critical text but lamentably falls far short of a proper exegesis.

One of the key failings of the amillennial and postmillennial views is the failure to see that Daniel 9:24f is concerned with the ultimate eschatological prophecy, the resurrection of the dead. Both schools insist that Daniel does deal with the end of the Old Covenant world of Judaism, but they fail to see that terminus as the eschatological consummation. As a result, we find the untenable posit that the seventy weeks were fulfilled circa AD 35 long before the events foretold in the text came to pass.

This work shows that Daniel 9 is eschatological to the core. It is not "just" about the end of Israel's history. It is the climax and consummation of salvation history and God bringing resurrection life to a reality in the everlasting kingdom of Messiah.

If Daniel 9 foretold the resurrection from the dead then this has profound implications for all futurist eschatologies.

The amillennialists and postmillennialists insist that Daniel 9 is fulfilled, yet still anticipate the resurrection. But if Daniel 9 predicted the resurrection this is patently misguided. If the resurrection has not occurred, and if Daniel 9 foretold the resurrection, this demands that God has not completed His covenantal dealings with Israel, the Torah remains valid, and there truly is a gap between the sixty-ninth and seventieth week after all.

If Daniel 9 foretold the resurrection, and the resurrection has not come, then the millennialists are on far more solid exegetical ground to affirm a gap between the final two weeks of the countdown. The problem is that the New Testament writers simply never affirmed or recognized any such gap, and more significantly, they affirmed that the climax of all prophetic expectation was near in the first century. In other words, they were looking for the fulfillment of the seventieth week of Daniel 9 in their lifetime, and this falsifies dispensationalism.

Daniel 9 did foretell the resurrection. Not in so many specific words, but the elements anticipated in the prophecy are so inextricably tied to the resurrection of the dead that the connection is undeniable. Sadly, too few commentators make the connection.

So, this book seeks to show that Daniel 9 did predict the resurrection of the dead. It will prove that the New Testament writers knew nothing of a past fulfillment of the seventy weeks, or of a postponed countdown. We will show that every single constituent element contained in Daniel 9:24-27, with the possible exception of one, is vitally connected to the resurrection event, and that this means *Seventy Weeks Are Determined...For the Resurrection.*

Finally, we will show that not only did Daniel predict the resurrection, at the end of the seventy weeks, but that the consummation of Daniel's prophecy was the end of the Old Covenant age of Israel. That age, *that symbolized sin and death*, was removed by the triumphant parousia of Messiah Jesus and the full glorious arrival of his kingdom and New Covenant world in A. D. 70.

Don K. Preston D. Div.
February 2007
November 2010

Acknowledgments

I must express my appreciation to a few key individuals for their assistance in this work.

My thanks to the producer of the excellent *Online Bible Study*, for his volunteer proofreading of the MSS. Naturally, any remaining errors are on my part. He has humbly requested I not give his name.

I encourage the reader to obtain a copy of the Online Bible Study. I have been using this resource for some years now and find it invaluable. Free downloads as well as CDs of the program itself can be purchased at www.onlinebibleusa.com.

In addition, my special thanks goes to Samuel Dawson, who is a fine author in his own right, for his work in producing the topical and scripture indices for the book. He was also a great help with the PDF formatting issues. I am somewhat limited in my computer expertise, but Sam's generous offer to do this menial task is a great boon to you the reader and greatly appreciated by me.

I must always mention the patience and support of my wife. She is a constant encouragement and sounding board as I share my research and thoughts with her, very often late at night when she is, in reality, too tired to pay good attention! Yet, she always gives me her careful attention and helpful insights to make the mss more readable and understandable.

There are other behind the scene individuals that continue to be a great encouragement to me, but who do not wish to be mentioned publically. To them, I offer my sincere gratitude.

Of course, I must thank you the reader, for your interest in God's word, and for your courage to dare to read something that goes against the tide. This book is for those who are not complacent, for those not satisfied to be pew packers. This book is for the proverbial inquiring minds. You want answers and are willing to ask questions, to do independent thinking, to do the research necessary to satisfy your hunger and thirst for righteousness. It is my prayer, hope, and intention that this book will help you in your search and your journey.

Table of Contents

SEVENTY WEEKS ARE DETERMINED...
FOR THE RESURRECTION

There is little doubt that Daniel 9:24f is one of the most pivotal prophecies in the entire Old Testament, even the Bible. It has been, and continues to be, the source of almost endless speculation and calculation. The questions about the seventy week countdown seemingly are numberless, and many of the "answers" are speculative at best, and fanciful at worst.

This book is not concerned with when the "countdown" began. I am not overly concerned here with mathematics. I will tell you right up front that this book operates on certain presuppositions that I hold to be essentially undeniable:

➡The prophecy is Messianic and predicted the total work of Jesus the Messiah.

➡That Jesus in his ministry, and that the NT writers, knew more about the prophecy of Daniel 9 than commentators today. Thus, if they comment on, cite, or allude to Daniel, and make any application, I take their comments as definitive and authoritative.

➡The prophecy terminates with the "overwhelming flood" of the destruction of Jerusalem that occurred in AD 70 (Daniel 9:27).

These are my presuppositions and operative principles in this book. For corroboration and confirmation of all of them I recommend that you read my other work on Daniel 9, *Seal Up Vision and Prophecy*, where I set forth a great deal of evidence to support the last of my presuppositions.

What I am doing in this book is demonstrating that Daniel 9 foretold the consummation of God's dealings with Old Covenant Israel and that consummation included the promised resurrection from the dead. This book will prove that the resurrection of the dead occurred at the time of the fall of Jerusalem in AD 70.

I understand that most who read this book have been raised, as I was, to believe that the resurrection is the raising of human corpses out of the ground.[1] However, resurrection to life is the restoration of the life lost in Adam: "As in Adam all men die, even so in Christ shall all men be made alive" (1 Corinthians 15:22). The life lost in Adam was not physical life and the death introduced by Adam was not physical death. The death introduced by Adam was sin-death, the loss of

1

fellowship with God. We cannot develop this at length here. See my internet article for a full development of this.[2]

Our purpose is to show what the Bible says about the *time and the framework* for the resurrection. We will not discuss a *lot* of questions about the resurrection because, although those issues are *important*, the focus of this work is confined to what the Bible says about the *when* of the resurrection.

Lots of good, honest Bible believers are unaware of the time problem in the Bible. By that we mean that while the Bible is very plain as to when the Second Coming, the judgment and resurrection were to occur, many believers are unaware of those time statements,[3] or, they have tuned them out because they don't have the answers. If Christ said he was coming back in the first century, did he not keep his word? How can we believe in Jesus if he lied, failed, or was mistaken? After all, he said himself that if he did not do the works that the Father gave him, they were not to believe him (John 10:37f) and most assuredly, *judgment and resurrection are the works the Father gave to him* (John 5:19f).

Is the Bible really inspired if the Biblical writers said the end of the age was coming in the first century and it did not happen? Clearly, if the Bible writers were wrong the Bible is not inspired. It is that simple. If Jesus said he was coming back in his generation and he did not come back, then he is not the Son of God. There is no way out of that conundrum. The only way to honor the Bible and maintain the Deity of Jesus is to maintain that he kept his word and that the Bible writers were right. The end of the age did come. Christ did come in judgment. The resurrection did occur.

If you were raised in one of the traditional views of eschatology, you are probably saying, "How could this be? How could Christ have come? Did every eye see him?" How did he come on the clouds of heaven, in flaming fire? For answers to these questions and more, we direct you to some of our other writings that discuss the nature of Christ's coming.[4] In the meantime, as food for thought, perhaps the words of Milton Terry, the noted author on hermeneutics is *apropos*:

"When we come to study the doctrines of biblical eschatology, how little do we find that is not set forth in figure or in symbol? Perhaps the notable confusion of modern teaching on the subjects of the parousia, resurrection and judgment is largely

2

due to the notion that these doctrines must needs have been revealed in literal form."[5]

My purpose, as just noted, is to focus on what the Bible says about *when the resurrection was to occur.* The framework for the resurrection was the last days of Old Covenant Israel, not the last days of time. The time for the resurrection was to be the time of the judgment of Jerusalem in AD 70.

Also, in this work we will be interacting with the book *When Shall These Things Be, A Reformed Response to Hyper-Preterism.*[6] That book purports to be a definitive response and refutation of the full, or true preterist view of prophecy.[7] As the reader of this work will soon see, *When* is built on shaky ground and is no refutation of preterism. I will also interact somewhat with some of the representatives of dispensational millennialism. By establishing our case for when the resurrection was to occur, the millennial view is also falsified.

As I stated, my focus is the *framework* and the *time* of the resurrection as set forth in scripture. My thoughts will be drawn from and based on the Seventy Week prophecy of Daniel 9.[8] My premise is simple:

1.) Daniel 9:24f is not concerned with the end of the Christian age, or human history. As Goldingay notes, "The concern of v. 24 is thus Israel and Jerusalem. It does not have a worldwide perspective; it is not speaking of the end of all history, or of the sin of the whole world."[9] Cline says, "The theme that pervades the entire chapter, is Yahweh's covenant with Israel, particularly the actualization of the covenant sanctions through the faithfulness of God."[10]

By and large, this is admitted by the semi-preterists. (I use the term "semi-preterist" synonymously with partial preterist). As Gentry says, "The prophecy's focus is on Israel."[11] The implications of this are significant, but not just for Gentry. If it can be shown that Daniel 9 predicted the resurrection, then that effectively proves that the resurrection must be posited at the end of Old Covenant Israel's aeon.

2.) The Seventy Week prophecy of Daniel 9 was completely fulfilled in the first century.[12] There is a consensus among partial preterists that this is true.[13]

3.) If, therefore, Daniel 9 is a prediction of the resurrection from the dead, then the resurrection is past.[14]

It may be objected that Daniel 9 does not use the specific word "resurrection," and of course this is true. However, as I will show, the *word* does not have to appear for the doctrine to appear. Further, the promised blessings of Daniel 9 are motifs inextricably linked to resurrection. Therefore, while the word "resurrection" is not found in Daniel 9:24f, the *doctrine* definitely is, as we shall demonstrate momentarily.

Daniel was told, "Seventy weeks are determined on your people and for your holy city, to finish the transgression, to make an end of sins, to make reconciliation for iniquity, to bring in everlasting righteousness, to seal up vision and prophecy and to anoint the Most Holy."

Let it be noted that one cannot extend the fulfillment of these promises beyond the seventy weeks. To suggest for instance that while seventy weeks are determined "to make atonement for sin," that the actual atonement would not occur for thousands of years beyond the terminus *(ad quem)* of the seventy weeks is to ignore the parameters of the time "determined." We will have much more to say on this issue as we proceed.

Gentry notes the millennial attempt to extend the seventy weeks 2000 years beyond the atoning work of Jesus, "The dispensationalist here prefers to interpret this result as *application* rather than effecting. He sees it as subjective appropriation instead of objective accomplishment." Gentry responds, "On the basis of the Hebrew verb, the passage clearly speaks of the actual *making reconciliation* (or *atonement*)." *(Dominion*, 315, his emphasis) Gentry's point is correct. The atonement promised in Daniel 9 was the *objective appropriation of atonement.*[15] The normal OT use of the term "make atonement" *never* refers to a later application of what the sacrifice was offered to make. It was the *cultic process* itself that is *always* referred to as "to make atonement for sin." If the millennialist posits the end of the 70th Week as yet future, then the accomplishment of the atonement has not even been made!

The problem for Gentry, however, is that he has the atonement accomplished before the time posited by Scripture. More on this below.

If the elements of Daniel 9:24f were not to be fulfilled *within the determined seventy weeks*, what was the point of saying, "Seventy weeks are determined on your people and on your holy city"? The significance of this will become more apparent as we proceed. Keep this vital fact in mind.

4

SEVENTY WEEKS ARE DETERMINED...
"TO PUT AN END TO SIN"

Gentry and Mathison believe that the prediction "to put away sin" is unrelated to Christ's redemptive work, but means, "Israel's sins were reserved for punishment until the generation of the Messiah." (*Hope*, 221) Gentry claims that the term means, "The sealing or reserving of the sins indicates that *within* the 'Seventy Weeks' Israel will complete her transgressions, *and* with the completing of her sin, by crucifying Christ, God will act to reserve (*beyond the seventy weeks*) her sins for judgment." (*Dominion*, 315). There are several problems with this.

It is wrong to say that Israel completely filled up the measure of her sin by crucifying Christ. While Matthew 21 posits the killing of the Son as "the straw that broke the camel's back," Jesus added additional information in Matthew 23. As he stood in the temple and recounted Israel's long history of persecuting the righteous, he said, "fill up then the measure of your father's guilt." (Matthew 23:32). How were they going to finally fill up that measure of sin? Verse 34 has the answer: "Behold, I send unto you prophets, wise men, and scribes. Some of them you will crucify, and some of them you will scourge in your synagogues, and persecute from city to city." Israel would finally fill up the measure of her sin by persecuting the apostles and prophets sent by Jesus. This was patently after the Cross.

Interestingly, some of the early church fathers understood this meaning of filling the measure of sin, but did not apply the term "put an end of sin" to that concept. Eusebius cites Aquilla on Daniel 9 that, "to finish the transgression" meant to fill the measure of sin.[16] He relates this to Matthew 23.[17] Neither Eusebius or Aquila applied the term "put an end to sin" to the filling up of the measure of sin. These are different concepts.

Paul did not believe that Israel had completely filled up the measure of her sin at the Cross. In 1 Thessalonians 2:15f, when, speaking of the internecine Jewish history he said they, "killed both the Lord Jesus and their own prophets, and have persecuted us, and they do not please God and are contrary to all men, forbidding us to speak to the Gentiles that they may be saved, so as always to fill up the measure of their sins, but wrath has come upon them to the uttermost." Take note that for Paul, the filling up of the measure of

Israel's sin was a then still ongoing process that had not yet reached its fulness.

Thus, the assertion that Israel would fill the measure of her sin at the Cross and that God would at that time "reserve her for punishment" *after the seventy weeks* is untenable. The filling up of the measure of Israel's sin extends *well beyond* the time when most partial preterists posit it. Yet, according to Daniel, the filling up of the measure of sin (i.e. the finishing of transgressions) *belongs to the seventy weeks*. And, it must not be forgotten that Daniel was told, "seventy weeks are determined... on your holy city." The fate of the city lies within the seventy weeks just as surely as "finishing the transgression" lies within the seventy weeks.

Paul emphatically said that it was his suffering that was filling up, "what is lacking in the afflictions of Christ" (Colossians 1:24f). O'Brien says: "The presence of the definite article τά suggests that the phrase 'what is lacking in Christ's afflictions,' refers to something well known and agrees with the apocalyptic notion of a definite measure of affliction to be endured in the last days. As God had set a definite measure in time (Mk. 13:5-27) and the limit of the tribulations at the end, so there is a definite measure of suffering that is to be filled up. That limit of messianic woes has not yet been reached. There are still deficiencies which Paul through his sufferings is in the process of completing."[18]

Very clearly, for Paul, the measure of sin was not yet full. He believed that fullness was to be fulfilled in his personal suffering and that of the apostolate, "God has displayed us, the apostles, last, as men condemned to death" (1 Corinthians 4:9). Historically, myriads have died after Paul and the other apostles. That was not Paul's concern. He was focused on the eschatological "measured suffering" and corollary "measure of sin."

Now, since the suffering of Paul and the apostolate are post Cross, it cannot be argued that Israel filled up the measure of her sin (i.e. finished the transgression) at the Cross. This falsifies the partial preterist view that "putting away of sin" is referent to "reserving the fate" as a result of filling the measure of sin. If the filling up of the measure of sin extends beyond the time posited by Mathison and Gentry, and it surely does, their paradigm is false.

We need to take note that the filling up of the measure of sin, the resultant judgment on the guilty (and vindication of the righteous,

6

contained within the prediction of "finishing the transgression") *belongs to the seventy week countdown* and does not lie outside of it. The implications of this for our understanding of Daniel 9 are great.

FINISHING THE TRANSGRESSION,
ISRAEL'S LAST DAYS,
AND THE SEVENTY WEEK COUNTDOWN

We will make this discussion as brief as possible, in order to concentrate on the main topic of this book, the resurrection. Nonetheless, it is important to see that the promise that the seventy weeks were determined to "finish the transgression" has profound implications for the terminus of the seventy weeks.

Daniel 9:26 foretold the death of Messiah. Furthermore, virtually everyone will admit that the AD 70 destruction of Jerusalem was also as a direct result of killing the Messiah. Wright correctly notes, "So closely do they belong together, in fact, that the destruction of the temple--predicted already in symbolic action, and here in prophetic oracle--is bound up with Jesus' own vindication, as a prophet and also as Messiah."[19] He adds, "The Destruction of Jerusalem on the one hand, and the rescue of the disciples on the other, would be the vindication of what Jesus had been saying throughout his ministry." (*Victory*, 338)

There is no doubt that Jesus posited the impending destruction of Jerusalem as the judgment on the persecutors and the vindication of the righteous martyrs. In Matthew 23:29f he uttered his prediction of that catastrophe and the reasons for it:

"Woe to you, scribes and Pharisees, hypocrites! Because you build the tombs of the prophets and adorn the monuments of the righteous, and say, 'If we had lived in the days of our fathers, we would not have been partakers with them in the blood of the prophets.' Therefore you are witnesses against yourselves that you are sons of those who murdered the prophets. Fill up, then, the measure of your fathers' guilt. "Serpents, brood of vipers! How can you escape the condemnation of hell? Therefore, indeed, I send you prophets, wise men, and scribes: some of them you will kill and crucify, and some of them you will scourge in your synagogues and persecute from city to city, that on you may come all the righteous blood shed on the earth, from the blood of righteous

Abel to the blood of Zechariah, son of Berechiah, whom you murdered between the temple and the altar. Assuredly, I say to you, all these things will come upon this generation. O Jerusalem, Jerusalem, the one who kills the prophets and stones those who are sent to her! How often I wanted to gather your children together, as a hen gathers her chicks under her wings, but you were not willing! See! Your house is left to you desolate."

There are several things to be noted here.

First, Jesus blames one people, and one people alone, for shedding the blood of the righteous martyrs. That one people was Old Covenant Israel. And this has *nothing* to do with modern Israel.

Second, while the locus of the judgment would be Jerusalem, the comprehensive nature of the judgment is affirmed. All of the blood, of all the martyrs, all the way back to creation, would be judged and avenged. This means that while the locale of the judgment was Judea and Jerusalem, the scope of the judgment was "universal." This was not to be simply a "local judgment on the Jews" as some affirm, for, there were no "Jews" in Genesis 4 when Cain killed Abel! There were no Jews, or Israelites even, for century upon century, while the righteous were being persecuted. Yet, Jesus posited the vindication / judgment of all the righteous blood at the judgment of Old Covenant Judah. This is *incredibly* significant.

Third, undeniably, Jesus posited that judgment in his generation, "Verily I say unto you, all these things will come upon this generation."

So, these three things, seen in light of Matthew 23 establishes certain facts.

Daniel 9:26 predicted the death of Messiah.

Daniel 9:26-27 predicted the destruction of Jerusalem.

**Matthew 23 predicted the destruction of Jerusalem
for killing the righteous martyrs–
*which of course includes Messiah Jesus.***

This means that Matthew 23 predicted
the fulfillment of Daniel 9:26-27.

Not only was the destruction of Jerusalem the fulfillment of Daniel 9, it therefore follows that the destruction of Jerusalem was *the fulfillment of Old Covenant Wrath in Israel's last days.* And this has a direct bearing on our understanding of the seventy weeks of Daniel 9.

Deuteronomy 32 is one of the greatest of the Old Testament prophecies. It is one of my personal favorites and I am currently working on a book on this magnificent chapter. I am convinced that the Song of Moses is paradigmatic for the eschatology of the New Testament. Yet few Bible students seem to see the connections.

Moses was predicting the ultimate fate, the last days, of his beloved nation:

"And when the LORD saw it, He spurned them, Because of the provocation of His sons and His daughters. And He said: 'I will hide My face from them, I will see what their end will be, For they are a perverse generation, Children in whom is no faith. They have provoked Me to jealousy by what is not God; They have moved Me to anger by their foolish idols. But I will provoke them to jealousy by those who are not a nation; I will move them to anger by a foolish nation.'" (Deuteronomy 32:19-21)

"Oh, that they were wise, that they understood this, That they would consider their latter end! How could one chase a thousand, And two put ten thousand to flight, Unless their Rock had sold them, And the LORD had surrendered them?" (Deuteronomy 32:29-30)

We do not have the space to do an in-depth exegesis of these texts. However, we can take note of a few critical factors.

◆The reference to Israel being a "perverse generation" in the last days, is echoed by Peter in Acts 2:40: "Save yourselves from this perverse generation."[20] Coupled with Peter's emphatic declaration, "This is that which was spoken by the prophet Joel" (Acts 2:15) that the last days of Israel foretold by Joel 2:28f were present, this is *prima facie* proof that for Peter and the apostles the time foretold by Deuteronomy had arrived.

✦ In Romans 10:19, Paul quotes directly from Deuteronomy 32:21 to speak of the calling of the Gentiles through his ministry. In chapter 11:11-14, he alludes once again to the Song of Moses and Jehovah's prediction that He would provoke His nation to jealousy by calling those who had never been called.

✦ The writer of Hebrews believed that the promised judgment of Israel and the vindication of the saints was coming "in a very, very little while." In Hebrews 10:33-37 he directly quotes from the Song of Moses to affirm the urgency of the impending judgment.

So, the New Testament writers affirm that the time foretold by Moses was present in their generation. What is the significance of this for our study of the seventy weeks?

Notice that in Deuteronomy 32, Jehovah twice affirmed that the focus of the chapter was Israel's latter end, i.e. *her last days*. So, in her last days, she would become perverse, (like *Sodom*! V. 32) and that terminal generation would be "the perverse generation" foretold by Moses. (Cf. Matthew 12:43-45). Peter called his generation the perverse generation. Therefore, Peter's generation was the generation foretold by Moses. Israel's last days were present when Peter spoke on Pentecost. And when Paul cited Deuteronomy to justify his gentile mission, this means that he also believed that the last days of Israel were present in his generation.

Of course, this is devastating to the millennial paradigm. It is insisted that due to the Jewish rejection of Jesus, Jehovah withdrew the kingdom offer, suspended the countdown of the seventy weeks and posited Israel's last days at the Rapture, when the church will supposedly be removed from the world and God resumes His covenantal dealings with Israel. Daniel's seventieth week will then be counted down in the critical Tribulation period of seven years. Thomas Ice says: "I believe the Scriptures teach that Israel could have obtained her much sought after kingdom, by recognizing Jesus as the Messiah. We all know the sad reality--the Jews rejected Jesus. As a result, the kingdom is no longer near, but postponed."[21] On page 117 he continues, "The sad truth is that the Jews rejected the offer and the kingdom was postponed."

The problem of course is that if what Moses foretold in Deuteronomy 32 was a reality in Acts 2–Israel being accused of being the terminal "perverse generation"-- then the seventy week countdown had not been postponed. Israel's "last days" were present. If Paul believed that Deuteronomy foretold his mission to the Gentiles, and if the author of Hebrews believed, through inspiration, that the prophesied judgment of Deuteronomy 32 was coming very, very soon, then the entire millennial paradigm is falsified. And now to drive this point home.

Notice that not only did Peter and Paul cite directly from Deuteronomy to speak of their generation, but Deuteronomy 32 foretold another event, for Israel's "last end" that definitively links the first century generation with Israel's last days. Notice :

"For I raise My hand to heaven, And say, "As I live forever, If I whet My glittering sword, And My hand takes hold on judgment, I will render vengeance to My enemies, And repay those who hate Me. I will make My arrows drunk with blood, And My sword shall devour flesh, With the blood of the slain and the captives, From the heads of the leaders of the enemy. Rejoice, O Gentiles, with His people; For He will avenge the blood of His servants, And render vengeance to His adversaries; He will provide atonement for His land and His people." (Deuteronomy 32:43).

The promise of Deuteronomy leads us to the following observation and argument.

In Israel's last days
God would avenge the blood of His saints.

The seventy weeks of Daniel 9
--inclusive of the seventieth week--
constitute Israel's last days.

Therefore, God would avenge the blood of His saints
within the seventy weeks of Daniel 9.

This leads us to this:

God would avenge the blood of His saints
within the seventy weeks of Daniel 9.

11

**But, God would avenge the blood of his saints
in the fall of Jerusalem in AD 70– Matthew 23:29f** .[22]

**Therefore, the destruction of Jerusalem in AD 70
occurred during, or at the end of,
the seventy weeks of Daniel 9**

Expressed another way, here is what we are saying:

**The avenging of the blood of the saints
belongs to the last days of Israel (Deuteronomy 32).**

**But, the last days of Israel
are confined to the seventy weeks of Daniel 9:24f.**

**Therefore, the avenging of the blood of the saints
is confined to the seventy weeks of Daniel 9**

The foregoing leads directly to this:

**The avenging of the blood of the saints
is confined to the seventy weeks of Daniel 9.**

**But, the avenging of the blood of the saints
would occur in the judgment of Jerusalem in AD 70
(Matthew 23).**

**Therefore, the destruction of Jerusalem in AD 70
occurred during, or at the end of,
the seventy weeks of Daniel 9**

You cannot divorce the avenging of the blood of the saints from
Israel's last days (Deuteronomy 32).

You cannot divorce the avenging of the blood of the saints from
the fall of Jerusalem in AD 70 (Matthew 23).

You cannot divorce the destruction of Jerusalem in AD 70, *as
direct result of cutting of the Messiah* (Daniel 9:26-27) from the
avenging of the blood of the saints.

It therefore follows inexorably that the destruction of Jerusalem belonged to Israel's last days, i.e. the seventieth week of Daniel 9.

There is something else at work here in regard to the fall of Jerusalem and the avenging of the blood. That is the relationship between the passing of the Mosaic Covenant and the outpouring of Covenantal wrath in the avenging of the blood of the saints.

It is the Mosaic Covenant *alone* that provided for the punishment of Israel. This is a *critical*, yet somewhat overlooked fact. David connected either victory or defeat for Israel directly to the nation's relationship with Jehovah: "By this I know that you are well pleased with me, when my enemies do not triumph over me" (Psalms 41:11). His ideas sprang directly from the Mosaic Covenant, the Blessings and Cursings of Deuteronomy 28-30. Likewise, Jehovah promised the nation that if they diligently observed their mandated feast days, that when they went to Jerusalem to worship Him, their enemies would not invade their land at those otherwise vulnerable times (Exodus 34:23f).

It is imperative to see Daniel 9 in the light of the Mosaic Covenant and its fulfillment in the ultimate, consummative outpouring of Covenantal Wrath. In sum, the Law of Blessings and Cursings said that if Israel was obedient: "The Lord will cause your enemies that rise against you to be defeated before your face" (Deuteronomy 28:7). On the reverse side, if they broke the covenant, He threatened, "It shall be that as the Lord rejoiced over you to do good and multiply you, so the Lord will rejoice over you to destroy you and bring you to nothing, and you shall be plucked from off the land which you go to possess" (Deuteronomy 28:63– cf, Leviticus 26 also). So, there you have it. Any attack and defeat of Israel signaled that Israel had broken the covenant, and Jehovah was exercising the covenant provisions of wrath against them.

Consider now *The Abomination of Desolation and The Great Tribulation*. There is virtual unanimity among dispensationalists that these two events fall on *Israel* during the seven year interim between the Rapture and the Second Coming.

The Abomination of Desolation is set up "in the holy place" (Matthew 24:15) which can refer to the land of Israel, Jerusalem or the temple area. According to Ice the Abomination of Desolation will be set up *in the temple* (*Tribulation*, 135).

13

In the midst of the seven week tribulation period the man of sin breaks the peace treaty and embarks on a catastrophic persecution of the Jews, resulting in the killing of 2/3rds of the nation in the Great Tribulation. Ice says this is the time of Israel's "greatest distress in which she is persecuted by her enemies." (*Tribulation*, 83). Of course, the dispensationalists argue that Israel is delivered from this persecution. Scripture however, says it is *the righteous remnant*[23] that is saved, not the nation.

Do you see the problem? According to the scriptures, the actions that the dispensationalists posit against Israel during the seven year tribulation period could only happen to Israel for *Israel's violation of the Mosaic Covenant*. These actions can only be seen as the outpouring of God's *Mosaic covenantal wrath.* Yet, I have yet to find a single dispensational writer that affirms this, much less acknowledges it! Why? Because according to the millennialists, Israel is "the good guys" in the last days scenario and it is the man of sin that is the persecutor of God's chosen (innocent) people. But there is more.

Dispensationalists do not believe that the Mosaic Covenant is effective today or will be effective in the period after the Rapture. According to the millennial school the Mosaic law, "has forever been fulfilled and discontinued through Christ" (Ice, *Watch*, 258). He also says: "The Mosaic Covenant (Exodus 20-23; the book of Deuteronomy), which contains the law of Moses for Israel was given to Israel's people after they were delivered from the land of Egypt to show them how they could please God as His redeemed people. *This was a conditional covenant.* (his emp) The New Testament makes it very clear that the Mosaic Covenant was temporary until Christ would come. Many passages teach that the law was done away with in Christ."[24]

So, according to the millennialists, the Mosaic Law passed away with the coming of Christ. And, we might add, most of them posit that passing of the Law at the Cross. However, there is a severe problem here, and as already noted, the dispensationalists are not acknowledging the problem. Furthermore, very few non-millennialists seem to be taking note. Allow me to express it as succinctly as possible.

Israel could only be invaded, desecrated and destroyed if they were in violation of *the Mosaic Covenant.*

Any invasion, desecration and destruction of Israel would be in fulfillment of the *Mosaic Covenant Wrath*

The Abomination of Desolation and the Great Tribulation are desecrations and destructions of Israel.

Therefore, the Abomination of Desolation and the Great Tribulation would come as a result of Israel's violation of the Mosaic Covenant and the outpouring of *Mosaic Covenant Wrath.*

Now do you see the problem? If the temporary Mosaic Covenant was forever removed, fulfilled in Christ, then how in the name of reason will the Mosaic Covenant provisions of wrath be valid and applicable in the Tribulation period? It cannot be argued that it is not the Mosaic Covenant that is in effect, for this raises the question: If the Abomination of Desolation and the Great Tribulation are not the result of Israel's violation of the Mosaic Covenant and the outpouring of Mosaic Covenant wrath, then what covenant will Israel violate that will bring such horrific suffering on them? What covenant will be in effect between Israel and God during the seven year tribulation period, that due to her sin, God allows (brings) another holocaust on her that makes WWII seem pale in comparison?[25] To be sure, the Abrahamic covenant, and the Davidic covenant has no such provisions for covenantal wrath.

The bottom line is that, Biblically, you cannot posit suffering, cataclysm and catastrophe on the nation of Israel outside of the parameters of the Mosaic Covenant.

15

> Biblically, Israel was only invaded, desecrated and destroyed for violation of *the Mosaic Covenant.*
> The Great Tribulation is supposedly a desecration and destruction of Israel.
> This demands that the Mosaic Covenant is still in force, or will be restored after the rapture.
> There is no judgment on Israel outside the Mosaic Covenant!

This relationship between catastrophic suffering and Mosaic Wrath is recognized by some millennialists, yet it is patently obvious that they have not thought through what they are saying.

Thomas Ice wrote that Luke 21:20-24 must be AD 70 because it speaks of the days of vengeance and this means,

"Those first century days are called 'days of vengeance' for Jerusalem is under the divine judgment of covenantal sanctions recorded in Leviticus 26 and Deuteronomy 28. Luke records that God's vengeance upon His elect nation is 'in order that all things which are written may be fulfilled.' Jesus is telling the nation that God will fulfill all the curses of the Mosaic covenant because of Israel's disobedience. He will not relent and merely bring to pass a partial fulfillment of His vengeance. Some of the passages that Jesus said would be fulfilled include the following: Lev. 26:27-33; Deut. 28:49f; 32:19-27; 1 Kings 9:1-9; Jeremiah 6:1-8; 26:1-9; Daniel 9:26; Hosea 8:1-10-10:15; Micah 3:12; Zechariah 11:6)." *(Tribulation*, 98)

As I often say in seminar presentations,[26] "You have to catch the power of this!" Take careful note of what Ice says.

✎ The destruction of Jerusalem in AD 70 would be the outpouring of Mosaic Covenant wrath for killing the Messiah.

✎ The destruction of Jerusalem would fulfill all things that are written.

✎ The destruction of Jerusalem would not be a *partial* fulfillment of covenant wrath, but a *complete fulfillment.*

✎ The destruction of Jerusalem would be the fulfillment of Daniel 9:26.

In these four admissions you will find the total refutation of the dispensational paradigm. And consider this.

If the destruction of Jerusalem in AD 70 was the fulfillment of Mosaic Covenant wrath (even though the Mosaic Covenant had been forever fulfilled and removed in Christ!) then why were not the pogroms against the Jews throughout history an outpouring of Mosaic Covenant wrath?

If the destruction of Jerusalem in AD 70 was the fulfillment of Mosaic Covenant wrath (even though the Mosaic Covenant had been forever removed!) then why were the atrocities against the Jews in WWII not an expression of Mosaic Covenant wrath?

If the destruction of Jerusalem in AD 70 was the fulfillment of Mosaic Covenant wrath (even though the Mosaic Covenant had been forever fulfilled and removed in Christ) then why should we not see the attacks in 1967, 1973 and the 2007 attacks against Israel by Hezbollah as the outpouring of Mosaic Covenant wrath?

Those today who insist that Israel remains as the chosen people of God must confront this issue. The 2007 war with Hezbollah was not merely a bloody conflict *if Israel remains God's chosen people*, it was a sign that Israel was in violation of the Mosaic Covenant! To affirm that Israel remains as God's chosen, covenant people, and then to ignore the relationship between *covenant and catastrophe* is misguided thinking.

The modern world needs, *desperately*, to understand that Israel is no longer God's chosen people, that they are not under any kind of Covenant Curse and that a way of peace grounded on solid humanitarian concepts is essential. Bad theology is shedding innocent blood in the Middle East and will continue to do so until politicians and the voters who elect them come to grips with this incredibly important theological truth.

So, if the destruction of Jerusalem was the fulfillment of Mosaic Covenant wrath, then undeniably, the provisions of the Mosaic Covenant were still valid and in force when these events took place. This refutes the millennial posit that the Mosaic Covenant had been removed at the Cross.

If the destruction of Jerusalem was the fulfillment of all things that are written then most assuredly there are no prophecies to be fulfilled post AD 70. Ice might rejoin that all that Jesus meant by "all things that are written" referred to the days of vengeance on Israel. This will not help, for most assuredly Ice believes that Isaiah 62 and its predicted Day of Vengeance of our God, remains unfulfilled to this day. If all things written concerning vengeance and Israel was fulfilled, then, patently, there is no yet future Abomination of Desolation or Great Tribulation.

If the fall of Jerusalem in AD 70 was the complete fulfillment of Covenantal Wrath against Israel, not just a partial fulfillment, then the previous point is confirmed. Remember, Biblically, the only way for Israel to be invaded, desecrated and destroyed– *as a covenant people*-- was for her to be in violation of the Mosaic Covenant. All destructions and desecrations of Israel must be seen in the light of Mosaic Covenantal Wrath. For Ice to affirm therefore, that AD 70 was the *complete fulfillment of Covenantal Wrath* against Israel totally strips the dispensational theology of any future Great Tribulation against Israel.

If the fall of Jerusalem in AD 70 was the fulfillment of Daniel 9:26, then without any doubt, the seventy weeks of Daniel are fulfilled, since, as we have seen, the avenging of the blood of the saints was to occur in the last days of Israel, i.e. in the seventy week countdown. So, since the destruction of Jerusalem was the fulfillment of Israel's last days prophecies and since Daniel 9:24-27- the seventy week countdown– is the countdown of Israel's last days, it therefore follows that since Ice says that the fall of Jerusalem fulfilled Daniel 9:26, this demands that the seventy weeks are fulfilled.

Furthermore, you will note that Ice claims that the fall of Jerusalem was the fulfillment of Deuteronomy 28:49f. However, in his debate with Gentry, Ice claimed that Deuteronomy 28:49f was a prophecy of *Israel's last days*. So, if the fall of Jerusalem in AD 70 was the fulfillment of Deuteronomy 28, and if Deuteronomy 28 was a prediction of Israel's last days, it therefore follows, irrefutably, that Israel's last days were present and fulfilled in the fall of Jerusalem in AD 70.

The same is true of Deuteronomy 32:19-27. Ice says that the fall of Jerusalem fulfilled that prophecy. Yet, as we will see, the Song of Moses was a prophecy of Israel's last days! So, for Ice to affirm that the fall of Jerusalem was the fulfillment of the last days prophecy of Deuteronomy 32 is fatal to his eschatology. *The last days of Israel were not supposed to be present in AD 70.* They had supposedly been suspended and postponed. This is no small issue. It strikes at the very heart of the millennial doctrine.

As suggested earlier, if the destruction of Jerusalem in AD 70 was the outpouring of Mosaic Covenant Wrath, *this demands that the Mosaic Covenant was still binding in AD 70.* How can it be argued that the Mosaic Covenant was no longer in effect, in fact had been *abrogated* almost 40 years beforehand, but its provisions for wrath were fulfilled in the destruction of Jerusalem? How are the provisions of a nullified covenant applied when the covenant that is the source of those provisions is no longer in force?

So, the millennial admission that the judgment of AD 70 was the fulfillment of Mosaic Covenant wrath nullifies dispensationalism.

The millennial admission that the judgment of AD 70 was the *complete*, not partial, *fulfillment of vengeance on Israel* falsifies dispensationalism.

The millennial admission that the judgment of AD 70 fulfilled "all things that are written" destroys dispensationalism.

Let me close this aspect of our discussion with the repetition of a few vital thoughts.

The seventy weeks of Daniel 9 constitute the "last days" of Old Covenant Israel.

But, the avenging of the blood of the martyrs would occur in Israel's last days (Deut. 32:19f, 43; Isaiah 2-4:4).

The destruction of Jerusalem in AD 70 would be the time of the avenging of the blood of the martyrs.

Therefore, the last days of Israel, the seventy week countdown, encompassed the fall of Jerusalem in AD 70.

What the foregoing proves is that the seventy weeks were not fulfilled in AD 34-35 as posited by the postmillennialists and amillennialists, and of course, it completely falsifies the idea that the seventieth week was postponed so far 2000 years.

It matters not whether we understand the "math" of the seventy weeks. If the elements foretold in the prophecy include the fall of Jerusalem in AD 70, then we must submit to that "calculation." This demonstrates that the seventy weeks were not to be calculated mathematically, but is a symbolic period of time marked by a beginning point, interim events, and a consummation point, the final destruction of the Old Covenant world in AD 70.[27]

Let me return now to a discussion of the putting away of sin.

There is a widespread consensus that the "putting away of sin" is referent to the atoning work of Jesus. The Hebrew writer says Christ appeared "to put away sin" (9:26) and this theme of "putting away of sin" in fulfillment of God's promises to Israel is found throughout the New Testament. Furthermore, *the time of the putting away of sin is the time of the resurrection.* Let's take a look at some critical NT texts that deal with the putting away of sin in the context of the resurrection.

ACTS 3:19F
Peter assuredly anticipated the removal of Israel's sin, at the time of the fulfillment of all of God's promises to her:

"Repent therefore and be converted, that your sins may be blotted out, so that times of refreshing may come from the presence of the Lord, and that He may send Jesus Christ, who was preached to you before, whom heaven must receive until the times of restoration of all things, which God has spoken by the mouth of all His holy prophets since the world began." (Acts 3:19f)

Peter was addressing a Jewish crowd, affirming that Jesus was the promised messiah, and that at the parousia, when all things written by all the Old Covenant prophets would be fulfilled, if they would repent, *their sins would be blotted out!* For Peter then, the blotting out of sin, in fulfillment of the promises made to Israel–and does that not include Daniel 9?– would occur at the parousia. The parousia here is without any doubt, the time of the resurrection. Thus, the time of the blotting out of the sins of Israel, the parousia and the resurrection are inseparably connected. But of course, the removal of Israel's sin is limited by Daniel 9 to the confines and parameters of the seventy weeks!

Did Peter anticipate:

1.) A salvation of Israel different from Daniel,

2.) A different time of fulfillment than foretold by Daniel,

3.) A different removal of sin than foretold by Daniel?

Peter was anticipating the fulfillment of God's promises to Israel. Those promises would be fulfilled at the parousia and resurrection. If the parousia and resurrection has not occurred, then the seventy weeks have been postponed, Israel remains God's covenant people, the Old Covenant remains valid.

However, if Peter was anticipating the fulfillment of Daniel 9:

➨ It is undeniable that the seventy weeks were not already fulfilled, because the putting away of sin is confined to the seventy weeks.

➨ It is undeniable that the seventy weeks would not be fulfilled until the fulfillment of all of God's promises to Israel.

➨ It is undeniable that the seventy weeks would be fulfilled in the parousia of Christ and the resurrection.

It needs to be stated again and re-emphasized, that you cannot place *any* of the events and blessings of the prophesied seventy weeks outside the confines and parameters of the seventy weeks. The efforts of Gentry, DeMar, Noe and others to posit the fate of the city outside the parameters of the seventy weeks suggests that you can also place *any or all* of the other elements of Daniel 9:24 outside the seventy heptads.

If the fate of the city can be placed outside the seventy weeks, then why can't the finishing of the transgressions, the putting away of sin, the making of the atonement, the bringing in of everlasting righteousness, the sealing up of vision and prophecy and the anointing of the Most Holy also be posited outside the seventy? It seems arbitrary at best to suggest that only the actual fate of the city lies outside the seventy week countdown, when the angel told Daniel that "seventy weeks are determined on your people and your holy city," and then listed every single one of the six elements. To my knowledge, none of the above men argue that the fulfillment of the other elements of Daniel 9:24 lie outside the seventy weeks. How is it then that *the fate of the city*, that is inextricably linked with the finishing the transgressions and the sealing of vision and prophecy, is posited outside the Seventy?

God did not say that seventy weeks are determined to begin a process that will not be completed for 2000 years. He did not say seventy weeks are determined to determine what will happen later. He did not say seventy weeks are determined to predict events to occur thousands of years later. Everything listed in Daniel 9:24 is confined to *within the seventy week period.*

Thus, Acts 3 and Peter's promise that *all that all of the prophets foretold* about the restoration of all things and the blotting out of Israel's sin, at the parousia (and resurrection) shows that the seventy weeks had not yet been fulfilled and would not be fulfilled until the parousia. If therefore, you attempt to divorce the parousia and resurrection from the context of the removal of Israel's sin and the fulfillment of the seventy weeks, you create a dichotomy that does not exist in scripture. Wherever you place the resurrection and the removal of sin, it is there that you posit the completion of the seventy weeks of Daniel 9. The removal of sin, resurrection and the consummation of Israel's seventy weeks all belong together.

Here then is our argument:

Seventy weeks were determined to put away sin, bringing Israel's salvation to completion (Daniel 9:24).
But, Israel's sin would be removed at the parousia/resurrection in fulfillment of God's promises to her (Acts 3:21f).[28]
Therefore, the parousia and resurrection foretold by Acts 3 would be the fulfillment of the seventy weeks.

Unless Peter was anticipating a *different salvation* than foretold by Daniel, a *different removal of sin* than foretold by Daniel, in fulfillment of *different OT promises to Israel,* then it is *prima facie* evident that Peter was anticipating the fulfillment of Daniel 9. But, if Peter was anticipating the fulfillment of Daniel 9, then the seventy weeks of Daniel 9 had not yet been fulfilled. And, since Peter was emphatic that all the prophets, "from Samuel forward

22

spoke of these days" (i.e. Peter's first century days) it is obvious that Peter did not believe the seventy weeks had been postponed. He expected the consummation of Israel's eschatological promises, including the seventy weeks, in his days.

ROMANS 11:25-27

Since we discuss Romans 11:25f in-depth below, we will not say much about it here, except to note that Paul affirms, repeatedly, that he preached *nothing* but the hope of Israel. And, in Romans 11 he anticipated the time when God would fulfill His promise to Israel[29] to "take away their sin." Paul was anticipating the completion of the promise of Daniel 9.

So, Paul said that God would fulfill His promise to take away Israel's sin at the parousia, i.e. the time of the resurrection, (Romans 11:26f). But, the time of the taking away of Israel's sin is confined to the seventy weeks of Daniel 9:24. *Therefore, the parousia and resurrection are confined to the seventy weeks of Daniel 9:24.*

Furthermore,

The parousia and resurrection are confined to the seventy weeks of Daniel 9:24.

But, the parousia and resurrection were still future to Paul in Romans 11 (circa AD 57-59).

Therefore, the fulfillment of the seventy weeks of Daniel 9:24 was still future to Paul.

This means of course, that the amillennial and postmillennial contention that the seventy weeks were completely fulfilled, circa 34-35 A. D. in the conversion of the Gentiles, is false.

1 CORINTHIANS 15

In 1 Corinthians 15 we find Paul's great discourse on the resurrection and in verses 23f he says that Christ had "put all things under his feet." The last enemy, Paul says, to be destroyed "is death." And when would death be conquered? It would be when "the sting of death," *sin*, would be finally put under Christ. Thus, the resurrection would be when the sting of death would be put down by Christ. But the sting of death is sin (1 Corinthians 15:55-56). Therefore, resurrection would be when sin would be put down by Christ. That leads to our initial argument from Daniel 9:

The time of the resurrection would be when sin would be put away (1 Corinthians 15:55-56).

But the time of the putting away of sin belongs to the seventy weeks of Daniel 9:24f.

Therefore, the time of the resurrection belongs to the seventy weeks of Daniel 9:24f.

This lead us to:

The time of the resurrection belongs to the seventy weeks of Daniel 9:24f.

But, the seventy weeks of Daniel 9:24f ended with the fall of Jerusalem in AD 70.[30]

Therefore, the resurrection belongs to the time of the fall of Jerusalem in AD 70.

At this juncture it is vital to be reminded again that *Paul's resurrection doctrine was the hope of Israel.* Notice the correlation between Daniel 9 and 1 Corinthians 15. Both deal with the fulfillment of God's promises to Israel. Both give a time referent for fulfillment.

Daniel 9	1 Corinthians 15
Time of the end (v. 27)	Time of the end (v. 23f)
Time of the kingdom (cf. Lk. 21:31)	Time of the kingdom (v. 50f)

24

Putting away of sin (v. 24)	Putting away of sin (v. 23f; 54f)
End of Old Covenant age	End of Old Covenant age (v. 54-56)**
Fulfillment of OT promises to Israel (v. 24)	Fulfillment of OT promises to Israel (v. 54f)
Consummated in AD 70 (v. 27)	"We shall not all sleep" (v. 50)

**Paul said the resurrection would be when "the law" that was the "strength of sin" was removed. In Paul, the term "the law," when used without modifiers, (110 times) is *invariably* the Old Covenant Law.[31] Thus, resurrection would be when the Old Covenant was removed.[32] Those who posit the resurrection at the end of the Christian age must take the position that *the gospel of Christ is the strength of sin*, since resurrection would/will be when "the Law" that is the strength of sin will be removed. Thus, if the resurrection is at the end of this age and the law which is the strength of sin is removed at the end of this age, this means that *the gospel is called the strength of sin*. This hardly agrees with Paul's assessment in Romans 8:1f.

It is clear that Daniel 9 and 1 Corinthians 15 are in fact speaking of the same time and the same event, the resurrection. This being true, since Daniel 9 posits the resurrection at the end of the Old Covenant world of Israel, this demands that 1 Corinthians 15 was fulfilled in the demise of the world and the Law that was "the strength of sin."

Notice now some important arguments.

The time of *the putting away of sin*, (the resurrection) would be within the confines of, and by the end of the seventy weeks of Daniel 9, the end of the Old Covenant world of Israel (Daniel 9:24f).

But, the time of the putting away of sin, (*the resurrection*) would be when the Law, that was "the strength of sin" was removed (1 Corinthians 15:54f).

The Law that was the strength of sin was the Mosaic Covenant, (the Old Testament).

Therefore, the resurrection would be when the Mosaic Covenant (The Old Testament) was removed.

Stated another way, we would express it like this:

The resurrection would be when the Law that was the strength of sin was removed (1 Corinthians 15:54f).

But, the Law that was the strength of sin was the Old Covenant of Israel (the Mosaic Law).

Therefore, the resurrection would be when the Old Covenant of Israel (the Mosaic Covenant) came to an end.

And to join 1 Corinthians 15 with Daniel again, we offer this:

The resurrection would be when the Old Covenant of Israel (the Mosaic Covenant) came to an end.

But, the Old Covenant of Israel would come to an end at the end of the seventy weeks of Daniel 9.

Therefore, the resurrection would be at the end of the seventy weeks of Daniel 9.

So, in Corinthians Paul discusses the coming resurrection, when sin would be put away, *strictly within the context of the fulfillment of God's promises to Israel.* Unless Paul has a completely different set of promises, concerning a different time of salvation, than that foretold by Daniel, then we must conclude that the seventy weeks of Daniel had not yet been fulfilled. After all, *Daniel said that the putting away of sin was confined to the seventy weeks.* Furthermore, if the resurrection has not occurred, the seventy weeks are unfulfilled, Israel remains God's covenant people and the Law that was the strength of sin– *the Mosaic Covenant*--remains valid and binding today.

The fact that Paul's doctrine of the resurrection– and the putting away of sin-- in 1 Corinthians 15 is tied inseparably to the fulfillment of God's promises to Israel demands that Paul was either anticipating the consummation of Daniel 9, or of some other eschatological prophecies made to Israel. If Daniel 9 is not related to 1 Corinthians 15, then patently, Daniel 9 and its promise of Israel's salvation is unrelated to the Old Covenant prophecies that Paul does specifically draw from, Isaiah 25 and Hosea 13. The reality is that one cannot divorce those prophecies from Daniel's promises, however. Therefore, Daniel 9 does lie behind 1 Corinthians 15.

Not only must we see Paul's discussion of the resurrection within the context of Daniel 9 and God's promises to Israel, we must see it within the context of *covenant transformation* as well.

As we will show, when we discuss the bringing in of everlasting righteousness, Paul's concept of the resurrection is posited within the framework of the changing of the covenants. Here is what we mean.

We have already shown that the resurrection would be when the Law that was the strength of sin, the Torah, was removed. Thus, resurrection is undeniably connected with covenantal transformation. What is so often overlooked is the relationship between resurrection, *forgiveness* and covenantal transformation.

The New Testament affirms that there was *no genuine forgiveness under Torah*: "For the Law, having a shadow of good things to come, and not the very image of those things, can never with these same sacrifices which they offer year by year continually, make those who approach perfect. For then would they not have ceased to be offered? For the worshipers once purged, would have had no more consciousness of sins. But in those sacrifices there a reminder of sins every year. For it is not possible that the blood of bulls and goats could take away sin." (Hebrews 10:3-4). This is the law that Daniel and Israel lived under.

Since there was no provision for true forgiveness under the Law, but instead a constant reminder of sin, those under the Law were acutely aware of their standing. Without forgiveness there was no life. But, the Law could give no forgiveness, therefore the Law could not give life. It was the ministration of death.

Paul said that the resurrection would occur when the Law that was the strength of sin was removed. That means that resurrection is the transformation from the Torah that condemned to the covenant that gave life. To say that the resurrection would occur when sin, the sting of death was overcome, was tantamount to saying that the resurrection would occur when the New Covenant of Christ, wherein there is true forgiveness, would fully arrive!

Consider this. Paul said that the resurrection would be when sin, the sting of death, was overcome (1 Corinthians 15:56). Does that mean that sin would be overcome by not being a reality in the world, or does it mean that sin would be overcome through *forgiveness*? Sadly, too many believe that the first option is what Paul had in mind. But if so, then that means that the Torah remains as the strength of sin until the material creation is revamped and sin is removed from the world. What then of forgiveness? Is it not a reality *now*?

If the resurrection happens when sin, the sting of death is overcome, then we must ask, "Is the child of God, redeemed by the blood of Christ, truly, genuinely forgiven of sin today?" If the answer is yes, then, *has not the sting of death been removed*? And if the sting of death is removed, is resurrection not a reality?[33] Further, Paul said that "the last enemy to be destroyed is death" (1 Corinthians 15:26). Question: *is physical death the enemy of the child of God that has been redeemed by the blood of Christ, today?* If physical death is not the enemy of the child of God, then has not the sting of death been removed? And if the sting of death has been removed through forgiveness, then has the resurrection not occurred?[34]

Leon Morris, although a futurist, nonetheless recognized some of the issues in the text:

"It is not death in itself that is the harmful thing. It is *death* that is the 'wages of sin' (Romans 6:23) that matters. For death, considered simply as the passing out of this life into the immediate presence of the Lord is a gain, not a loss (Phil. 1:21,23). Where sin is pardoned, death has no sting. But where sin has not been dealt with, there death is a virulent antagonist. The *sting* is not death, but in *sin*. By *the strength of sin is the*

28

law Paul turns us to such thoughts as those expounded in Rom. v. 12ff, vii.7ff. The law, though it is 'holy' and just and good' (Rom. vii.12) is quite unable to bring men to a state of salvation. Indeed, by setting before men the standard that they ought to reach and never do, it becomes sin's stronghold. It makes sinners of us all. It condemns us all."[35] (His emphasis)

Morris sees that the problem is not physical death *per se*, even though he seems to mix the references. It is sin death, the death of the Garden. Further, Morris sees that *forgiveness is the solution to the death of 1 Corinthians 15!* He even sees that Paul identifies the *Torah as the strength of sin.*

The problem is that Morris fails to see that if the New Covenant has been established, bringing forgiveness, then Torah has been removed and death has been destroyed. For Morris to consistently hold to a futurist eschatology he must believe, as he seems to, that the *Torah is in fact still the strength of sin.* One can only wonder then, how Paul could exclaim, *as he ministered the New Covenant*: "There is therefore, now no condemnation for those in Christ Jesus, who do not walk after the flesh, but after the Spirit. For the law of the Spirit of life in Christ, has made me free from the law of sin and death. For what the law could not do, in that it was weak through the flesh, God sent forth His son, on account of sin: He condemned sin in the flesh" (Romans 8:1-4).[36]

The point is that in Corinthians as in the other New Testament books, forgiveness and resurrection are inextricably connected.[37] Furthermore, forgiveness and the New Covenant, as opposed to death and the Old Covenant is also a pervasive theme.

When we realize that Daniel was writing from the perspective of life under Torah, anticipating the time when sin would be put away through forgiveness, then its relationship with 1 Corinthians 15 becomes crystal clear. Daniel was anticipating a new order in which God would remove man's sin. The atonement would bring true forgiveness, something Torah could never do.

Let me put it like this:

➤1 Cor. 15 anticipated the time of the resurrection when the Torah that was the strength of sin would be removed.

➤By removal of the Law that was the strength of sin, the sting of death would also be removed.

➤The Law that was the strength of sin was the Mosaic Covenant, as we have shown abundantly in this study.

➤When Daniel wrote, he was living under the Torah that was the ministration of death and the strength of sin.

➤The Torah under which Daniel lived could never put away sin.

➤When Daniel wrote he was anticipating the arrival of the world where sin would be put away.

➤Jeremiah and many other Old Testament prophecies foretold the time, the Messianic kingdom, when God would make the New Covenant. The key aspect of that New Covenant would be: "their sins and iniquities will I remember no more" (Jeremiah 31:29f).

➤Thus, the New Covenant would not be the strength of sin. And because it would bring forgiveness of sin, the New Covenant would also *remove the sting of death.*

➤The New Covenant therefore, would bring resurrection life.

➤It follows that since Daniel was anticipating the putting away of sin, that he was anticipating the full arrival of the New Covenant world of the Messiah.

➤It also follows that since Paul was still anticipating the putting away of sin in 1 Corinthians 15, that he was still looking for the full arrival of the New Covenant world of Messiah, but expected it before the Corinthians died. (cf. 1 Corinthians 15:50-51).

The book of Hebrews was fully aware of the failings of the Old Law, "the Law made nothing perfect; on the other hand, there is the bringing in of a better hope through which we draw near to God" (Hebrews 7:19). This better hope and drawing near to God conjured up ideas of entering the Most Holy Place, something unthinkable under Torah. But for the author of Hebrews, the reality of forgiveness would open up that most Holy Place, "having boldness to enter the Holiest by the blood of Jesus, by a new and living way which he has consecrated for us, through the veil, that is, His flesh, and having a High Priest over the house of God, let us draw near with a true heart in full assurance of faith, having our hearts sprinkled from an evil conscience and our bodies washed with pure water." (Hebrews 10:19f).

These statements all have to do with *covenantal transformation.* There is no concern here with the transformation of rocks and trees into being better rocks and trees. It is all about standing before God justified and forgiven. The contrast is between the world of Torah that could never take away sin, and the New Covenant world of Messiah, where: "their sins and iniquities will I remember no more." Let me express a few thoughts to clarify this issue of the relationship between the putting away of sin, the New Covenant and resurrection.

☦ Seventy weeks were determined for the putting away of sin, i.e. forgiveness.

☦ The putting away of sin demanded the death of Christ (which occurred *after the sixty ninth week,* Daniel 9:26) and that is the purpose of his passion (Hebrews 9:26).

☦ However, according to prophecy, the forgiveness of sin would come through the *New Covenant* (Jeremiah 31:29f): "For this is the covenant that I will make with them says the Lord...their sins and iniquities will I remember no more."

☦ Jesus' death was for the purpose of confirming that New Covenant (Matthew 26:26f; Galatians 3:15; Hebrews 9:15f).

☦ Jesus' death, while it confirmed the New Covenant, was in fact, the "surety (ἔγγυος- *guarantee*) of a better covenant" (Hebrews 7:22). His death *initiated* the process of bringing the New Covenant, but it did not *finalize* that process.

☦ As we show below, there was a transitional period of time, a time in which the Old Covenant world was passing away and the New Covenant was being delivered (Hebrews 8:13).

☦ The transformation from the Old Covenant world of the ministration of death, the Torah that was the strength of sin, and that did in fact bring death, was the distinctive, personal commission and mission of Paul the apostle through the ministry of the Spirit: "God who made us ministers of the New Covenant" (2 Corinthians 3:6; 4:1-2).

31

✝ Since the putting away of sin was directly related to the New Covenant, then, until the New Covenant world was perfected, the promise of the putting away of sin was not fulfilled.

✝Since the putting away of sin and the New Covenant are inseparably linked, then since the New Covenant world was not yet perfected / completed when Hebrews was written, it therefore follows that the seventy weeks had not yet been competed when Hebrews was written.

✝ The putting away of sin–and thus the perfection of the New Covenant world-- is tied specifically and emphatically to the parousia of Christ (Romans 11:25-27) and to the resurrection (1 Corinthians 15:55-56).

The promise of Daniel 9 then, of the time when God would take away sin, *is the promise of the New Covenant world of the Messiah* to be fulfilled at the resurrection and parousia. The redeemer would establish the New Covenant in fulfillment of Jeremiah 31:29f. Whereas the Old Covenant could never take away sin, when the New Covenant world was fully established, forgiveness would be real. The Law that was the strength of sin would pass, and through forgiveness the sting of death would be removed. *The New Covenant and resurrection go hand in hand.*

Paul was still anticipating the removal of sin at the resurrection, when the Torah that was the strength of sin was removed and sin would find its "final solution." But, since the end of Torah and the overcoming of sin belongs within the confines of the seventy weeks of Daniel 9, then this means that the seventy weeks were not already fulfilled and it means that the seventy weeks had not been postponed.

If the resurrection has not occurred therefore:

1.) The Torah remains valid as the strength of sin.

2.) Sin is still the sting of death, *even for those in Christ.*

3.) The New Covenant, that was to bring forgiveness is not established.[38]

4.) The seventy week prophecy of the removal of sin has not been fulfilled.

5.) If the seventy week prophecy has not been fulfilled, then Israel remains as God's chosen covenant people, the Torah remains valid, sin still reigns.

6.) If the seventy week prophecy *has been fulfilled*, then sin has been removed and resurrection life is a reality today.

HEBREWS 9:26F

Notice the correlation with Hebrews 9:26: "Now, once, at the end of the ages he has appeared, *to put away sin*, by the sacrifice of himself." (My emphasis) Where did the Hebrew writer get the idea of the "putting away of sin" in fulfillment of God's promises to Israel? Could he have gotten that idea from Daniel 9:24? And notice that just as Daniel 9 anticipated the putting away of sin by the consummation of God's determined time on the people and the city, Jesus appeared at "the end of the ages" (*suntelia ton aionion*)[39] *to put away sin*. Daniel foretold the time of the end, Jesus appeared at the time of the end. This is not just coincidental usage of language. This is not just similarity of language. Hebrews is discussing what Daniel foretold.

Would it be argued that the seventy weeks are unrelated to "the time of the end"? Surely not. Virtually all conservative students would affirm that the time of the end is in fact the focus of Daniel 9. This is especially true of the millennialists. So, in other words, the time of the end was designated to "put and end to sin." Jesus appeared in the appointed time, the time of the end and he appeared for the express purpose of accomplishing what Daniel foretold for the time of the end.

However, Jesus' appearing was also for the express purpose of *dying, to put away sin in fulfillment of Daniel 9*. But, in Daniel, the putting away of sin is confined to the seventy weeks and the death of Messiah would occur after the sixty-ninth week. The putting away of sin and the death of Messiah are inextricably linked. This is undeniable, especially in Hebrews 9. So, since the putting away of sin and the death of Messiah are inseparably connected, it therefore follows that the death of Messiah–after the sixty-ninth week–in Daniel 9 did not postpone the countdown but was an integral part of the countdown.

It is impossible to honor the text of Daniel 9 and divorce the death of Messiah from the countdown of the seventy weeks. If the putting away of sin belongs to the seventy weeks, then since the death of Messiah is fundamentally linked with the putting away of sin, it therefore follows that the death of Messiah does not lie outside of the seventy weeks.

Seventy weeks were determined to *put away sin*.
The death of Jesus was to "put away sin."
Therefore, the death of Jesus belongs to the seventy week countdown.
The death of Jesus was after the sixty-ninth week.
The death of Jesus did not, therefore, postpone the seventy week countdown, but was a vital part of it.

Jesus did not appear at the end of *the Christian age* to put away sin. He came, in the fullness of time, *at the end of the Old Covenant age of Israel* (Galatians 4:4; Hebrews 1:1) to put away sin, just as Daniel said seventy weeks were determined to put away sin. The Messiah was to die *after* the sixty ninth week (Daniel 9:26). The Passion was the power by which the removal of sin began (He triumphed over his enemies in the Cross, Colossians 2:15f) but the parousia would be the consummation of the process begun (cf. 1 Corinthians 15:21-28). This is the "already-but-not-yet" of the putting away of sin. But remember, Daniel said only seventy weeks were determined to put away sin. He did not say the process would begin within the seventy weeks but not be consummated for 2000 years!

If the putting away of sin is the time of the resurrection, and if seventy weeks were determined to put away sin, then it must be true that the resurrection must be confined to, and fulfilled by the time of the completion of the Weeks. If the semi-preterists were to argue that the initiation of the putting away of sins began in the seventy weeks, but that the consummation has not yet taken place, since the resurrection, per their paradigm has not occurred, *then they are guilty of inserting a 2000 year gap in the text of Daniel 9!* But Daniel 9 does not say, nor indicate that seventy weeks were determined to start a process that would not be completed for two millennia. It says, "Seventy weeks are determined on your people and on your holy city...to put away sin." That means that unless resurrection is totally unrelated to the promise of putting away of

34

sin, that the resurrection had to have occurred by the end of the seventy weeks, in A. D. 70.

One final thought here. Many futurists insist that the putting away of sin was accomplished strictly at the sacrifice of Jesus and point to Hebrews 9:26. However, to confine the discussion of the putting away of sin to just the death of Jesus is misguided and fails to consider the "already-but-not-yet" nature of Christ's work.

Notice a parallel situation. In Hebrews 2:14f it says that Christ was manifested in the flesh, "that through death, he might destroy him who had the power of death, that is, the devil." So, Jesus was manifested to destroy the devil through his death. Did Jesus' death destroy the devil? Well, Paul affirmed that *through* the Cross, Jesus did triumph over the principalities and powers (Colossians 2:14f). However, it surely was not finalized at the Cross! Paul's referent to the Cross includes the *resurrection*, does it not? Paul was using *synecdoche*, i.e. a figure of speech in which a part stands for the whole. In other words, the Cross stands for not only the death of Jesus, but the resurrection of Jesus as well.

The reality is that had Jesus not been raised from the dead Paul could not have said that he triumphed. The Cross (alone) was the symbol of humiliation; the empty tomb was the symbol of his victory.

But of course, our point is that although Paul said Jesus was manifested in the flesh to destroy the devil through death that the destruction of the devil was not accomplished, even at the resurrection of Jesus. Paul was still awaiting the destruction of Satan at Christ's parousia (Romans 16:20): "The God of peace shall crush Satan under your feet shortly." Likewise, John anticipated the final defeat of the Devil in Revelation and like Paul affirmed that the victory was coming very soon (Revelation 20:10f; 22:10-12).

The reality is that the Cross *initiated* the victory over Satan and in a sense guaranteed it, but the actual consummation of that victory awaited the parousia. This is the same situation with the putting away of sin. Jesus appeared, "to put away sin, by the sacrifice of himself" (Hebrews 9:26), but he was to be manifested to put away sin, at his parousia.

Note that in Romans 11:26-27 written *long after the death of Jesus to put away sin*, Paul was anticipating the parousia of Christ to fulfill God's promise to Israel *to take away her sin*. So, Daniel 9 said seventy weeks were determined to put away sin. Christ appeared at the end of the age to put away sin, but he was coming again to definitively fulfill the prophecy of Daniel to put away sin. This demands that either Romans and Hebrews were speaking of different putting away of sin, in fulfillment of Israel's promises, or, more correctly, that the death of Jesus began the process that was to be perfected at his parousia. But if this is true, this demands that the seventy weeks would not end until the parousia of Christ, when he returned to put away sin. This is definitive proof that the seventy weeks did not end prior to AD 70. Unless we want to maintain that sin has not yet been taken away we must acknowledge that Christ did come in fulfillment of Israel's hope.

DANIEL 9, FORGIVENESS,
THE END OF EXILE AND RESURRECTION

We need to take note that by virtually any measure, Daniel 9 is a prediction of resurrection. For simplicity and brevity, we want to make the following points:

1.) In scripture, sin was the cause of "death" to Israel: "When Ephraim spoke trembling, he exalted himself in Israel: But when he offended through Baal *worship*, he died" (Hosea 13:1). The death in view was not biological death, but separation from God, the temple and the land.

2.) In scripture, *exile is synonymous with death*. That is, to be exiled from the land, captive in a foreign land, was, to the Jewish mind, the equivalent to *death*.[40] As Watts says, commenting on the Assyrian captivity, "The exiles in Assyria and Egypt are said to have been perishing. But they will be gathered by God to come and worship him on his holy mountain in Jerusalem (v. 13). Separation from the temple is equivalent to death. Being allowed to participate again in Jerusalem is like coming back to life."[41] When Judah apostatized, even worse than Israel, she also "died," and was in the "graves" of Babylonian captivity (Ezekiel 37:1-14).

3.) As a direct corollary to the above points, *forgiveness is seen as the return from exile*. Petri notes that in response to Daniel's prayer for the forgiveness of Israel's sins and the end of the Exile, the prophet was given the prediction of the death of the Messiah that, "will not only bring about the forgiveness of sins, but also its biblical corollary: the end of the Exile."[42] Forgiveness is paramount in Daniel's mind, "O Lord, hear! O Lord, forgive!" (Daniel 9:19). Other scholars have noted this motif in scripture.[43]

The scriptures are very clear about this relationship between forgiveness and the return from exile. See Leviticus 26:33; 26:43; 1 Kings 8:33-34; Lam. 4:22; Is. 40:1-11; Jeremiah 31:10-12, 31f; Ezekiel 36:24f; 37:15-28, etc.

4.) As a direct corollary to #3, return from exile was considered and described as *resurrection from the dead*. See Ezekiel 37 especially: "They indeed say, 'Our hope is lost, and we ourselves are cut off' Therefore, prophesy and say to them, 'Thus says the Lord God: 'I will open your graves and cause you to come up from your graves, and to bring you into the land of Israel. Then you shall

37

know that I am the Lord, when I have opened your graves, O my people, and brought you up from your graves."

What this means is that when Daniel was given the promise of *the taking away of Israel's sin*, through the atoning work of the Messiah, *this cannot be viewed as anything but the eschatological resurrection from the dead.*

Wright argues convincingly that in Jesus' ministry, both in his actions and in his verbal teaching, he conveyed the message that, "Israel would return, humbled and redeemed: sins would be forgiven, the covenant renewed, the Temple rebuilt, the dead raised. What her god had done for her in the exodus–he would at last do again-and more gloriously. The story of the prodigal son says, quite simply: this hope is now being fulfilled–but it does not look like what was expected. ...But this is a highly subversive retelling. The real return from exile, including the real resurrection from the dead, is taking place, in an extremely paradoxical fashion, in Jesus' own ministry."[44]

It is strange to see Wright affirm that in Christ's ministry the promised resurrection was already taking place and then to read him claim that the Old Testament promises of the resurrection involved the raising of biologically dead bodies.[45] When Jesus affirmed, "The hour is coming, and now is, when the dead shall hear the voice of the Son of Man, and live" (John 5:24f) this cannot be construed to be a statement that the raising of the physically dead was underway.[46]

As already noted, the context of Daniel 9 is the exile in Babylon. Daniel understood that Judah was in exile as a result of her sin. His prayer, a *Rib Todah* prayer,[47] called on Yahweh to remember His covenant with Israel, to fulfill His covenant promises, and restore the people. It is important to see that Daniel was not simply concerned with Judah. He was focused on the restoration of those taken in the Assyrian captivity as well (Daniel 9:7– "All Israel."). This theme of the restoration of all twelve tribes, is clearly a "kingdom prophecy."

Remember that Daniel and Ezekiel were contemporaries. Daniel foretold the restoration of Israel at the end of the seventy weeks, when the kingdom would be established. Ezekiel foretold the resurrection of Israel when Jehovah poured out the Spirit, under the

Messiah, when the New Covenant was established, and God dwelt among His people in the New Tabernacle (Ezekiel 37:22-28).

To state it another way, what Daniel foretold as the ultimate end of Israel's exile, was, in the words of Ezekiel, *the resurrection.* This relationship between the salvation of Israel at the ultimate return from exile, *and the resurrection,* is found in numerous other resurrection prophecies. *This fact is critical for understanding the New Testament doctrine of resurrection.* Yet, most commentators either do not see the relationship, they ignore it, or, even in the case of those who see it, misconstrue the nature of the resurrection being predicted.[48]

In fact, there is an inseparable bond between the promises of Israel's salvation through restoration and the resurrection.

In Isaiah 25-27, we find a major discourse on Israel's last days and ultimate salvation. Space will not allow a full exegesis, but some of the more salient points are as follows.

➡ Israel's judgment for covenant violation (24:1-10).

➡ The promise of God ruling on Zion (24:19f; 25:6f).

➡ The Messianic Banquet (25:6f).

➡ The resurrection (25:8– the ground for Paul's discourse in Corinthians).

➡ The time of Israel's salvation (25:9) at the coming of the Lord to avenge the blood shed on the earth (26:19-21).

➡ The restoration of Israel when the great trumpet would be blown to gather the dispersed (27:6-13; Cf. Matthew 24:31).

So, like Daniel, Isaiah foretold the ultimate restoration of Israel and couched it in resurrection terminology.

Likewise, Hosea 13 foretold the restoration of Israel after her "death"[49] (v. 1-2). Hosea foretold the time when Jehovah would be Israel's king once again (v. 9-10) when Jehovah destroyed the power of the grave (v. 14f). Verse 14 is the second of the verses utilized by Paul for his discourse on the resurrection in 1 Corinthians 15.

Several things are clear from these texts. The first is that they are Messianic. The second is that they predicted the restoration of all twelve tribes, just like Daniel 9. The third is that the death discussed in the *texts has nothing to do with biological death.* The fourth is that the resurrection in view is, therefore, the restoration to the fellowship of God through forgiveness, just like Daniel 9.

The other significant thing about the two passages just noted is that they are the key passages of appeal for Paul, in his *magnum opus* on the resurrection. This means that not only does Isaiah 25 and Hosea 13 lie behind 1 Corinthians 15, but Ezekiel 37 and Daniel 9 also serve as Paul's prophetic anticipation.

5.) The points above bring us to this: Daniel is about Israel's ultimate salvation. He was predicting forgiveness and return from exile. Daniel is parallel with other prophecies of Israel's ultimate salvation, i.e. Isaiah and Hosea. The prophecies of Isaiah and Hosea foretold Israel's resurrection from the dead, through restoration to fellowship with her God. Daniel 9 therefore, predicted the resurrection.

Isaiah and Hosea serve as the foundation of Paul's discourse on the "final" resurrection. Therefore, since Daniel is parallel with Isaiah and Hosea, this means that Daniel 9 also lies behind 1 Corinthians 15.

If Daniel 9 lies behind 1 Corinthians 15, this means that for Paul, *the seventy weeks were not fulfilled.* Furthermore, if the seventy weeks lie behind 1 Corinthians 15, then the seventy weeks had not been postponed, since Paul said, "Brethren, I tell you a mystery, we will not all sleep" (1 Corinthians 15:51). The climax of Paul's eschatology was near! Let me state my argument as succinctly as possible.

Daniel 9, Isaiah 25-27, and Hosea 13 all predicted the same time and event, the final salvation of Israel–the resurrection of the dead.

But, Daniel 9 would be fulfilled within the parameters of the seventy week countdown.

Therefore, Isaiah 25-27, and Hosea 13 would be fulfilled within the parameters of the seventy week countdown.

That leads to this:

Isaiah 25-27, and Hosea 13 being parallel with Daniel 9, would be fulfilled within the parameters of the seventy weeks of Daniel 9.

But, Isaiah 25-27, and Hosea 13 serve as the source of Paul's discourse on the resurrection in 1 Corinthians 15.

Therefore, Paul's discourse on the resurrection in 1 Corinthians 15 would be fulfilled within the parameters of the seventy week countdown.

As we will see later, virtually all amillennialists and postmillennialists affirm the past fulfillment of the seventy week countdown of Daniel 9. But you cannot affirm the past fulfillment of Daniel 9 without thereby affirming the past fulfillment of 1 Corinthians 15 and the resurrection.

Daniel 9, Isaiah 24-27 and Hosea 13 all foretold the same time and events.

This means that Isaiah and Hosea would be fulfilled within the seventy weeks of Daniel 9.

But when Paul wrote 1 Corinthians 15, he was expecting the fulfillment of Isaiah and Hosea, in his generation.

Therefore, the seventy weeks had not yet been fulfilled and had not been postponed!

Allow me now to correlate this concept of the salvation of Israel, Daniel 9 and the resurrection, with 1 Corinthians 15.

Clearly, Paul was anticipating the resurrection in fulfillment of Isaiah 25:8, "When mortal has put on immortality...then shall be brought to pass the saying, 'Death is swallowed up in victory'" (1 Corinthians 15:54f).

Note now, Isaiah 25:9,

"It will be said in that day (the day of resurrection, the Messianic Banquet, on Mt. Zion, etc. v. 6-8), 'Behold, this is our God; we have waited for Him, and He will save us. This is

41

the Lord; We have waited for Him; we will be glad and rejoice in His salvation."

In brief form, here are the points we want to see:

The resurrection of 1 Corinthians 15 would be in fulfillment of Isaiah 25:8f.

The resurrection of Isaiah 25:8f would be the time of Israel's salvation (Isaiah 25:8-9).

The time of Israel's salvation would be the coming of the Lord in judgment of Israel for shedding innocent blood (Isaiah 26:19f; 59:3-20).

The judgment of Israel for shedding innocent blood was in AD 70 (Matthew 23).

Therefore, the resurrection of 1 Corinthians 15 occurred at the judgment of Israel for shedding innocent blood, in AD 70.

Let me follow up on that with the following:

The resurrection of 1 Corinthians 15 would be in fulfillment of Isaiah 25:8f.

The resurrection of Isaiah 25:8f would be the time of Israel's salvation (Isaiah 25:8-9).

The time of Israel's salvation is confined to, and would be fulfilled at the time of the fulfillment of the seventy weeks of Daniel 9:24-27.

The seventy weeks of Daniel 9:24-27 would be consummated in the fall of Jerusalem in AD 70.
Therefore, the resurrection of 1 Corinthians 15–the time of Israel's salvation--would be fulfilled in the fall of Jerusalem in AD 70.

As is illustrated by this set of arguments, unless one grasps the Biblical connection between Israel's ultimate salvation, the return from exile, and the resurrection, Biblical eschatology will not be understood. It is because of the failure to keep Biblical eschatology within its proper framework, and context, i.e. God's promises to Israel and her last days, that confusion continues to reign in the discussion of the last days.

The amillennialists and postmillennialists, by and large have divorced all eschatology from its covenantal roots belonging to Israel. The premillennialists see the indivisible connection between Israel and the last days, yet, openly reject the emphatic declarations that Israel's last days had arrived in the first century. The result is rampant eschatological speculation about the end being near on the part of the millennialists, and in many, many cases, open apathy or disinterest on the part of the amillennialists and postmillennialists[50] due to the long delay in the fulfillment of God's eschatological schema.

Before summarizing and finalizing this section, I want to address some of the claims in regard to Daniel 9 found in *When Shall These Things Be*, and particularly the comments by Richard Pratt Jr.. Pratt's comments have to do with Judah's return from exile and Daniel's prophecy.

Pratt claims that the prophecy of the seventy weeks was actually given to inform Daniel that Jeremiah's prophecy of the return from Babylon had *failed* due to Judah's failure to repent, and so, "Gabriel said that the Exile had been extended from the seventy years to seventy weeks of years, or about 490 years. Because the people had refused to repent, God decided to multiply the length of the exile by seven....at a time when other prophets were speaking of the imminent fulfillment of eschatological expectations, Daniel learned that the eschaton had been postponed because of a lack of repentance." (*When*, 145)[51] We want to briefly note some of the many errors of these comments.

First, Pratt's argument makes Jeremiah a false prophet, just like the prophets of the "imminent fulfillment of eschatological expectations." Notice the conflict between Jeremiah and Hananiah, presumably one of the false prophets of the imminent eschatological fulfillment alluded to by Pratt. In Jeremiah 27-28, Hananiah responded to Jeremiah's prediction that the captivity

43

would be long, i.e. seventy years long (Jeremiah 29:10). Hananiah proclaimed, ostensibly as the voice of the Lord, that "within two full years, I will bring back to this place all the vessels of the Lord's house" (Jeremiah 28:3).

Jeremiah stated that whichever prophecy came true confirmed the prophet as the spokesman of God (Jeremiah 28:9). He then confronted Hananiah, telling him that if his prediction came true, that he, Jeremiah, was a false prophet. However, he issued a foreboding warning to Hananiah, "This year you shall die, because you have taught rebellion against the Lord" (Jeremiah 28:17). See also Jeremiah's similar conflict with Shemaiah in Jeremiah 29:24f.

Now, patently, Hananiah was proven to be a false prophet. Nebuchadnezzar was more powerful in two years and Jerusalem was in deep trouble. Hananiah died just as Jeremiah foretold (Jeremiah 28:16).

The failure of Hananiah's prophecy proved he was a false prophet. However, per Pratt, the failure of Jeremiah's prediction should not concern us and has no bearing on his prophetic status! Furthermore, the failure of fulfillment of Daniel 9 has no bearing on Daniel as a prophet either.

It should be more than obvious that had Jeremiah espoused Pratt's paradigm, Jeremiah could not have challenged or falsified Hananiah's prediction. Hananiah could have said, "Well, I predict that things will be better in two years, but if things don't work out that way, it is just because of historical contingencies that postponed fulfillment." In effect then, Pratt's view of prophecy mitigates any possibility of testing the prophets.

Second, Pratt unequivocally posits the *failure* of Jeremiah as a prophet. Jeremiah stated in no uncertain terms that Judah would return from Babylonian captivity after seventy years (Jeremiah 25:11f; 29:10f). After seventy years, Babylon would be destroyed and Judah would return home.

Pratt would undoubtedly rejoin that Jeremiah himself provides us with the definitive statement of the conditional nature of prophecy, in chapter 18. Simply stated, if the Lord spoke condemnation of a nation, and they repented, He would relent and not punish them. If, however, He spoke of good intentions toward a nation, but they became disobedient, then He would not bless them as promised. No one doubts this is true. However, *it is not applicable to Daniel 9!*

Pratt's paradigm poses an interesting situation. He suggests that due to Jewish unbelief Jeremiah's prophecy was postponed and Daniel was given another prophecy of the seventy weeks. When Jesus came, he said, "The time is fulfilled, the kingdom has drawn near" (Mark 1:15; Matthew 4:17). As Bruce notes, Jesus' proclamation would have indicated to his listeners that the time foretold by Daniel had arrived.[52]

So, both John the Immerser (Matthew 3:2) and Jesus claimed that the time for the kingdom, i.e. the consummation of Daniel's promises had drawn near. However, the Jews undeniably rejected Jesus' offer of the kingdom. So, as Pratt argues, "Even if the New Testament does predict an imminent return of Christ, intervening historical contingencies make it unnecessary that the imminent return take place." (*When*, 149).

In other words, just like Jeremiah's eschatological prophecy was postponed, the New Testament eschatological predictions were postponed as well. *We thus have a two-fold postponement of God's promises.* This naturally raises the question, how many times might man's rebelliousness and disobedience postpone the fulfillment of God's prophecies? After all, according to many Bible students, "evil men will wax worse and worse." (2 Timothy 3). So, if man gets worse and worse, and if man's sin prevents the fulfillment of God's promises, it stands to reason that God's eschatological promises can never be fulfilled.

Third, Daniel most assuredly believed that the time for the fulfillment of Jeremiah had arrived (Daniel 9:2) and Pratt concurs that it had: "he (Jeremiah, DKP) recognized that he lived in Jeremiah's seventieth year"(*When*, 144). Now, contra Pratt, the angel never said, "Judah has failed to repent, therefore, the prophecy of Jeremiah has been postponed." Pratt claims that in verses 13-14 Daniel acknowledges Judah's failure to repent. This simply is not true. Verses 13-14 are Daniel's confession of Judah's *past sins*, that led them to their current captivity. Daniel was not confessing that they were still in a state of rebellion.

As we have seen just above, Daniel offered a *Rib Todah* prayer on the behalf of the nation and that is a prayer of *confession and repentance, the very conditions necessary for return from exile.*

Notice that Daniel petitioned Jehovah "with fasting, sackcloth and ashes" (Daniel 9:3):

"and made confession...we have sinned and committed iniquity, we have done wickedly and rebelled, even by departing from Your precepts and Your judgments...O Lord, righteousness belongs to You, but to us shame of face as it is this day–to the men of Judah, to the inhabitants of Jerusalem and all Israel, those near and those far off in all the countries to which You have driven them, because of the unfaithfulness which they have committed against You. O Lord, to us belongs shame of face, to our kings, our princes, and our fathers, because we have sinned against You."

Undeniably, this is a prayer of *confession* and *repentance* on behalf of the entire nation. Daniel knew that there was no promise of return from exile if there was no repentance. However, in his prayer he was confessing Israel's sin and asking for the return from exile. This is *prima facie* evidence that Daniel fully expected the fulfillment of Jeremiah's promise, *not its postponement*.

Gabriel the angel was sent and told Daniel, "At the beginning of your supplications the command went out, and I have now come to tell you that you are greatly beloved; therefore consider the matter and understand the vision." (Daniel 9:23). If we accept Pratt's claims, it means that in direct response to *a prayer of confession and repentance*, Gabriel told Daniel that Jeremiah's prophecy of Judah's return from captivity had *failed*, because of a failure to *confess and repent*. In truth, Judah was about to return. And in addition to that predicted and promised return, Gabriel now shared with Daniel the prophecy of Israel's true, ultimate return, the time of her salvation in the Messianic kingdom.

Fourth, *Judah did return from exile*, as stated in Ezra 1:

"Now in the first year of Cyrus king of Persia, that the word of the LORD by the mouth of Jeremiah might be fulfilled, the LORD stirred up the spirit of Cyrus king of Persia, so that he made a proclamation throughout all his kingdom, and also put it in writing, saying, 'Thus says Cyrus king of Persia: All the kingdoms of the earth the LORD God of heaven has given me. And He has commanded me to build Him a house at Jerusalem which is in Judah.'"

46

So, Pratt's claim that Daniel was informed that Jeremiah's prophecy had failed, due to Judah's failure to repent, flies in the face of inspired scripture. There could hardly be a more emphatic denial of Pratt's claims. He says Daniel was told that Jeremiah's prophecy was being postponed, yet, Ezra says that God stirred up the heart of Cyrus "that the word of Jeremiah might be fulfilled."[53]

Pratt argues "The imminent eschatological expectation of Jeremiah had been realized in part, but it had also been delayed." (*When*, 146). One can only wonder at such a statement.

If repentance and obedience were the prerequisites for the fulfillment of prophecy, then if Jeremiah's prophecy was partially fulfilled does this not indicate that Judah had repented, at least partially? Just how much repentance had to take place for fulfillment? If God could recognize that Judah had repented sufficiently for Him to fulfill the prophecy of Jeremiah, then perhaps Pratt could help us to understand how much more repentance was needed for a full return? Ezra 1 tells us that *Cyrus, through God's motivation, authorized a full and complete return.* Does this not demand that the conditions had indeed been met?

It is significant that in *When,* Mathison concurs with Pratt's claim that Jeremiah's prophecy failed:

"It should be noted that the precursor to Daniel 9:24-27 is Jeremiah 25:11-12 and 29:10. Jeremiah provided a specific time text (seventy years; cf. Daniel 9:2) that is extended sevenfold in Daniel 9:24-27 because of Israel's failure to repent. In other words, Jeremiah provided a specific time text that was greatly extended in Daniel." (*When*, 164). This is more than a little remarkable.

It is not coincidental that Mathison avoids using the word "postponement" for the "re-calculation" if you will, of Jeremiah's prophecy. Whereas Pratt unabashedly avers that Jeremiah's prophecy failed and was postponed, Mathison avoids the term, in favor of "extended." And why is this? It is because Mathison, on virtually all other occasions, at least when not addressing preterism, condemns the idea of failed or postponed prophecy.

You have to know that Mathison, and Gentry, have been, and we can only assume still are (although one has a right to wonder) adamantly opposed to the millennial view of a gap of 2000 years between the 69th and 70th Week of Daniel 9:24-27.

Dispensationalist Thomas Ice, whom Gentry has debated, maintains that there is a gap of so far 2000 years between the 69th and 70th Week of Daniel. Without that gap, dispensationalism ceases to exist, per Ice.[54] And what created that gap? Ice says: "I believe the scriptures teach that Israel could have obtained her much sought after messianic kingdom by recognizing Jesus as the Messiah. We all know the sad reality, the Jews rejected Jesus. As a result the kingdom is no longer near but postponed, awaiting Jewish belief, which will occur at the end of the Tribulation."[55]

In another work dedicated to the refutation of preterism, Ice asserts that the Second Coming of Christ is contingent upon Jewish faith. Since, "that nation refused Him, it became impossible to establish the kingdom."[56] In other words, to use the words of Pratt, "The historical contingency of human choice can (and did, DKP) make a difference in the way God fulfills a prophecy." To put it yet another way, God postponed the kingdom due to Israel's rejection of Jesus.

Does Mathison, and the wider postmillennial community, agree with the millennial gap theory? Does he believe that Israel's rejection of Jesus postponed the kingdom and made a difference in the way God fulfilled, *or did not* fulfill prophecy? As we have just seen, Mathison agrees that Jeremiah's prophecy of the seventy years failed and was therefore "extended." Also, in *When*, (181, n. 36) he says that Jesus' predictions about his coming should possibly be seen in the light of Pratt's explanation, so, perhaps he *does* ascribe to the gap/postponement theory!

However, if Mathison does believe what Pratt says, his earlier writings do not suggest it. In an earlier book, Mathison discusses the millennial contention of whether the Jewish rejection of Jesus caused a postponed kingdom: "If God intended that Christ establish an earthly Jewish kingdom, and Satan prevented that, then Satan defeated God. But Satan never defeats God. Had Christ come to establish an earthly Jewish kingdom, all the forces of heaven and hell combined could not have stopped God from accomplishing that purpose. The plans of God cannot be thwarted by man or Satan."[57]

Gentry, commenting on the millennial gap theory, says: "It is only by hermeneutic gymnastics and a suspension of reason that a massive gap may be imported into Daniel in order to interrupt the otherwise chronologically exact time-frame."[58] Boettner wrote concerning the dispensational view that man's rebellion can alter God's prophetic plan: "The idea that unregenerate man can frustrate the purposes of God is so contrary to clear Scripture teaching and to all right ideas of God that it is almost unbelievable that it could seriously be put forth by any who claim to be students of the Word."[59] Obviously, the concept is not so "unbelievable" that it prevented Mathison from including–and endorsing--that possibility in *When Shall These Things Be?*.

Which Mathison do we believe? Do we believe the Mathison that ascribes to Pratt's view of the *failure and postponement of prophecy*, or do we believe the Mathison that affirms that neither man nor Satan can cause God to change His plans? This is quite a conundrum for Mathison. It seems sadly true that Mathison is arguing out of both sides of his keyboard. When arguing against Covenant Eschatology he is willing to make dispensational arguments. When arguing against the dispensationalists, he is willing to make preterist arguments. Which position does he *really* believe?

Mathison is arguing out of both sides of his keyboard. When arguing against Covenant Eschatology he is willing to make dispensational arguments. When arguing against the dispensationalists, he makes preterist arguments. Which position does he *really* believe?

This contradiction between Pratt and Mathison's views is no small issue. Everyone understands that scholars and Bible students differ on some issues. That is not the point. Some differences are minor, some are major. We are dealing here with an issue that strikes at the very heart of hermeneutics, at the very idea of the Sovereignty of God. It strikes at the very nature of prophecy itself.

If Pratt's contention is true, *Mathison's objections to millennialism fall to the ground.* Indeed, if Pratt's contention is true, Strimple's chapter on the resurrection in *When*, is negated, for if prophecy does not have to be fulfilled in the *manner* foretold, and *when* it was predicted, then, even if the Bible did predict the raising of physical corpses out of the grave at the end of time, the Lord could have altered that promise so that resurrection is actually a spiritual resurrection that did occur in AD 70! (Of course, we also cannot help but wonder if Mathison agrees with Strimple that prophecy does not have to be fulfilled in the time or the manner foretold).

On the other hand, if Mathison's claims contra the postponement doctrine are true, then Pratt's entire chapter is negated. If Mathison, Gentry, et. al. are right to affirm that man's disobedience could never alter or negate God's Sovereign intent,[60] then surely, Pratt's contention that, "even if the Scriptures did predict that Jesus' return would take place within a few years, his return could still be in our future, even two thousand years later" (*When*, 122) is totally nullified and refuted. This is no minor problem in the pages of *When*. It is a *critical* issue.

When Peter, in Acts 2, cited by Pratt, affirmed that the outpouring of the Spirit was the fulfillment of God's promises for the last days restoration of Israel, had Israel repented at that time? Patently not! How then could God fulfill part of the promise? Pratt argues that Acts 2 was partial fulfillment, but that in Acts 3 Peter said the parousia was dependent on Israel's repentance, and that later, in 2 Peter 3, the apostle had come to grips with the reality of a postponed parousia. (*When*, 150f).[61]

The reality of the situation is that, while Israel as a whole did not obey, *the remnant did*. According to Paul, writing at a time when the parousia was supposedly now delayed, the remnant was entering into the promises made to Israel (Romans 11:7f). God's promises to Israel were not being delayed or postponed. They were being *fulfilled* in Christ and the church.

It was in full light of Israel's national rejection of the gospel that Paul affirmed the nearness of the end (Romans 8:18f; 13:11f; 16:20).[62] He did this, fully cognizant we can be sure, of what happened in Jesus' ministry when he sent out the seventy to preach, "The kingdom of heaven has drawn near" (Luke 10:9). Jesus *knew* that his disciples would be rejected. However, in spite of that rejection, they were to proclaim, "Nevertheless know this, that the kingdom of God has come near to you" (Luke 10:11).

That word "*nevertheless*" is a falsification of Pratt's paradigm. It says that in spite of Israel's rejection, God was going to fulfill

His word. It echoes Psalms 2 and God's statement that in spite of Israel's rejection of His Messiah, that He would laugh at them and enthrone His king anyway.

> The failure to see the Jewish rejection, and subsequent judgment, *as part of God's plan all along*, leads directly to a belief in a postponed and failed eschatology. Judah's unbelief did not postpone God's purposes, it brought that plan to its fulfillment.

Pratt, like so many others, sees the Jewish unbelief as a barrier to fulfillment. This is lamentable. What many Bible students fail to realize is that the Jewish rejection and subsequent judgment, was always, in prophecy, *part of the plan*. While it is often claimed that Israel failed to receive her promises due to her unbelief, God had always foreseen this situation, predicted it. It was *through that unbelief* that He was justified in bringing the old shadow world to its end through judgment, while revealing the spiritual body of Christ. Thus, Jewish rejection of Christ did not postpone the parousia, it was *necessary for these things to happen*!

Pratt's attempt to negate Covenant Eschatology fails, badly, for it posits the repeated postponement and failure of God's prophets. While we cannot develop the thought, his view negates any possibility of "testing the prophets" for, per Pratt, if a prophet's predictions did not come to pass, he could very quickly claim "mitigating circumstances." Jeremiah rejected this approach, insisting that it was fulfillment of the predicted word that verified prophetic standing (Jeremiah 28:9f).

What we have seen then is that the prediction of Daniel 9 was not to be postponed into an indeterminate, unknown future subject to repeated postponements. Daniel was told "seventy weeks are determined" and this means that God would fulfill His word, in spite of, and in full foreknowledge of Judah's rejection of His Messiah. After all, the death of Messiah was part of the countdown and it is impossible to believe that if Jehovah knew of the rejection of His Son, that He had to postpone His eschatological plans when that predicted rejection took place!

51

Summary of This Section.

In this section we have demonstrated that the theme of the removal of sin is positively linked with the idea of the resurrection, both in the Old Testament and the New.

We have shown that the putting away of sin is tied inextricably to the parousia of Christ and the end of Israel's Old Covenant age.

We have proven that the idea of the removal of sin is tied directly to the arrival of the New Covenant promised in so many places in the Old Testament. Therefore, the arrival of the New Covenant and the arrival of the resurrection are, at the very least, synchronous events, and at most, synonymous events.

We have shown that the New Testament writers were eagerly awaiting and expecting the consummation of the hopes of Israel with the arrival of the end of the "ministration of death," and the bringing in of "the ministration of life."

We have shown Daniel 9 is parallel with the other Old Testament prophecies of the resurrection, but that the other resurrection prophecies are concerned with the return of Israel from sin exile.

We have proven that since Daniel 9 is parallel with the verses that serve as the basis of Paul's resurrection discourse in 1 Corinthians 15, that this means that the seventy weeks of Daniel 9 could not have been fulfilled as maintained by the amillennial and postmillennial paradigms. However, this also proves that the seventy weeks had not been postponed as affirmed by the millennialists, since Paul stated unequivocally that not all of the Corinthians would die before the occurrence of the resurrection.

The concept of the putting away of sin, therefore, as promised by Daniel 9, is an referent to the resurrection. It delimits the resurrection to the first century. It links that event with the consummation of Israel's covenant history. It effectively demands that the resurrection occurred with the AD 70 destruction of Jerusalem with "an overwhelming flood."

The only way to counter our argument in this section is to divorce the putting away of sin motif in the New Testament from the promise of Daniel 9. This cannot be done since the New Testament writers affirm repeatedly that their eschatological hope was nothing but the hope of Israel.

To falsify our argument one would have to prove that Daniel's prophecy predicted something totally different from the prophecies of Isaiah 24-27, Hosea 13 and Ezekiel 37. Yet, the motifs and themes of all these texts are identical.

Since these things cannot be proven, our premise stands that Daniel 9 foretold the resurrection from the dead. And that means that the resurrection of the dead had to have occurred at the end of the Old Covenant age of Israel that transpired with the destruction of Jerusalem in AD 70.

SEVENTY WEEKS ARE DETERMINED...
TO MAKE AN ATONEMENT FOR SIN

There is no disagreement, in conservative commentaries, that this promise in Daniel 9 is referent to the atoning work of Jesus Christ. The tragedy is that the great majority of commentaries stop the atoning process at the Cross, whereas Scripture posits the consummation of the atonement at the parousia of Christ. Gentry says of the promise to make an atonement for sin, "It clearly speaks of Christ's atoning death, which is the ultimate atonement to which all the temple rituals looked (Hebrews 9:26). This also occurred during his earthly ministry-at his death." (*Dominion*, 315). Mathison likewise argues: "This was fulfilled in Christ's atoning death." (*Hope*, 221)

Gentry is correct to say that Christ's atoning death is what all the temple rituals anticipated and foreshadowed. Furthermore, *Christ's high priestly function*, in offering himself as a sacrifice, is also pointed to by those Old Covenant rituals. It is here that the partial preterists and all futurists abandon the text.

Notice the chart that shows the direct type/anti-type relationship between Jesus in his High Priestly service and that of the Old Covenant High Priest on the Day of Atonement.

OT HIGH PRIEST ON DAY OF ATONEMENT	CHRIST, HIGH PRIEST TO MAKE ATONEMENT
PRIEST KILLED THE SACRIFICE	CHRIST APPEARED TO "PUT AWAY SIN" BY HIS SACRIFICE (26)
PRIEST ENTERED THE MOST HOLY PLACE	"CHRIST ENTERED THE HOLY PLACE" (24)
RETURN OF HIGH PRIEST FROM MHP FINISHED ATONEMENT & DECLARED SALVATION	TO THOSE WHO EAGERLY LOOK FOR HIM, HE SHALL APPEAR A SECOND TIME, FOR SALVATION (28)

It will be noted that after describing these actions by Christ, so perfectly picturing the Old Covenant Day of Atonement, that the writer of Hebrews says Christ would appear a second time... *"for* the law, having a shadow of good things to come, can never by those sacrifices which they make year by year continually, perfect" (Hebrews 10:1). In other words, the Old Law and its typological functions were a shadow, and Christ in his High Priestly function was the fulfillment. Just as the High Priest killed the sacrifice, entered the Most Holy Place and came back out, Jesus offered himself, entered the Most Holy Place, and was set to appear "a second time, for salvation" *for*, the law was a shadow of good things about to come. It was necessary for the fulfillment of the Old Covenantal liturgical cultus that Christ fulfill *every aspect* of the High Priest's Atoning function and that included the coming out of the Most Holy Place to declare the atonement accepted. Simply stated, if the High Priest did not come back out of the Most Holy Place *there was no atonement.*

However, virtually all futurist paradigms say the atonement was finished *at the Cross*. This in spite of the fact that Christ's Priestly function *demanded* that he *enter* the Most Holy Place, just as the Old Covenant High Priest had to enter the MHP.

Was the atonement completed before Christ even offered his blood in the Most Holy Place? Hebrews 9:24 says he entered there to appear "in the Presence of God for us." Just like the High Priest under the Old Covenant had to enter the Most Holy to appear in the Presence of God on the behalf of Israel and offer the sacrifice, Jesus had entered the Most Holy Place there to offer his blood.

The idea that the atonement was finished at the Cross also overlooks the fact that, just like the Old Covenant High Priest, Jesus had to return from the Most Holy Place before the atonement was finished. This leads to the following argument:

The atonement work of Christ would be perfected and consummated at his "Second Coming" (Hebrews 9:28).

But the Second Coming is the time of the resurrection of the dead (1 Corinthians 15).

Therefore, the atonement work of Christ would be perfected and consummated at the resurrection of the dead.
The atonement work of Christ would be perfected at the resurrection of the dead.

But the seventy weeks were determined to make the atonement (Daniel 9:24).

Therefore, the resurrection of the dead, at the perfection of the atonement work of Jesus, would occur within, or by the end of, the seventy weeks.

We should be reminded that, "On the basis of the Hebrew verb, the passage (Daniel 9:24, DKP) clearly speaks of the actual making of reconciliation (or atonement). (*Dominion*, 351). Thus, since Christ's parousia was the crowning act in the atonement process, one cannot say as Gentry and others do, that the atonement was perfected at the Cross prior to the parousia. This short-cuts the typological fulfillment of Christ's High Priestly function and violates Hebrews 9.

Unless one can prove definitively that the atonement was unrelated to the coming of the High Priest out of the Most Holy Place, then it is *prima facie* proof that the atonement was not completed until that "return." But if the atonement was not completed until the High Priest came out of the Most Holy Place,[63] then this is indisputable proof that the parousia, to complete the atonement, is confined to the seventy weeks of Daniel 9:24. Since the "Second Coming" is the time of the resurrection, the resurrection must have occurred by the end of the seventy weeks of Daniel 9.

Take note again that Gentry, DeMar and others argue that the seventy weeks actually ended circa 35 AD while the destruction of Jerusalem was only "determined" within the Heptads. However, the atonement refutes that idea.

The atonement would not be complete until the coming of the High Priest out of the Most Holy Place (Hebrews 9:28). The atonement belongs, *totally*, to the seventy weeks. You cannot have the atonement *initiated* within the Heptads, and then *consummated* outside those parameters, without denying the text of Daniel 9. However, since the coming of the High Priest was still in the future from Hebrews 9–yet was coming in "a very, very little while" (10:37)– this means that the seventy weeks had not been consummated years before. And, since the coming of Christ out of the Most Holy is set within the context of the imminent judgment of Israel (Hebrews 10:26-37) this means that the resurrection, the consummation of the atonement and the seventy weeks, was to occur in that judgment.

The only way to negate this argument is to argue:

1.) That the making of atonement is unrelated to the "final coming" of Christ at the time of the resurrection. Yet, Hebrews 9 posits the "Second Coming" which is universally posited as the time of the resurrection, as the time when the atonement would be perfected. Atonement was not finished without the return of the High Priest. That would be a violation of the type/anti-type *imagery* and the *text* of Hebrews 9.

2.) That the atonement was made within the seventy weeks, but that it would/will be *applied* at the parousia. This is the millennial view that partial preterists deny. The problem is that there is no textual justification for this argument in the text of Daniel.

One caveat here. It is certainly true that the application of atonement is inextricably linked with the consummation of the atonement process. No *application* without *consummation*. So, in that sense, the application would come at the parousia. Yet, it cannot be argued that the perfection of the atonement was accomplished before the very act of perfecting the atonement i.e. the parousia, was in fact completed.

The fact that there could be no application of the atonement

> **If forgiveness in Christ is objectively real today, then *the atonement is completed*. Forgiveness is the direct result of the completed atonement. But if the atonement is complete, Christ has returned, the resurrection has occurred!**

---

until the atonement was consummated has incredible implications. Do we, today, have the true forgiveness of sin? If so, *then the atonement is applied.* Forgiveness is the application of the *completed atonement*! So, if the atonement blessings are *applied*, then *the atonement is perfected*. This means that *Christ has come out of the Most Holy Place!* If Christ has not come, then the atonement process is not completed. But if the atonement is not completed there is no forgiveness of sin today!

3.) That the making of the atonement in Daniel 9 is unrelated to the high priestly atonement work of Jesus in Hebrews 9. Yet it is from the typological Old Covenant world of Daniel's promise of the atonement that the Hebrew writer makes his argument about Christ's Atoning work.

The Hebrew writer is writing about the consummation of the atonement work of Christ. This is indisputable. The atoning work of Christ is the atonement promised by Daniel. Therefore, the consummation of Christ's atonement work in Hebrews 9 is confined to the seventy weeks of Daniel 9. But the consummation of Christ's atonement work is the Second Coming, i.e. the time of the resurrection. Therefore, the resurrection is confined to the seventy weeks of Daniel 9.

The bottom line is, where ever you posit the consummated work of Christ's atonement it is there you place the finishing of the seventy weeks of Daniel 9. And, where ever you place the consummation of Christ's atonement work it is *there* that you place resurrection. If the resurrection has not occurred *the seventy weeks are not yet fulfilled*. If the seventy weeks are fulfilled, meaning Christ's atonement work is perfected, then resurrection has occurred.

It is interesting to note the common beliefs of the evangelical world in this regard. In formal debates, I have asked my opponents the following question: "When the faithful child of God dies physically today, where do they go? Do they go directly to heaven, or into the Hadean realm to await judgment and the parousia?" My amillennial opponents very often answer, "They go to Hades and Abraham's bosom, to await the judgment and resurrection."[64] Other opponents, affirm, "They go directly to heaven to be with the Lord." These answers, both of them, reveal a disturbing failure to deal with Hebrews 9, Daniel 9, and the Biblical doctrine of the atonement. We can only deal with this ever so briefly but there are two major problems in the respective answers.

First, if, when the faithful child of God dies physically today, they go into the Hadean realm, Abraham's bosom, but not heaven itself, then patently, according to Hebrews, the Old Covenant remains valid and binding today.

Notice that the writer affirms that as long as that cultus had standing,[65] that man could not enter the Most Holy Place. This is incredibly significant for those who believe that today, the faithful child of God cannot and does not enter the presence of God in heaven. Here is the argument in simple form:

As long as the Old Mosaic Covenant stood valid and binding, no man could enter the Most Holy Place, i.e. the presence of God and heaven (Hebrews 9:6-10).

But today, no man may enter the Most Holy Place, i.e. the presence of God and heaven, when they die, instead, having to go to the Hadean world of Abraham's bosom when they die, to await judgment and the resurrection. (amillennialism)

Therefore, it must be true that the Old Mosaic Covenant stands valid and binding today.

Since the writer of Hebrews affirms unequivocally that it was the Mosaic Covenant and its cultus that stood between man and God, between man and the Most Holy Place, then it is undeniably true that if the child of God cannot and does not enter the Most Holy Place, *then the Mosaic Covenant and its cultus remains valid and a barrier between man and God.*

Why is this true? It is true because as the writer affirms, that Old Cultus could never make the worshipper perfect; it could never take away sin (Hebrews 9:11f; 1:1-4). It is sin that separates man from God. It is sin that *kills* (Romans 6:23). So, consider this.

What is the one thing that has always separated man from God? Is it not sin? Read Isaiah 59:1f. So, sin is what separates man from God, that always prevented man from entering the presence of God even under the Torah, because the Law could not give life and righteousness. It could never take away sin. Without forgiveness, man could not enter the Most Holy, the presence of God.

If you ask those who believe that the faithful child of God goes to Abraham's bosom in Hades upon death, whether they are *truly forgiven* by the blood of Christ, (i.e. whether they have received the benefits of the Atoning work of Christ) they will zealously affirm, "Yes!" The question must therefore be asked, "If the child of God is *forgiven*, having received the benefits of the atonement, then since sin is the one thing, *the only thing*, that keeps man out of the presence of God, why is it that when they die, forgiven in Christ, that they still cannot go to the Most Holy Place? Are they, after all, *not forgiven*? Do they believe that they have not in fact received the benefits of the atonement because deep down, they do not believe that the atonement is completed?

> **YOU CANNOT, CONSISTENTLY AND BIBLICALLY, CLAIM THAT FORGIVENESS IS A CURRENT REALITY AND DENY THAT THE PAROUSIA HAS OCCURRED!**

Likewise, you cannot, consistently and Biblically, claim that forgiveness is a current reality and deny that the parousia has occurred! This is a fundamentally important issue that has seemingly escaped the majority of most believers. The question has to be asked, at what point in time was forgiveness a reality in the atonement process. Just like the question concerning the atonement and when it was completed, the question of forgiveness is indivisibly connected with the atonement. So, if the atonement was not considered perfected until the return of the High Priest out of the MHP, then likewise, forgiveness did not become a reality until his return either. This is where the conundrum for modern believers comes in.

How is it possible to affirm the current reality of the forgiveness of sin, as most believers do, and at the same time claim that Christ has not returned to complete the atonement? Expressed simply and succinctly, here is the argument.

Forgiveness of sin would become a reality as the direct result of the completed atonement when the High Priest (Jesus) came from the MHP.

But, forgiveness of sin is a reality today (affirmed by most believers today.)

Therefore, it must be true that Christ has come out of the MHP.

The question of course is, how the majority of Christian believers can affirm *the present reality of forgiveness*, and yet deny that Christ has consummated the atonement process through his parousia. This is a *huge* issue!

The bottom line is that you cannot, consistently and logically, affirm that forgiveness is a reality now, in Christ, and yet affirm that the believer does not enter the Most Holy Place. You cannot affirm the reality of forgiveness and deny the reality of the parousia. You cannot affirm that the faithful child of God must go to Hades and await judgment, without thereby affirming that the Mosaic Covenant, with its animal sacrifices, remains valid and binding today.

On the other hand, what does it mean to affirm that the faithful child of God does enter the Most Holy when they die? Well, it certainly means that the atonement is completed, that man is genuinely forgiven and that there is nothing to keep man from the presence of God. It affirms that everything that the old world symbolized and prophesied has now become a reality. The High Priest's work is finished. The atonement is finished and man can now enter into its benefits.

However, if the atonement is completed and man can enter the Most Holy Place, then this demands that Christ's coming, the second time, "apart from sin, for salvation" has occurred. Remember, the atonement was not completed until the High Priest came out of the MHP and signified the acceptance of the atonement sacrifice.

To help see the relationship between the end of the Old Covenant age, the consummation of the atonement and the

61

relationship with the end of the seventy weeks of Daniel, we need to take a closer look at the idea of entering the Most Holy Place..

As we have seen, in Hebrews 9, the writer posits access and entrance into the Most Holy Place at the end of the Mosaic world, when all that it typified and foreshadowed was fulfilled, i.e. at the time of reformation.[66] So, the time when all that the Old Covenant anticipated, the realization of Israel's eschatological and soteriological hopes, would be when the system that stood only in animal sacrifices, carnal washings and ordinances, *reached its terminus through fulfillment.* In other words, the time of reformation--when man could enter the MHP--would come at the end of the Mosaic covenant world! This is not the only time we find this motif.

In Luke 21, Jesus predicted the fall of Jerusalem (v.7f). He tells the disciples that when they see Jerusalem surrounded they are to know that her desolation is nigh (v. 20-24). He describes the fall of Jerusalem, "These be the days of vengeance, in which all things that are written must be fulfilled" (v. 22). Jerusalem's fall would be the consummation of God's vengeance. Furthermore, in the events of those days, they were to "look up, for your redemption draws nigh," and to know that the kingdom of heaven had drawn near (Luke 21:28-31). Thus, in the destruction of the temple and the removal of the cultus the saints were to see *the fulfillment of all things that are written,* the coming of their *redemption* and the arrival of the *kingdom!*

Note also that in Revelation 15, John sees a vision of the temple in heaven. Remarkably, the veil is gone and *the Most Holy Place is open* (Revelation 11:19; 15:8)! This signified that man could now approach God—but there was a problem. No man could actually enter the Most Holy Place until, "the seven plagues of the seven angels were completed" (15:8). Man could not enter the Most Holy Place until the wrath of God was consummated. God's wrath would be completed *when judgment fell on Babylon* (Revelation 16:17f). Therefore, access to God would be opened when God's vengeance was completed against Babylon.

We cannot develop this at length here, but suffice it to say that Babylon of Revelation was none other than Old Covenant Jerusalem.[67] It is the great city where the Lord was slain (Revelation 11:8), the city that killed the prophets (16:6f) and the city guilty of shedding the blood of the apostles and prophets (18:20-24) and all the blood shed on the earth. Compare Jesus' words in Luke 11:49f and Luke 13:33f.

So, here is what have in Revelation.

John saw the Most Holy Place open, but no man could enter until God's wrath was completed in the outpouring of the Seventh Vial.

But, God's wrath would be finished in the outpouring of wrath *against Babylon* (Revelation 16:17f).

Babylon was Old Covenant Jerusalem.

Therefore, entrance into the Most Holy Place would be opened when God's wrath was completed in the judgment of Old Covenant Jerusalem.

The chart will help visualize the comparison of Luke 21, Hebrews and Revelation and the concept of entering the MHP.

Luke 21	Hebrews 9-10	Revelation 15-19
Fall of Jerusalem (v. 20f)	End of Old Covenant system (v. 6)	Judgment on Babylon (16:7f) (Jerusalem)
Days of Vengeance fulfilled (v.22)	Time of Vengeance (10:26-37)	Completion of God's Wrath (15:8; 16:17f)
Coming of Redemption, Kingdom (v. 28, 32)	Entrance into Most Holy Place (9:6f)	Entrance into Most Holy Place (15:1, 8)
At Coming of the Lord (v.26f)	At Coming of the Lord (10:37)	At Coming of the Lord (chapter 19)

In Jesus' generation (v.32)	In a very, very little while (10:37)	"Behold I come quickly" (22:12, 20)

In Luke the judgment against Jerusalem would fulfill God's vengeance and bring redemption. Hebrews (10:26-37) depicts the removal of the Old Covenant system (at the time of Christ's coming in judgment) as opening the way to the Most Holy Place. In Revelation, God's wrath is consummated in the judgment against *Babylon* resulting in access to the Most Holy Place! The parallels positively demonstrate that the time when entrance into the Most Holy Place would be opened was at the end of the Mosaic Covenant world with the removal of the City and the Temple.

Daniel 9 said, "seventy weeks are determined for your people and for your holy city," and the end of that vision would bring the atonement, the putting away of sin and the arrival of everlasting righteousness. It would bring in the realization of the hopes of Israel. But the end thereof would be with an overwhelming flood. The arrival of the new world of righteousness would signal the end of the old world of sin, death and futility. Or, as Eusebius stated it, "It is quite clear that the seven times seventy weeks...was therefore the period determined for Daniel's people, which limited the total length of the Jewish nation's existence."[68]

Unless Luke, Hebrews and Revelation were anticipating the arrival of a totally different salvation in fulfillment of Israel's promises, then we must see that their referent to "the time of reformation," the time of redemption and the kingdom (Luke 21) and the time when man could enter the Most Holy Place (Revelation) as the same identical time. All three of them posit the arrival of these blessings at the parousia of Christ as the chart shows. Those blessings would arrive at the time of the parousia– *and thus the resurrection.*

So, if they were in fact anticipating the fulfillment of Daniel's prophecy, that meant that Daniel's seventy weeks were not completed previously, but that they would be filled up at the cataclysmic removal of the cultus that had stood as a barrier to man for 1500 years. And, this means, without doubt, that the parousia and resurrection belong inseparably to the coming of Christ at the end of the seventy weeks of Daniel 9, when Christ came and brought that old system to an end in the "overwhelming flood" of destruction in A.D.70.

Finally, the millennialists have a severe problem in regard to their fundamentally important gap theory, the making of the atonement and the death of Jesus. There is no question that Daniel was told "seventy weeks are determined, to make atonement for sin." As we have seen, this involves not the subjective appropriation of the atonement, but the objective process of making the atonement. Boutflower well notes that the Hebrew word that is translated here in Daniel 9, is the identical word, "that occurs so frequently in the Book of Leviticus." (*Daniel*, 183). His point is that the making of atonement does not refer to an event divorced from *the process of atonement*. It is in fact *the process of making the atonement* that is the focus. In other words, it involved Christ fulfilling the typological high priestly atonement practices. That means his death, the offering of his blood in the MHP *and his parousia*. But this is where the difficulty comes in.

The millennialists tell us that the death of Jesus does not belong to the seventy weeks of Daniel 9. They point out, correctly so, that the death of Jesus would be after the 69th week. While that would *seem* to demand that his death occurred in the pivotal 70th week, it is insisted that the death of *Jesus actually postponed the prophetic countdown*! Thus, Jesus' death, *which is for the atonement*, does not, per the millennialists, belong to the seventy weeks at all! Exactly how *the atoning death of Jesus* does not actually belong to the seventy week countdown the millennialists do not explain. Indeed, some even argue that the words "make reconciliation for iniquity," "seems to be a rather clear picture of the cross of Christ in which Christ reconciled Israel as well as the world to himself (2 Cor. 5:19)."[69] However, Walvoord and other millennialists insist that the application of what Christ did on the Cross still awaits the parousia. It is then argued that the consummation of the seventy weeks has been postponed.

> How can you say that the *application* of the atonement
> belongs to the seventy weeks, but that the *making* of the
> atonement, through the death of Jesus *after the sixty-ninth
> week* does not belong to the seventy week countdown?

The question is however, how can one confine the *application*
of the atonement to the seventy weeks, and exclude the *making* of
the atonement from the seventy weeks? Again, Daniel was not told
that the *application* of the atonement belongs to the seventy weeks,
but that the *appropriation* of the atonement is unrelated to the
seventy weeks. To reiterate the point, the atonement –*every aspect
of it-- is confined to the seventy weeks.* Not *after*, not *before*, but
within the seventy weeks (Daniel 9:26)– "Seventy weeks are
determined, to make atonement." You cannot argue that the death
of Jesus, which was to appropriate the atonement, does not belong
to the seventy week countdown, and stay true to the text of Daniel
9. *Yet, if the atoning death of Jesus belongs to the seventy weeks,
millennialism is falsified, for the death of Jesus occurs after the
sixty ninth week.*

THE COMMUNION TABLE
AND THE SEVENTY WEEKS

It seems to me that the significance of the "the last supper" is
often ignored in discussions of the seventy weeks of Daniel 9. Our
millennial friends of course, insist that by the time of the institution
of the Supper Israel's kingdom offer had been postponed, and
Jesus was establishing the Supper strictly for the hastily conjured
up church. However, nothing could be further from the truth.
Daniel 9 establishes that very firmly.

I will keep my comments on this very brief, but hopefully these
few thoughts will provoke and promote further consideration of the
significance of the Communion table in its relationship to the
seventy weeks.

There is no doubt that the death of the Messiah was predicted
in Daniel 9:26: "And after the sixty-two weeks Messiah shall be
cut off, but not for Himself." *This means that the rejection of Jesus*

was no surprise to God– it was a necessary part of the countdown. Since this is true, it cannot be argued that as a result of that rejection God had to postpone the kingdom. The rejection of Jesus is part of the warp and woof of Daniel's seventy week prophecy.

What also needs to be understood is that in light of the rejection of Jesus, *God had determined not to change the kingdom plan.* Indeed, the rejection of Christ was integral to the kingdom plan: "Ought not the Christ to have suffered these things and to enter his glory?" (Luke 24:26). This is *hugely* important, yet millennialists seem not to notice. Take note of some truths in this regard.

☛ God foretold the rejection of His Messiah (Psalms 2; Daniel 9:26). Yet, God said He would laugh at man's attempts to thwart His plan.

☛ God said that His servant would not fail in his mission (Isaiah 42:5).

☛ God said that He would not alter His plan to seat Messiah on the throne of David (Psalms 89:34f). It goes without saying that a 2000 year postponement of the seventieth week would be an alteration of the plan.

The fact that in Daniel 9 God foretold the rejection and death of Messiah, but nonetheless gave the seventy week countdown, serves as powerful testimony that the seventieth week was not postponed. You cannot logically argue, as some do,[70] that there is a gap, *in the text* of Daniel 9, between the 69th and the 70th week of Daniel 9, and at the same time argue that the kingdom was supposed to be established at the time of its offering in the ministry of Jesus. See my *Seal Up Vision and Prophecy*[71] for a full refutation of the millennial "Gap Theory." But what about the Supper and Daniel 9?

Let's briefly summarize. The goal of Daniel 9 was the New Covenant kingdom of the Messiah. Intrinsic in the prophecy of Daniel 9 is the death of Messiah. It therefore follows, again, that the death of the coming King would be essential to, and *part of the countdown* to the kingdom, to the New Covenant. More specifically, the death of the Messiah would *confirm* the coming New Covenant. Since the death of the Messiah would be indispensable for the bringing in of the New Covenant, it follows

67

that the death of the Messiah had to have been included in the countdown to the New Covenant.

As we have seen, the fulfillment of Jeremiah's prophecy of the New Covenant would be occur at the end of the seventy week countdown. That New Covenant would bring the forgiveness of sin and righteousness. So, again, the death of Messiah, the New Covenant and the kingdom go hand in hand.

Notice now Matthew 26:26f,

"And as they were eating, Jesus took bread, blessed and broke it, and gave it to the disciples and said, 'Take, eat; this is My body.' Then He took the cup, and gave thanks, and gave it to them, saying, 'Drink from it, all of you. For this is My blood of the new covenant, which is shed for many for the remission of sins. But I say to you, I will not drink of this fruit of the vine from now on until that day when I drink it new with you in My Father's kingdom.'"

It will be helpful to recognize the symbolism of what happened at the Supper. Jesus had his specially chosen twelve apostles with him at the Passover. The Passover was pre-eminently *a covenant meal*. As Stallings notes, "In the Jewish experience, Passover prepared the Jews to become the people of God, but it was at Mount Sinai that God actually made them his people.[72] It was the Covenant that made the escaped slaves into a holy nation and a kingdom of priests (Exodus 19:6)."[73]

Not only was Passover a covenant meal, the fact that Jesus specifically chose to have the twelve apostles present is suggestive that he intended for them to realize the covenantal significance of what was unfolding before them. As Stallings says, "The Twelve Apostles are the twelve witnesses to the institution of the Eucharist and the Lord's Supper, and they are also the required twelve witnesses to the institution of the New Covenant. They stood in place of the twelve memorial stone pillars that stood as the twelve tribes of Israel as Moses instituted the Sinai Covenant." (*Passover*, 256). In other words, Jesus gathered the twelve apostles around him at Passover[74] for them to be the legal witnesses for institution and establishment of the New Covenant promised to Israel.

We must remind ourselves that Jesus came "to confirm the promises made to the fathers (Romans 15:8). He came to fulfill the prophecies of Israel, and they *were* being fulfilled in his ministry

(Matthew 13:16f). Furthermore, the prophecies of the Old Testament were emphatically said to be being fulfilled in Christ and the church long after the time when the millennialists insist that the kingdom had been postponed.[75]

Our point is that when Jesus established the Supper, he was not instituting an ordinance unrelated to the kingdom promises of Israel. This means that his statement that the Cup represents the blood shed for "*the* New Covenant"[76] can be nothing less than the promised New Covenant anticipated by Jeremiah and Daniel. To put it another way, Isaiah also foretold the coming New Covenant "I will make an everlasting covenant with you, the sure mercies of David" (Isaiah 55:3-4). And Paul affirmed in the most positive way of God's actions in Christ, "God has fulfilled this for us their children, in that he has raised up Jesus. As it is written in the second Psalm...and that he raised him from the dead, no more to see corruption, He has spoken thus, I will give you the sure mercies of David." (Acts 13:33-34).

The sure mercies of David are linked directly to the New Covenant, and Paul believed that through the power of Jesus' resurrection that promise was being fulfilled.

Notice now Luke 22:17f,

"Then He took the cup, and gave thanks, and said, 'Take this and divide it among yourselves; for I say to you, I will not drink of the fruit of the vine until the kingdom of God comes. And He took bread, gave thanks and broke it, and gave it to them, saying, 'This is My body which is given for you; do this in remembrance of Me.' Likewise He also took the cup after supper, saying, 'This cup is the new covenant in My blood, which is shed for you.'"... "And I bestow upon you a kingdom, just as My Father bestowed one upon Me, that you may eat and drink at My table in My kingdom, and sit on thrones judging the twelve tribes of Israel."

Space will not allow in-depth exegesis of this significant text. However, it is indisputably true that both the disciples and Jesus have the establishment of the Messianic kingdom in mind at the Supper.[77] The disciples are arguing about the places of honor in the kingdom, perhaps indicative of the fact that they still do not quite understand the *nature* of the kingdom (cf. Jesus' response in v. 24f). Jesus does not deny that they will have places of honor in the kingdom, they will sit on twelve thrones judging the tribes of Israel!, but that their position will also demand servitude and humility. The kingdom would not be what they had *envisioned*, but it would be what was *promised* nonetheless.

The important thing is to see the direct parallels between Daniel's seventy week prophecy and what Jesus was saying and doing in the institution of the Supper.

The *goal* of the seventy weeks was the establishment of the New Covenant that would bring forgiveness, in the kingdom of the Messiah, when the redeemed would enjoy the Messianic Banquet (Isaiah 24-27). Prior to the consummation of the seventy weeks, Messiah had to be killed, but his death would be after the sixty-ninth week.

In Luke, Jesus told his disciples that while *the kingdom was not like they envisioned it*, he was nonetheless endowing them with the kingdom and they were to eat with him at the Messianic Banquet. However, he, *and they*, had to first suffer. His death however, was to establish the longed for New Covenant that would bring the forgiveness of sin.

We see therefore, a point by point parallel between Daniel 9 and the institution of the Supper. The implications of this are, needless to say, profound.

Daniel was told that the seventy weeks were determined to put an end to sin, make atonement and bring in everlasting righteousness. Each of these promises is inseparably connected to the Passion of Jesus, although as seen, not finished at the Cross. What should never be overlooked is that these things are all directly linked to *the New Covenant.*

The death of Jesus was fundamentally essential to the accomplishment of putting an end to sin, making the atonement, and bringing in of everlasting righteousness through the establishment of the New Covenant world. Jesus' establishment of the Supper, therefore, based on his passion, stands firmly within the seventy week countdown. His statement, "this is my blood of the New Covenant," his references to the table in the kingdom and the promise of the twelve sitting on thrones ties the institution of the Supper to the seventy week countdown. That being true, this means that the countdown had not been postponed. It had not been altered.

70

Jesus' institution of the Supper was a profound proclamation that God's plan was firmly, irrevocably, on course, that the cutting off of Messiah, so essential for him to "enter his glory," and, "the glories to follow" (1 Peter 1:10-12) was now at hand. There is therefore, no justification for positing a two millennia gap between the sixty-ninth week and the seventieth based on the misguided view that the death of Jesus caused that postponement.

It cannot be argued that the death of Messiah postponed the seventy week countdown if the death of Messiah is part and parcel of the seventy week prophecy, i.e. after the sixty ninth week, "Messiah shall be cut off." (Daniel 9:26).

It cannot be argued that the death of Messiah postponed the New Covenant world, if the death of Messiah is essential to the establishment of the New Covenant world.

It cannot be argued that the death of Messiah would postpone the putting an end to sin, if the death of Jesus was essential to the putting away of sin (Hebrews 9:26).

It cannot be argued that the death of Messiah would postpone the making of atonement, if the death of Messiah is part of the atonement process.

It cannot be argued that the death of Messiah would postpone the bringing in of everlasting righteousness if the death of Messiah is vital to the establishment of everlasting righteousness.

The fact is that the very things Daniel's prophecy posited within the seventy weeks, are all indubitably tied to the death of Jesus, which of course, the millennialists try to set outside the seventy weeks.

If the death of Jesus *to establish the New Covenant (kingdom) (Luke 22)* which is the goal of Daniel 9, was to be after the sixty-ninth week how can it be argued that the death of Messiah postponed the very thing his death was to accomplish? If the New Covenant world would arrive at the end of the seventy weeks, and the New Covenant would be confirmed by the death of Messiah–as even the millennialists agree-- then why does the death of Messiah not belong to the seventy week countdown?

There is a great deal more that could be said about the relationship between the institution of the Supper and Daniel 9. However, this should suffice to demonstrate that the Supper instituted by Jesus played a vital role in signifying that the

71

fulfillment of Israel's promises was near. Jesus' promise to the disciples that he was appointing them a table in his kingdom, to rule the twelve tribes, through the New Covenant for which he was about to die, is nothing less than a positive affirmation that the fulfillment of the seventy weeks was near.[78]

A final thought. Notice that Jesus said he appointed a table for the disciples to eat in his kingdom. This means that the Supper would be a vital, integral part of the kingdom, *when the kingdom fully arrived.* The kingdom would fully arrive at the end of the seventy week countdown and that includes the destruction of Jerusalem, which as we have shown, was the time of Christ's parousia. Thus, the kingdom *–and the kingdom Communion table* -- would achieve its full meaning at the time of the parousia. It would then be taken in the kingdom, with the Lord.

This stands diametrically opposed to the mistaken concept that Paul said the *Supper* would be taken only until the parousia. That is not what Paul said. He maintained that the first century church would *show forth the death (sufferings) of Jesus until he came.* This has nothing to do with the continuance or cessation of the Supper.

"You do shew forth the Lord's death til he comes," has nothing to do with whether the Supper itself would continue after the parousia. It speaks to the fact that the pre-parousia church was sharing in Christ's suffering in order to fill up the measure of eschatological suffering. They, not us, manifested that suffering and their sharing in it when they partook, anticipating the consummation of their salvation hopes. We today do not "shew forth the Lord's death," because the measure of suffering was fulfilled, and Christ brought salvation. The Supper is now the memorial of that perfected salvation, and that is the ultimate purpose for which it was established: to memorialize deliverance from death and bondage.

The pre-parousia church had become "partakers of the sufferings of Christ" (1 Peter 4:13). They were always bearing about, "in the body the dying of the Lord Jesus" (2 Corinthians

4:10) which was an eschatologically loaded concept of filling the measure of sin. *The early church matched Christ's sufferings.* They died with him (Colossians 3), so that his "body" might be raised, vindicated and glorified at the parousia and resurrection.[79]

So, the Corinthians and the first century church did, "shew forth his death until he comes," because they were sharing in his eschatological sufferings[80] (1 Corinthians 4:9f; Colossians 1:24f– specifically Paul and the apostolate). However, through that end times suffering and sharing the kingdom was being established, "we must through tribulation enter the kingdom" (Acts 14:22). The kingdom fully arrived at the end of the Old Covenant world in the destruction of Jerusalem (Luke 21:31). The Supper is now for all those delivered from death. It is now truly taken "new," and "fulfilled," as a celebration of deliverance from sin and death. *In other words, the Supper was not to cease at the parousia, it was to be perfected, and henceforth celebrated in the everlasting kingdom.*

SEVENTY WEEKS ARE DETERMINED...
TO BRING IN EVERLASTING RIGHTEOUSNESS

Daniel was told that the seventy weeks were determined to "bring in everlasting righteousness." Gentry says: "The final, complete atonement establishes righteousness. This speaks of the objective accomplishment, not the subjective appropriation of righteousness." (*Dominion*, 316) We agree, but unfortunately, semi-preterists like Gentry once again stop short of proper application, and they fail to see that the bringing in of everlasting righteousness is definitely related to the resurrection. As Boutflower noted: "'Everlasting righteousness' is a description of the coming salvation, which contains within it a promise of victory over death and the grave."[81] Contra Gentry, Mathison, et. al. it is clear that the New Testament writers were still awaiting the consummation of the work of righteousness and did not see that work as finished at the Cross.

WHY WAS ISRAEL PROMISED
EVERLASTING RIGHTEOUSNESS?

In order to properly understand Daniel's prophecy of the arrival of the world of everlasting righteousness, we must understand Daniel, and thus Israel's standing under Torah, the Mosaic Covenant world.

When Daniel wrote, he and Israel, was living under Torah, the law that could not give righteousness. It was under that system that Isaiah lamented, "Justice is turned back, and righteousness stands afar off; truth is fallen in the streets" (Isaiah 59:14) and, "all of our righteousnesses are like filthy rags" (Isaiah 64:6).

In the Jewish mentality, righteousness was inextricably related to the Torah (Luke 1:6). As a faithful Jew, Paul wrote of the Torah, "If a law could have been given that could have given life, then, verily, righteousness would have been through the Law." (Galatians 3:20-21).

So, living under that system that could never impart righteousness, Daniel was told of a new order when righteousness would be the order of the Day.

Paul spoke of the Torah, written and engraven in stone, as, "the ministration of death" (2 Corinthians 3:6f) because it not only could not give life, but it made sin abound (Romans 5:20f). And, "sin, taking opportunity by the commandment, produced in me all manner of evil desire. For apart from the law sin was dead" (Romans 7:8). Thus, "I was alive once, without the Law, but the commandment came, sin revived, and I died" (Romans 7:9). As a result, "The commandment, which was to bring life, I found to bring death" (Romans 7:10). In other words, the Torah was "the strength of sin."[82]

While the Torah was indeed glorious, Paul acknowledged and affirmed that when it was compared to the New Covenant of Jesus, the Torah had no glory at all. It was after all, *the difference between life and death.*

It identified sin.
It accused the sinner.
It made sin abound.
It brought death.
It was the ministration of (the) death.

That means that the goal of Daniel 9 was the New Covenant world of Messiah.

It must be emphasized that the seventy week countdown included the time when the Mosaic Covenant was still in effect. In other words, the Mosaic Covenant as the strength of sin and the ministration of death would remain valid during the seventy week countdown.[83] But lying on the horizon, at the climax of the countdown, lay the wonderful New Covenant world of Messiah, the ministration of righteousness and life (2 Corinthians 3:9).

WHAT IS THE WORLD
OF EVERLASTING RIGHTEOUSNESS?

Was Daniel's anticipated world of righteousness a renewal of material creation, the restoration of physical Edenic utopia, or was it the giving of a New Covenant relationship, wherein righteousness was given, where life was possible? Notice the strongly covenantal context of Daniel. The covenantal context cannot be ignored. In reality, *righteousness* is a *covenantal concept and is not a matter of rocks and trees*. It has to do with *man's standing before God*, not how green the grass is or how clean the water is.

While we do not think that Gentry understands the gravity and implications of his own statement, we nonetheless agree with what

75

he says: "Recognizing the covenantal framework of the Seventy Weeks is crucial to its proper understanding." (*Dominion*, 311). Not only must we understand that Daniel was written within a covenantal context, it foretold the coming of a New Covenantal world. Daniel 9 is all about the covenants! And because this is true, Daniel is a prediction of the resurrection.

This covenant concept and context is demonstrated by a comparison of Daniel 9 and Ezekiel 37. At the consummation of the seventy weeks lay the restoration of Israel, the kingdom of David, the *everlasting covenant of peace* and the restored tabernacle of Jehovah (Ezekiel 37:19f). And here, we find proof that at the end of the seventy weeks lay the resurrection!

In Ezekiel's famous prophecy of the restoration of Israel the prophet foretold how Jehovah would pour out his Spirit on Israel and *raise them from the dead*, "I will open your graves and cause you to come up out of your graves, and bring you to the land of Israel. Then you shall know that I am the Lord when I have opened your graves, O My people, and brought you up from your graves. I will put my Spirit in you, and you shall live" (Ezekiel 37:12-14).

There is little doubt that this passage, along with Daniel 12, serves as the source for John 5:25-29. For our purposes, we can only note a couple of important facts:

☛ Both Daniel and Ezekiel are unmistakably concerned with the consummation of God's promises to Israel.

☛ Daniel 9 and Ezekiel 37 both predicted the same time and events. The restoration of Israel.

☛ Thus, the events of Ezekiel would occur at the end of the seventy week countdown.

☛ This means that the *resurrection*[84] would take place at the end of the seventy week countdown. Stated simply, here is what we are saying:

The *restoration of Israel* would occur at the end of the seventy weeks of Daniel 9.

But the restoration of Israel would be *the resurrection of Israel* (Ezekiel 37; see also Romans 11:15f).

Therefore, the resurrection of Israel would occur at the end of the seventy weeks of Daniel 9.

As a very important point, and one to be expanded on later, we need to note that God's resurrection promises to Israel are the fountain for the New Testament doctrine of the resurrection (Acts 24:14f; 26:21f; Romans 8:23-9:5; 1 Corinthians 15:54-56). Thus, unless the resurrection of Ezekiel, *which patently is not a prediction of a resurrection of physical corpses out of the ground*,[85] is a resurrection different from that foretold by, say, Isaiah 25-26, then this has tremendous implications for our understanding of resurrection in the entirety of the New Testament.

☛ This also means that the arrival of the New Covenant world of Messiah, and the resurrection are synchronous if not fully synonymous events.

There is something else to consider from the comparison between Daniel and Ezekiel. It is, as just noted, widely admitted that Daniel 9 and Ezekiel 37 foretold the same time and events, the consummation of Israel's Messianic hope. However, what many do not seem to realize is that in 2 Corinthians 3-6, virtually every constituent element foretold in Ezekiel 37 is expounded on by the apostle. This means that Ezekiel 37 was the source of Paul's eschatological expectation in those chapters. This is proven definitively by the fact that he quotes, virtually verbatim, from Ezekiel 37:26 in 2 Corinthians 6:16 and states that the church at Corinth was what Ezekiel foretold! So, what does that mean?

Daniel 9 and Ezekiel 37 foretold the same time and events. They are parallel prophecies of the consummation of Israel's Messianic hopes. But, 2 Corinthians 3-6 is drawn from, and based on Ezekiel 37. Therefore, 2 Corinthians 3-6 anticipated the fulfillment of Daniel 9 and the fulfillment of the seventy weeks. If this is true, then there can be no doubt that the seventy weeks had not been postponed and the seventy weeks had not already been completed when Paul wrote.

If the resurrection and the New Covenant of Ezekiel 37 are synchronous with the end of the seventy weeks, as just suggested, then the crucial nature of *Paul's ministry as a whole* takes on added eschatological significance. Since Paul was still anticipating the resurrection foretold by the prophets, as well as the full arrival of the New Covenant creation, the end of the seventy weeks was still future to him. But more on that in a moment.

OUT WITH THE OLD, IN WITH THE NEW!

For the New Covenant world to fully arrive, *the Old Covenant world had to be removed* (Hebrews 8:13; 12:25f) through fulfillment (Matthew 5:17-18). At least part of the "offence of the Cross," as proclaimed by Paul, was that the New Covenant and the new world that he proclaimed as fulfillment of Israel's promises, was not in any way what Israel had anticipated (Galatians 5:5). As Wright says, "One of the central tensions in Paul's thought, giving it again and again its creative edge is the clash between the fact that God always intended what has in fact happened, and the fact that not even the most devout Israelite had dreamed that it would happen like this."[86]

Paul's expression of the hope of Israel was not the end of the time-space world. As Longenecker says:

"What Paul has in mind when he envisages the inauguration of a new world is not, of course, the establishment of a completely new physical universe of matter– a world of cause and effect relationships, held together by forces of gravitational attraction at the molecular level. Instead he envisages the establishment of a new realm of existence. It is the sphere of life wholly different from the 'cosmos' that has been crucified to Paul, a domain where distinctive patterns of life are operative. As his comments in 6:14-15 highlight, Paul belongs to this new world, where different standards apply, different rules are followed, different habits are formed, different ways of life are practiced, and a different ethos exists. The world in which he used to live was characterized by many things, one of which was fundamental distinctions between those who were circumcised and those who were not, those who observed the law of God and those who did not. But Paul has seen the death of that world and now lives in a world where that distinction is not applicable."[87]

Longenecker is saying that the new creation that Paul speaks about is a *New Covenant Creation*. See his comments on page 46 for instance, where he continues his discussion of the new creation envisioned by Paul: "This eschatological perspective has to do first and foremost with the triumph of God, a triumph that is taking effect in the establishment of a new world. It is a world where matters of circumcision and uncircumcision are irrelevant."

So, if what stood at the end of the seventy week countdown was the kingdom of the Messiah, and it was, and if what Paul and the NT writers were awaiting was the hope of Israel, and it was, then since they, like Jesus, did not offer or preach the kind of kingdom that the Jews expected, then perhaps it is time for the modern exegete to come to grips with the possibility that the kingdom, *and thus eschatology*, is not what has traditionally been believed.

Undeniably, the NT writers did anticipate the fulfillment of the Old Covenant prophets. They expected their hopes to be fulfilled very soon. And, they realized that this meant the demise and destruction of the Old Covenant world. The New Covenant world could not come into full bloom until the shadow world of Israel was realized in the revelation of the "body" of Christ.

While the Torah was the strength of sin and the ministration of death, *it foretold its own demise* through the promise of the coming of the New Covenant that would not condemn, but justify and give life. This is why Paul could say, "But now, the righteousness of God *apart from the law* is revealed, being witnessed by the Law and the prophets, even the righteousness of God which is through faith in Jesus Christ to all and on all who believe." (Romans 3:21-22, my emphasis). The apostle even appeals to the declining glow of Moses' face after receiving the Torah, as a prophetic foreshadowing of the passing of the Old Covenant (2 Corinthians 3:13). In anticipation of the completion of the promise of the New Covenant, the Hebrews author says that Old Covenant was "nigh unto passing away" (Hebrews 8:13).

Was not this New Covenant world of the "righteousness of God" what Daniel was predicting? Was not this marvelous righteousness of God what the Torah foretold, and in foretelling the coming of a world wherein righteousness would dwell, did that not necessitate *the passing of the world wherein there was no righteousness*? Is this not what Paul meant when he said, "I through the Law died to the Law" (Galatians 3:19)? Paul was saying *that contained in the Law itself* lay the promise of the end of Torah! Is this not what Daniel was seeing?

As Daniel foretold, the atonement and putting away of sin was necessary for, and part of the process of, the bringing in of everlasting righteousness. Daniel said everlasting righteousness would arrive by the end of the seventy week countdown. Thus, the law that was the strength of sin and the ministration of death, would find its end at the end of the seventy weeks.

PAUL, THE HOPE OF ISRAEL AND DANIEL 9

The apostle Paul was eagerly anticipating the arrival of Daniel's promises. He says in Galatians, "We through the Spirit, eagerly await the hope of righteousness" (Galatians 5:5). We must understand that what Paul was writing about was the hope of Israel. So, whatever Paul had in mind as he awaited, "the hope of righteousness" it was in fact, the hope of Israel.

The context makes it clear that Paul was contrasting the futility of the Old Law, the world that could never give righteousness (Galatians 3:20f) with the Gospel of Jesus Christ that does give righteousness and life. Notice the direct correlation between the Torah and its failure to give life and righteousness. While Paul laments the inability of the Torah to give life, he contrasts that with the New Covenant of Christ. Paul's focus is on the Abrahamic promise of the new creation (Galatians 3:26-29—>6:15f). It is in the new creation, even then being brought to reality,[88] that those things that the Torah could never give would become reality.

So, in Galatians, we find the very themes of Daniel 9. The anticipation of the coming world of everlasting righteousness.

Thus, the new world that had broken into the old world, abolishing the significance of circumcision and the Torah, was, in fact *the hope of Israel*. This is easily understood when one realizes that part of the hope of Israel was *the New Covenant world* (Jeremiah 29:29f). This New Covenant world was the goal of the seventy weeks of Daniel 9, for, the New Covenant world is nothing less than the kingdom of the Messiah.

Stated simply we would express it like this:

The New Covenant kingdom was the hope of Israel.

The hope of Israel would be realized at the end of the seventy weeks of Daniel 9:24f.

80

Therefore, the New Covenant kingdom would be fully realized at the end of the seventy weeks of Daniel 9.

Thus, when we come to the New Testament and read that Paul, who preached nothing but the hope of Israel, affirms that he was the *specially chosen instrument* to bring about the transformation to the New Covenant the apostle knew the consummation of Daniel was near.

That Paul saw himself as the pivotal end times player, in a multi-faceted mission, has been the source of a great deal of scholarly discussion. Munck, commenting on Paul's statement that the transformation from the Old Covenant to the New was his personal stewardship and ministry, stated, "Paul is not only the one who knows what God's plan is and can tell of it, but the one by whose action this fulness is to be brought about." .... "Paul's work was more important than that of all the apostles who went to the Jews and were turned away by that impenitent nation. Where their work failed, the way of salvation provided for Israel will become a reality through Paul's work for the Gentiles. This also means that the apostle's work is more important than that of all the figures in Old Testament redemptive history, because he has been appointed by God to fill the key position in the last drama of redemption."[89] (See my extended discussion of Paul's distinctive, covenantal and eschatological role in my *Who Is This Babylon?*).

There are three factors that force us to see the fulfillment of Daniel 9 as occurring in the first century and not at some supposed end of the Christian age.

First, the one just stated, and that is that Paul saw himself as the crucial, specially chosen vessel to, "Fulfill the word of God, the mystery" (Colossians 1:24-27) and to serve as the minister and steward of the covenantal transformation from the Old Covenant to the New. If it was Paul's distinctive role to bring these things to reality, and if the New Covenant world was the goal of Daniel's seventy weeks, as just shown, then it is manifestly true that the end of the seventy weeks and the consummation of Paul's ministry would dovetail.

Second, the first point agrees with the fact that Paul undeniably anticipated the imminent parousia: "The night is far spent, the Day is at hand, now is our salvation nearer than when we first believed"

(Romans 13:11f). Paul could write "the end of the ages has come upon us" (1 Corinthians 10:11)[90] because he believed with all of his heart that through the Spirit, the consummation of his, and Israel's, hopes was very near. Paul was in the process of helping deliver and minister the New Covenant of Messiah (2 Corinthians 4:1-2). He envisioned the consummation of that New Covenant world as coming very soon.

Third, Paul says it was "through the Spirit" that they were "eagerly" (from *apekdekomai*) awaiting the full arrival of that righteousness (Galatians 5:5). In Galatians 3f Paul reminds them that it was the miraculous Spirit that was "perfecting" them in Christ, not through the Law. So, this "waiting through the Spirit" must be seen as a referent to the charismata, since it was that miraculous Spirit that was transforming (from *metamorphe*) the righteous remnant of Israel "from glory to glory" i.e. from the Old Covenant glory to the New (2 Corinthians 3:12-16). This miraculous element of the transformation was the *guarantee*, the *arrabon*, of the completion of the transformation, and in this miraculous ministry we see again the direct relationship between resurrection and covenant transformation.

Paul said it was through the ministry of the Spirit that they were being transformed "from glory to glory," from the "ministration of death" to the ministration of righteousness (life) (2 Corinthians 3:16-18). Likewise, he said the Spirit was the guarantee (*arrabon*) of the *resurrection* (2 Corinthians 5:5). Paul did not have a temporal disconnect of so far 2000 years in mind between the covenant transformation work of the Spirit and the resurrection work of the Spirit. That was *one* temporally confined work, the transformation from death to life.

Of course, what this means is that if the *arrabon* truly was the miraculous work of the Spirit,[91] then, those who deny that the resurrection has occurred, but who also are cessationists, have a severe problem. For instance, Gentry, believes that the age of the charismata ended by the end of the seventy weeks as we document below. This is a self destructive theology.

Stated logically, the argument would be:

The miraculous gifts of the Spirit were the guarantee of the resurrection, and would be operative until the Day of Redemption (2 Corinthians 5:5; Ephesians 1:12-13; 4:32).

But, the resurrection has not occurred. (Gentry and futurists).

Therefore, the miraculous gifts of the Spirit should be operative today.

It is self-contradictory to hold that the *arrabon* was the charismatic gifts of the Spirit, given to guarantee the resurrection and then to insist that while the resurrection has not occurred, the charismata have ceased to function.

On the other hand, if the charismata was the *arrabon* and the agent of the transformation from the Old Covenant world to the New, then if the miraculous gifts remain active today that means that the transformation from the ministration of death, the Torah of Moses, remains on-going.

So, the relationship between the *arrabon*, the resurrection and covenant transformation is direct. You cannot separate one from the other. And this covenantal transformation is precisely the point of Daniel 9:24f! It would be the atoning work of Jesus the Messiah (Daniel 9:26) that would bring about the New Covenant world of "everlasting righteousness." The death of Jesus would confirm the New Covenant (Galatians 3:15; Hebrews 9:15-16). The parousia would complete and perfect it. This establishes Daniel 9:24f as a prophecy of the resurrection.

Our point is that the "hope of righteousness" eagerly anticipated by Paul was the bringing in of everlasting righteousness foretold by Daniel 9:24. It was the New Covenant "ministration of righteousness" (2 Corinthians 3:5f) that was in the process of revelation, confirmation, identification and glorification through Paul's ministry. What Paul was anticipating, in fulfillment of Daniel, was the *New Covenant world* not the physical world turned into a utopian society. The Old Covenant world did not and could not bring *righteousness*. The New Covenant world of Christ, initiated at the Cross, but awaiting perfection at the parousia, would and does give that longed for righteousness and life.

83

This contrast between covenant worlds, and the contrast between death and life, is found in 2 Corinthians 3-6. Paul spoke of the Torah, the Old Law written and engraven in stone, and called it "the ministration of death" (2 Corinthians 3:6f). It was called the ministration of death because it not only could not give life, as we have just seen, it made sin abound (Romans 5:20f). And, "sin, taking opportunity by the commandment, produced in me all manner of evil desire. For apart from the law sin was dead" (Romans 7:8). Thus, "I was alive once, without the Law, but the commandment came, sin revived, and I died" (Romans 7:9). As a result, "The commandment, which was to bring life, I found to bring death" (Romans 7:10). In other words, the Torah was "the strength of sin."[92]

As we noted earlier, the Torah was the strength of sin, and the ministration of death, and *it foretold its own demise.* It promised the coming of the New Covenant that would not condemn, but justify, and give life. This is why Paul could say, "But now, the righteousness of God *apart from the law* is revealed, being witnessed by the Law and the prophets, even the righteousness of God which is through faith in Jesus Christ to all and on all who believe." (Romans 3:21-22, my emphasis).

Notice the resurrection motif of 2 Corinthians 3-5 in light of the Romans passages. The Torah was "the ministration of death, written and engraven in stones," but the gospel is, "the ministration of *righteousness.*" The Torah was the strength of sin. The resurrection would be when the Law that was the strength of sin was removed (1 Corinthians 15:54f). Paul *was not contrasting biological death with spiritual righteousness or spiritual life.* He was contrasting the *relational death* that he spoke of in Romans, and the *relational life* of the New Covenant. For Paul, righteousness and life were virtually synonymous.

Was not this world of the "righteousness of God" what Daniel was predicting? Was not this marvelous righteousness of God what the Torah foretold, and in foretelling the coming of a world wherein righteousness would dwell, did that not necessitate *the passing of the world wherein there was no righteousness offered*? Is this not to a degree what Paul meant when he said, "I through the Law died to the Law" (Galatians 3:19)? Furthermore, is this not what Daniel was seeing?

> The law that was the strength of sin and the "ministration of death," would find its terminus at the end of the seventy weeks. Paul was serving as personal steward and minister of the coming "ministration of righteousness," the triumph of life over death!

Since what Paul was administering was the promised New Covenant world, but since that world was patently not yet completed, it demands that the seventy week countdown was not yet terminated. Everlasting righteousness was not yet a full reality, "We through the Spirit eagerly await the hope of righteousness."

The coming of the New Covenant world of righteousness would demand the passing of the Old Covenant (Hebrews 8:13; 12:25f): "If righteousness comes through the Law, then Christ died in vain" (Galatians 2:21). Patently, the world of everlasting righteousness did not, and could not, in Paul's thought, include the Torah.

So, Daniel foretold the total demise, the overwhelming flood, that would come on his people, city and world, at the climax of their age (Daniel 9:26-27).[93] Likewise, Paul said the ministration of death was passing away when he wrote 2 Corinthians 3:8-16. He said the transition from the Old Covenant world to the New was taking place, "But we all, with unveiled face, beholding as in a mirror, the glory of the Lord, are being transformed into the same image from glory to glory, just as by the Spirit of the Lord" (2 Corinthians 3:18).

Let me express a few thoughts here:

The Torah was the strength of sin (1 Corinthians 15; Romans 7).

The Torah was the ministration of death (2 Corinthians 3:5f).
The resurrection would occur when the Torah that was the strength of sin was removed (1 Corinthians 15:54f).

The resurrection (life) would be when the Law that was the ministration of death passed.

85

Therefore, the resurrection would be at the end of the age of the Torah, i.e. when the New Covenant world of everlasting righteousness arrived, *at the end of the seventy weeks*.

Here is what this means:

It proves that Daniel 9, in its prediction of the coming of everlasting righteousness, is positively *a resurrection prophecy*.

It proves that resurrection belonged to the end of the Old Covenant world of Judah.

It proves that since Paul was the minister of the covenantal change from the ministration of death to the ministration of life, that the end of the seventy weeks belongs to Paul's ministry.

It proves that the seventy week countdown was not postponed by the Cross.

It proves that the countdown of the seventy weeks was not completed prior to the end of the ministry of Paul.

Now, if the New Covenant world of righteousness, glory and life of which Paul spoke was not the world of everlasting righteousness anticipated by Daniel, what was it? It most assuredly was not some distorted, perverted, alien theology, if we are to believe Paul. It was instead the "hope of Israel" and, Paul affirmed that he preached this gospel "through the prophetic scriptures" (Romans 16:25-26). In other words, the New Covenant of life and righteousness was foretold by the Old Testament prophets, and was the fulfillment of Israel's prophecies of the New Covenant.

Of course, this flies in the face of the modern dispensational world that insists that Paul's gospel was no where predicted in the Old Testament.[94] It is claimed that Paul's doctrine of the church, and Jew and Gentile equality, was unknown by any of the prophets, and that the gospel of Christ is *not* the New Covenant world of righteousness anticipated by Daniel. Nothing could be further from

86

the truth. If the gospel of Christ and the church was no where found in the Old Testament, how could Paul have preached those things from "the prophetic scriptures"? Did he just make up his message as he went along? Was he guilty of perverting the prophetic scriptures, or of "allegorizing them" beyond recognition?

The answer is, emphatically, No! The trouble was, as already noted, the Jews of Jesus' and Paul's day did not think for a moment, it never entered their minds that the things they hoped for were the things that Jesus and Paul proclaimed! They wanted something tangible, empirical, earthly. They wanted the restoration of national glory, "the return from exile." But, expressed in their own scriptures and in the mind of Jesus and Paul, "return from exile, in this period, *meant* 'forgiveness of sins,' and vice versa."[95] Thus,"Israel has not obtained that for which she sought, but the elect has, and the rest were blinded" (Romans 11:7). For the Jews, restoration meant nationalistic glory. For Jesus and the inspired writers, restoration meant fellowship restored.

Those who accepted Jesus as Messiah came to understand that the countdown of Daniel and the coming of "everlasting righteousness" did not entail nationalistic restoration. Kingdom life was the deliverance from bondage to "the ministration of death." The Torah could not give them life and could never be the ministration of righteousness. Instead, "Through this Man is preached to you the forgiveness of sins; and by Him everyone who believes is justified from all things from which you could not be justified by the Law of Moses" (Acts 13:38-39). Daniel's promised world of righteousness was about to come into full bloom!

So, the New Covenant (world) of Christ was the goal of the seventy weeks.[96] The New Covenant of Christ is now a reality, therefore, the goal of the seventy weeks has been reached. If the New Covenant promised by Jeremiah and Daniel has not been established, it therefore follows that the seventy weeks has not been fulfilled. I am currently working on a manuscript demonstrating the fallacy of the millennial posit that the New Covenant world promised by Daniel and Jeremiah has not been established. Many sincere believers deny that the New Covenant has been established. I am convinced that the great majority of dispensationalists do not realize the implications of saying that the gospel is not the promised New Covenant, and that another, *different covenant* will be established in the millennium, a covenant that will demand animal sacrifices.

Notice Paul's discussion of *righteousness and resurrection* life in Philippians 3. In that chapter, he contrasts the true circumcision and the true worshipers, with those who worship after the flesh. It is the contrast between the Old Covenant world and the New. Paul spoke of his former "glory" as a zealot under the Law, but how he now counted that former glory as "rubbish" (literally, *dung*, v. 8f). He then spoke of his desire:

> "That I might be found in Him, not having my own righteousness which is from the Law, but which is through faith in Christ, the righteousness which is from God by faith, that I might know him, and the power of his resurrection, and the fellowship of His sufferings, being conformed to his death, if, by any means, I might attain to the resurrection from the dead."

There is no doubt that Paul was contrasting the Old Covenant, with its inability to provide life and righteousness, with the New Covenant world of the Christ. Notice that Paul was still anticipating the arrival of the righteousness of God, that he longed to be "found"[97] in, and his desire to, "attain to the resurrection of the dead." Just as in Galatians 3:20-21, Paul was saying that the Old Covenant world of Moses and Torah could not give life and righteousness, but that the soon coming New Covenant world was to be a world of righteousness by faith.

This anticipated coming righteousness is certainly what Daniel predicted. During the seventy week period, the utter futility of Israel under the Law would be manifest, as Israel filled up the measure of her sin, and thus, the purpose of the Law, "that sin might abound" (Romans 5:20-21) was magnified. Daniel foretold a world of righteousness that would come after the total abolition of the old world: "the end thereof shall be with a flood" (Daniel 9:27). This was not simply to be the end of a city. It was to be the end of the futility of life under the Torah. It was to be the end of *the ministration of death* and the ushering in of the New Covenant, so that, "by Him, everyone who believes is justified from all things from which you could not be justified by the Law of Moses" (Acts 13:38-39).

It is undeniably true that in Philippians 3, Paul was still awaiting the full arrival and consummation of the city of his true citizenship, "Our *home city* (our citizenship, DKP) is in heaven, from whence we eagerly await[98] for the Savior" (Philippians 3:20). He then affirmed, "The Lord is near!" (4:5).

Of course the great question is, was that coming world of righteousness, the heavenly Jerusalem, the same world of righteousness anticipated by Daniel? As we have seen, Paul affirmed that his eschatological hope was nothing but the hope of Israel. So, if Paul's anticipation of the coming of righteousness at Christ's parousia was not from Daniel, where is it to be found in the O. T.? Did the OT predict the coming of two different worlds of righteousness, at the Day of the Lord? For Paul, there was but "one hope," and that hope was grounded firmly in the OT prophets. Daniel undeniably foretold the coming of the world of everlasting righteousness and confined the fulfillment of his promise to the seventy weeks. If we are going to delineate between Daniel and Paul one must prove several things.

First, Paul was anticipating a world of righteousness different from that foretold by Daniel.

Second, if Paul, in Philippians 3, was still anticipating the arrival of the world of righteousness foretold by Daniel, then this is *prima facie* evidence that the end of the seventy weeks had not come. It also proves that the end of the seventy weeks was near since Paul uses such strong language of imminence when speaking of the coming consummation (Philippians 4:5).

Third, if Paul was anticipating the soon coming fulfillment of the seventy week prophecy, then patently, not only was the seventy week prophecy not already fulfilled, *but it had not been postponed for 2000 years either!*

So, Philippians 3, like Galatians 5, shows us that Daniel's prophecy of the seventy weeks was very much in the mind of the NT writers as they longed for the bringing in of everlasting righteousness.

The world of righteousness foretold by Daniel would be fulfilled by the end of, but *within*, the seventy weeks of Daniel 9 (Daniel 9:24). *There is no justification for saying that the world of righteousness would arrive long after the seventy weeks.* Thus, again, if the world of righteousness anticipated by Peter and Paul was the world of righteousness foretold by Daniel, this is *prima facie* proof that the seventy weeks of Daniel 9 were not fulfilled in AD 35.

Daniel: The world of everlasting righteousness would come within the confines of the seventy week countdown.

Paul and Peter, writing in the 60s AD were eagerly awaiting the soon arrival of the world of righteousness foretold by the prophets.

Therefore, unless Paul and Peter were awaiting a world of righteousness different from that foretold by Daniel, then the seventy weeks had not been fulfilled, but was about to be!

Notice that Peter believed that the New Temple of God[99] was already under construction (1 Peter 2:5). And, he was eagerly "looking for (*prosdokao*) and hasting the Day of the Lord" and the arrival of "the new heavens and earth" as promised by the Old Covenant prophets (2 Peter 3:1-2, 13). Was the world of righteousness eagerly awaited by Peter a different world of righteousness from that foretold by Daniel? Did Daniel foretell one world of "everlasting righteousness," but Peter believe that the Old Testament prophets foretold another? Keil and Delitzsch says that Daniel's promise to "bring in everlasting righteousness" is the promise of 2 Peter 3, the new heavens and earth.[100] Most commentators are agreed that Peter's referent to the new heavens and earth is taken directly from Isaiah 65. This being true, then it must be true that Peter was anticipating the new creation to follow the judgment on Israel, for that is exactly what Isaiah 65 taught.

Some partial-preterists argue that Isaiah 65 and 2 Peter 3 and Revelation 21 foretold different New Creations. Gentry, (*Dominion*, 363) delineates between Isaiah 65 and 2 Peter 3. Interestingly however, he says that Revelation 21:2-5: "Is the bride of Christ that came down from God to replace the earthly Jerusalem in the first century. With the shaking and destruction of the old Jerusalem in AD 70, the heavenly (re-created) Jerusalem replaced her." But, if Revelation 21:1f is referent to the events of AD 70, *then since they follow the millennium* that means that *Gentry is forced to say that the millennium ended in AD 70!* Furthermore, if Revelation 21f is AD 70, that means that it is referent to the arrival of "everlasting righteousness" of Daniel 9. That in turn demands that the 70th Week ended in AD 70 and not 35 years earlier as Gentry suggests.

Isaiah foretold that the new creation would come when Israel filled the measure of her sin (v. 6-8) and was destroyed, "the Lord God will destroy you and call His people by a new name" (v. 13f). As a consequence of that destruction, Jehovah would, "create a new heavens and a new earth" (v. 17). So, if 2 Peter 3 was predicting the arrival of the world of righteousness foretold by Isaiah 65, then he was anticipating the destruction of Old Covenant Israel, followed by the New Covenant world of Messiah.

Is this not what Daniel 9 predicted? Daniel foretold the consummation of Israel's Old Covenant existence and the New Covenant world of Messiah. But, the consummation of Israel's history meant the destruction of "the city and sanctuary" (Daniel 9:26). So, Daniel and Isaiah foretold the arrival of the new world of righteousness–the new heavens and earth--at the time of the judgment of Israel.

Peter was anticipating the arrival of the world of righteousness foretold by the prophets (2 Peter 3:1-2; 13). Daniel 9 foretold the coming of the world of righteousness. Therefore, Peter was anticipating the coming of the world of righteousness foretold by Daniel, unless Daniel foretold a world of righteousness different from Isaiah. However, if Peter was anticipating the arrival of the world of righteousness foretold by Daniel (and Isaiah) then of necessity that means that the seventy weeks of Daniel 9 had not yet been fulfilled.

Gentry knows that the arrival of everlasting righteousness is inseparably bound to the seventy weeks, "This was effected by Christ within the seventy-week period." (*Dominion*, 316). If Christ effected the arrival of everlasting righteousness during his personal ministry, i.e. his passion, then what world of everlasting righteousness was Peter longing for, that was foretold by the Old Testament prophets? What was Paul still eagerly anticipating? *What world of righteousness* foretold by the prophets were the

91

inspired writers still eagerly awaiting, and predicting its *imminent* arrival? Only by severing the apostolic expectation of the coming world of righteousness from Daniel's prophecy can the postmillennialists claim that the end of the seventy weeks arrived in the third decade of the first century.

The new creation of 2 Peter 3 is the new creation of Revelation 21-22. Most semi-preterists concur.[101] Furthermore, the arrival of the new creation of 2 Peter 3 and Revelation 21 is the time of the resurrection (Gentry, Mathison, Bahnsen, et. al.). However, the arrival of the new creation of 2 Peter 3 and Revelation 21-22 is the world of righteousness foretold by Daniel. That new creation is confined to the time of the seventy weeks. That means that the fulfillment of the resurrection world of righteousness of 2 Peter 3 and Revelation 21-22 is confined to the seventy weeks of Daniel 9.

The resurrection world of righteousness of 2 Peter 3 and Revelation 21-22 is confined to the seventy weeks of Daniel 9. But the seventy weeks of Daniel 9 was fulfilled no later than the destruction of Jerusalem in AD 70. Therefore, the resurrection world of righteousness of 2 Peter 3 and Revelation 21-22 was fulfilled no later than the destruction of Jerusalem in AD 70.

Furthermore, the coming righteousness anticipated by Paul in Galatians and Philippians is inextricably linked with the parousia and the resurrection. But, the world of righteousness anticipated by Paul in Galatians and Philippians was the world of righteousness that is confined to the seventy weeks of Daniel 9. The seventy weeks of Daniel 9 would terminate with the utter desolation of Jerusalem and the end of the Old Covenant world. Therefore, the time of the resurrection and parousia, the bringing in of everlasting righteousness at the end of the seventy weeks, would occur at the coming of the Lord in the destruction of Jerusalem and the end of the Old Covenant world in AD 70.

The only way to counter our argument is to prove that the world of righteousness foretold by Daniel is not the world of righteousness foretold by Paul, Peter or John. Yet, the apostles all say their hope was from the Old Covenant prophecies. Paul said his eschatology was nothing but the hope of Israel. Where then are the Old Covenant prophecies of the destruction of literal heaven and earth followed by a literal new creation, if this is what Peter and Paul actually anticipated? It certainly is not in Daniel 9!

Finally, if the new creation of Revelation is, as Gentry suggests, the full arrival of the promise made in Isaiah 65, then Revelation is the promise of the full arrival of the world of righteousness foretold by Daniel 9, for these are parallel prophecies. But, if Revelation 21 anticipated the fulfillment of Isaiah 65 and Daniel 9 at AD 70, then it most assuredly anticipated the resurrection at that time, for *the new creation of Revelation 21 is the resurrection world of chapter 20:12f!*

What we are affirming is that in the key texts we have examined, the inspired writers spoke of the Old Covenant as a world of death, but they anticipated the New Covenant of life and righteousness. Likewise, Daniel, living under the ministration of death, anticipated the arrival of the new order. What is it called when one is delivered "from death to life?" Is this not a resurrection motif in its purest form? So, in the anticipation of "everlasting righteousness" Daniel 9 looked forward to the coming of the New Covenant world of the Messiah. He did not look for a utopian, transformed material creation. He looked forward to a transformed *covenant world* of relationship with God.

The fact that the New Covenant writers tell us they were anxiously expecting the fulfillment of the promises made to Israel, that the time of fulfillment had come and was about to be consummated, is powerful proof they did not believe the seventy week countdown had been postponed. And, they did not believe the seventy weeks were already over. They were still anticipating the climactic removal of the old world and the triumph of the new.

So, what have we seen in this section? Let me summarize as succinctly as possible.

✔ We have seen that the climax of the seventy weeks was to be the New Covenant kingdom. This is all but universally admitted.

✔ We have seen that the countdown of the seventy weeks was under the Mosaic covenant, the ministration of death. The deliverance from the ministration of death, the Law that was the strength of sin, is nothing less than resurrection.

✔ We have shown that the New Testament writers, almost all Jews, anticipated the fulfillment of God's Old Testament promises to Israel. They were eagerly awaiting the arrival of the world of righteousness.

✔ Since the New Testament writers were awaiting the arrival of the promised world of righteousness, then unless they were awaiting something different from what Daniel foretold this means that they were eagerly awaiting the soon coming fulfillment of Daniel 9.

✔ If the New Testament writers expected the near fulfillment of Daniel 9 this proves that the seventieth week of Daniel 9 had not been postponed.

✔ If the New Testament writers expected the near fulfillment of Daniel 9 this proves that the seventieth week of Daniel 9 had not yet been fulfilled in AD 34-35 as posited by postmillennialists and even some preterists.

✔ We have shown that if the anticipated New Covenant world has arrived, that the resurrection has occurred. If however, the seventieth week has been postponed, the New Covenant has not yet been established and the ministration of death and Torah, the strength of sin, remains valid.

✔ If however, one argues that the New Covenant has been established and that the end of the seventieth week has come, it must be admitted that the resurrection has come. Resurrection, the end of the seventy weeks and the New Covenant are all inextricably interwoven. You cannot have one without the other.

The *spiritual significance* and implications of the fulfillment of Daniel 9 cannot be over-emphasized. Daniel was foretelling far more than the fall of a city or the end of an Old Covenant world. He was foretelling the establishment of a world where man could be in a New Covenant that would *bring him to God*, bring him into *fellowship*, bring him to *Life*! This spiritual dimension of the fulfillment of Daniel must always be kept in mind and not lost in the shuffle of theological controversy.

SEVENTY WEEKS ARE DETERMINED...
TO SEAL UP VISION AND PROPHECY

The fourth element of Daniel 9 is the promise that the seventy weeks were determined, "to seal up vision and prophecy." Mathison, probably following Mauro,[102] has a unique view of this term: "The eyes and ears of the Jews were 'sealed' from understanding the prophecies of God."(*Hope*, 221). There is no proof for this rather eccentric offering. This makes "vision and prophecy" to refer to the people of Israel, rather than the prophetic revelation. I know of no passage, or commentator for that matter, that has ever suggested that Israel (or their eyes and ears!) be identified as "vision and prophecy."

Gentry vacillates. He says the term means, "By this is meant that Christ fulfills (and thereby confirms) the prophecy (Luke 18:31; cf. Luke 24:44; Acts 3:18)." (*Dominion*, 316). However, in his monograph contra Gruden, commenting on "that which is perfect" of 1 Corinthians 13, he says, "there is coming a time when will occur the completion of the revelatory process of God."[103] He offers a footnote to that comment that reads, "We even believe that this idea is contained in a proper understanding of Daniel 9:24 statement regarding the "sealing of the vision and prophecy." (N. 4) So, on the one hand seal up vision and prophecy refers to Christ's atoning work, and on the other hand it refers to the completion of the revelatory process.

Perhaps Gentry "saw the train coming" after he wrote against Gruden. If he takes the position that "seal up vision and prophecy" is referent to the revelatory process, then if he posits the completion of the seventy weeks in AD 35 (as he does) *the revelatory process must have been finished and sealed up through fulfillment, by AD 35!*[104]

So, it *seems* as if Gentry has retreated to the view that Daniel's prediction that vision and prophecy would be sealed up by the end of the 70th Week is referent to the fulfillment of Daniel's prophecy of Christ's atoning work. This does not help.

As already seen, the putting away of sin and the atonement were not consummated at the Cross.[105] That process *included the resurrection* since the parousia is the consummation of atonement *to put away sin.*

Gentry tries to limit the definition of "vision and prophecy" to the specific prophecy of Daniel 9 instead of the comprehensive prophetic corpus. The reader will notice that he says seal up vison and prophecy refers to the fulfillment of "*the* prophecy" i.e. the prophecy of Daniel. As I show in my other work on Daniel 9 there is no definite article in the Hebrew.[106] Gentry is not justified to argue that the seventy weeks were determined to fulfill "the" prophecy of Daniel 9. Further, there is a widespread consensus across all eschatological borders that "seal up vision and prophecy" is a comprehensive term referring to the prophetic corpus as a whole (*Seal*, 1f).

With that said, we could allow Gentry's position that seventy weeks were determined to fulfill Daniel 9, since properly understood *Daniel 9 is a prophecy of the resurrection.* As we have shown, the putting away of sin, the making of the atonement and bringing in of everlasting righteousness are eschatological and soteriological ideas inextricably linked with resurrection. You cannot argue that the atonement was consummated at the Cross because Hebrews 9 says it would be finished at the "Second Coming." But if the atonement was to be finished at the "Second Coming," that means that *sin was to be put away* then and this is *resurrection.* Since Daniel confines the putting away of sin and the making of atonement to the seventy weeks it is possible for one to argue that seventy weeks were determined for the fulfillment of *the specific prophecy of Daniel 9,* but that would *still* confine the resurrection to the seventy weeks.

The correlation between Daniel 9 and the Olivet discourse must be examined. As Pitre has illustrated, (*Exile*, 227-228) Daniel 9:26f contains virtually every constituent element found in Jesus' discourse. In Daniel we find the death of Messiah, the destruction of the city and sanctuary, the time of the end, the abomination of desolation and the determined desolations. It hardly needs pointing out that in the Discourse, Jesus mentions each of these, within the backdrop of the knowledge of his own martyrdom.

So, in Matthew 24 Jesus has Daniel 9 in mind (cf. Matthew 24:15). This means that when Jesus said, "this generation shall not pass until all of these things be fulfilled" (Matthew 24:34) *the seventy weeks were definitely to be fulfilled within his generation.*

And of course, this means that all prophecy was to be fulfilled within that generation.

Daniel was told seventy weeks were determined to "seal up vision and prophecy." This means the confirmation through fulfillment, of all vision and prophecy. This is well attested in virtually all the literature, ancient and modern. Jerome even noted that the Jews believed that "seal up vision and prophecy" meant, "And so shall the vision and the prophecy be sealed, with the result that there shall be no more any prophet to be found in Israel, and the saint of Saints shall be anointed."[107]

Jesus agreed that all prophecy would be fulfilled in the fall of Jerusalem. In Luke 21:22 Jesus spoke of the catastrophe to come on Jerusalem: "These be the days of vengeance in which all things that are written must be fulfilled."

It is fascinating, to say the least, that Thomas Ice (inadvertently of course) concurs that all prophecy was to be fulfilled in the destruction of Jerusalem in AD 70. Note again his comments from above: "Luke records that God's vengeance upon His elect nation is 'in order that all things which are written may be fulfilled.' Jesus is telling the nation that God will fulfill all the curses of the Mosaic covenant because of Israel's disobedience. He will not relent and merely bring to pass a partial fulfillment of His vengeance." *(Tribulation*, 98). To say the least, if all of the Mosaic Covenant provisions for wrath were fulfilled in AD 70, and if "all things that are written" were fulfilled in AD 70, then there is patently no room left for a future outpouring of wrath against Israel in fulfillment of that which is written!

How much of prophetic "vision and prophecy" would be left out of the fulfillment of "all things that are written"? Remember, Jesus in Luke is describing his coming, the coming *to finish the atonement* (Hebrews 9:28; 10:35-38) that is confined to the seventy weeks. But, that coming, and that atoning work, is to "seal up vision and prophecy." Thus, Daniel, and Jesus drawing from Daniel, posited the fulfillment of the entire prophetic corpus at the time of the fall of Jerusalem in AD 70. That means that the resurrection had to occur at that time.

Jesus earlier posited the fulfillment of all prophecy, "Verily I say unto you, until heaven and earth passes away, not one jot, nor one tittle shall pass from the Law, until it is all fulfilled" (Matthew

5:17-18). Notice that Jesus placed the passing of "heaven and earth" at the time of the fulfillment of all things in "the law and the prophets." And what do we find in the Olivet Discourse? We find the passing of "heaven and earth"(Matthew 24:29f, the Old Covenant world of Israel)[108] at the time when, "all things that are written must be fulfilled."

Should we ignore the perfect correlation between Daniel, Matthew 5:17-18, and the Olivet Discourse? Daniel was told that the end of the seventy weeks would see the fulfillment of vision and prophecy. The end of that vision would be the fall of Jerusalem. Jesus said none of the Old Law could pass until heaven and earth passed at the fulfillment of every jot and tittle of the Law. And in the Olivet Discourse, Jesus said, "all things that are written" would be fulfilled at the destruction of the Temple, Israel's "heaven and earth."[109]

Jesus said not one jot or tittle of the Law would pass until it was all fulfilled.[110] Resurrection was part of "the law" (Acts 24:14-15). Daniel said "vision and prophecy," *the entire prophetic corpus*, would be fulfilled by the end of the seventy weeks. The end of the seventy weeks was no later than AD 70. Therefore, the resurrection was fulfilled no later than AD 70.

Revelation 10:7f also anticipated the fulfillment of the prophetic corpus at the sounding of the seventh trump. Gentry posits the sounding of the seventh trump in the first century and says that it's sounding meant: "Israel's time is up: 'There shall be no more delay.'" (*Dominion*, 407). Significantly, at the sounding of the seventh trumpet, *the resurrection occurs*. Read Revelation 11:15f: "Then the Seventh angel sounded, and there were loud voices in heaven, saying, 'The kingdoms of this world have become the kingdoms of our Lord and His Christ, and He shall reign forever and ever....the nations were angry and Your wrath has come, and the time of the dead that they should be judged, and that You should reward your servants the prophets and saints.'"

So, Daniel 9 and 12 predicted *the fulfillment of all prophecy* (Daniel 9:24). We have the prediction of the *resurrection* (Daniel 12:2). We have the promise of *the rewarding of the dead, including prophets* (Daniel 12:13) at the time of the end. And, Gentry and Mathison acknowledge that *you cannot extrapolate Daniel 9 beyond AD 70*. (As we have shown, Daniel 12 and Daniel 9 are parallel, thus Daniel 12 cannot be protracted beyond the termination of Israel's aeon, as Daniel 12:7 shows). Finally, both Daniel 9 and Daniel 12 are dealing with the fulfillment of the eschatological *hope of Israel*, not the end of time or the end of human history as we know it.

Likewise, in Revelation, we find *the fulfillment of the prophetic corpus* (Revelation 10:7f). We find the time of the *resurrection* (11:15f). We find the *rewarding of the dead including the prophets and saints* (11:18). And, per Gentry and Mathison, (*Hope*, 151+) *all of this was fulfilled at the time of the fall of Jerusalem in A. D. 70!* Furthermore, Gentry and Mathison agree that the sounding of the Seventh Trump, with its climax at the resurrection, is dealing with the consummation of *Israel's history*, not the end of time.

Is not the resurrection, *according to all eschatological paradigms*, the time of the fulfillment of all prophecy? Surely! Is not the "final" resurrection the time of the rewarding of the dead, including the prophets and saints? Yes! And, Gentry and Mathison posit the time for *the rewarding of the dead*, including the prophets and saints, at AD 70!

Now, if the *dead*, including the prophets *received their reward at AD 70, what further reward would they now be waiting for*? Where in Revelation is there any indication of more *or different* reward after the sounding of the Seventh Trump? Is not the Seventh Trumpet the "last trump" of 1 Corinthians 15:52? The last trump of Revelation 10-11 *consummates Israel's history*, and the "last trump" of 1 Corinthians 15 brings Israel's eschatological hope to its climax. And, this is critical, in Revelation the resurrection occurs at the end of the millennium (Revelation 20:10f)! This is extremely consequential for postmillennialism.

Notice that in Revelation 10-11 we have the consummation of all prophecy, "the mystery of God would be finished as He declared to His servants the prophets" (10:7). This would be accomplished in the sounding of the seventh trumpet. Then, in chapter 11, we have the resurrection and the rewarding of the prophets and saints, and the perfecting of the everlasting kingdom of God (v. 15f) at the sounding of the seventh trump.

As we have seen, Gentry and Mathison believe that this involves the end of the Old Covenant age of Israel in AD 70.

99

But, what do we have in Revelation 20-21? We have the time of the resurrection! How do Mathison and Gentry delineate between the resurrection, judgment and kingdom of chapter 11, and the resurrection and judgment of chapter 20? Frankly, I have been unable to find a definitive answer to that question in their writings. All I have found is unsubstantiated, unsupported *assertions* that these are two different events. And yet, what is apparent is that both Gentry and Mathison, as well as other postmillennialists, view Revelation 21, as the new world that came in with the dissolution of Old Covenant Israel in AD 70.

So, in Revelation 11, the resurrection, judgment and kingdom arrived at the sounding of the seventh trumpet, when the mystery of God foretold by the prophets would be consummated. And, in Revelation 20-21, we have the time of the resurrection, the judgment and the New Creation!

Consistency begs to know the difference between the resurrection of chapter 11 and chapter 20. Logic compels us to inquire as to the difference between the time of consummation of chapter 11 and that of chapter 20. *Analogia Scriptura* seemingly *demands* that the *kingdom* of chapter 11 is the *New Creation* of chapter 21. *And Gentry and Mathison concur with this.* Yet, they tell us that the judgment and the resurrection of chapter 20 is different! We find no logic or harmony in such a view.

Both Gentry and Mathison insist that Revelation 10-11 is dealing with *the climax of Israel's history*, not the end of the Christian age. This being so, how can they delineate between Revelation 11 and *1 Corinthians 15?* Paul is dealing with the climax of Israel's history in 1 Corinthians 15. So, if Revelation 10-11 is about Israel's eschatological consummation, and if 1 Corinthians 15 is about Israel's eschatological consummation, *how many times is Israel's eschatological hope brought to perfection?* How many "last trumps" are there, anyway? How many resurrections to reward the dead are there? As we shall see below, this alone is devastating to the partial preterist paradigm, since Paul posits the "final resurrection" at the sounding of the "last trump" at the time of the fulfillment of "the hope of Israel" i.e. the time of the fulfillment of God's promises to Old Covenant Israel (1 Corinthians 15:54f). Take a look at the chart to see the perfect parallelism between these significant eschatological prophecies, and the problems presented to the partial preterist paradigm.

Daniel 9 / 12	1 Corinthians 15	Revelation 10 /11
Time of the fulfillment of prophetic corpus (9:24)	Time of the fulfillment of prophetic corpus (54-56)	Time of the fulfillment of prophetic corpus (10:7f)
Time of the end (12:4, 9f)	Time of the end (15:20f)	Time of the end 10:7f; 11:15f)
Time of the resurrection (putting away of sin / resurrection (9:24; 12:2)	Time of the resurrection	Time of the resurrection (11:15f)
Rewarding of the dead (including the prophets, 12:13)	Rewarding of the dead (15:52-54)	Rewarding of the dead (including the prophets, 11:16-18)
	At the last trump (15:52)	At the Seventh (last) trump (11:15f)
At the climax of God's promises to Israel, not the end of time (9:24; 12:7)	At the climax of God's promises to Israel, not the end of time (15:54–fulfillment of Isaiah 25 / Hosea 13:14)	At the climax of God's promises to Israel, not the end of time (when the city "where the Lord was slain" was judged (11:8)

Fulfilled in AD 70	Fulfilled when "the law"[111] that was the "strength of sin" removed. (v. 55-56)	Fulfilled in AD 70 (Gentry and Mathison)

The chart shows the perfect correspondence between these passages. Interestingly, Mathison and Gentry have no problem positing Daniel 9 and Revelation 10-11 at the same time. What they fail to see is the perfect correspondence with 1 Corinthians 15. Daniel 9 posits the fulfillment of all prophecy at AD 70. Mathison and Gentry posit the fulfillment of all prophecy at the time of the resurrection of 1 Corinthians 15. Mathison and Gentry posit the resurrection of Revelation 11 at AD 70. But the resurrection of Revelation 11 would be the fulfillment of all that the prophets had foretold (Revelation 10:7). Therefore, the fulfillment of all prophecy, at the time of the resurrection, was in AD 70.

I must digress to make an additional point in regard to, "the mystery of God as foretold by the prophets" in Revelation 10:7.

Gentry says that Revelation 10:7 means "the Gentiles are fully accepted by God" (*Dominion*, 407). If this is so, how can he argue that the seventy weeks were fulfilled in AD 35, however? The fulfillment of the seventy weeks would bring in the kingdom of God, which means that all men, i.e. the "Gentiles" would now be brought into the salvation of Christ. In other words, it is at the end of the seventy weeks that the Jew and Gentile equality would be realized as the accomplished work of Christ, in the kingdom.

That Jew/Gentile equality was the specific and personal work of Paul and his ministry. In Colossians 1:24-27, the apostle makes it clear that he was *specially chosen, specially commissioned, and personally responsible* for bringing the word of God, *the mystery,* to fulfillment. Here is what that means:

The fulfilling of the mystery was Paul's personal commission.

The fulfilling of the mystery would come at the end of the seventy weeks.

The fulfilling of the mystery belongs to the seventh trumpet of Revelation.

Therefore, the seventy weeks of Daniel 9 were not fulfilled before the end of Paul's ministry–neither were they postponed for 2000 years.[112]

Now back to our discussion of the resurrection.

To maintain their futurism, Gentry and Mathison must discover in scripture a resurrection *unrelated to the fulfillment of Israel's hope*. But and that would exclude 1 Corinthians 15, or Revelation 20 for that matter. Paul is emphatic that the resurrection he was anticipating was that foretold by the OT prophets.

Jesus earlier posited the fulfillment of all prophecy, "Verily I say unto you, until heaven and earth passes away, not one jot, nor one tittle shall pass from the Law, until it is all fulfilled" (Matthew 5:17-18). Notice that Jesus placed the passing of "heaven and earth" at the time of the fulfillment of all things in, "the law and the prophets." And what do we find in the Olivet Discourse? We find the passing of "heaven and earth" (Matthew 24:29f, the Old Covenant world of Israel)[113] at the time when, "all things that are written must be fulfilled."

If *the dead*, including the prophets and saints, received their reward in AD 70, according to Gentry and Mathison, how much more reward are they now waiting for? What kind of reward are *the dead* waiting for? How many rewards do the dead get, and how many resurrections to reward the dead are there?

Are we supposed to ignore the perfect correlation between Daniel, Matthew 5:17-18 and the Olivet Discourse, not to mention 1 Corinthians 15 and Revelation? Daniel was told that the end of the seventy weeks would see the fulfillment of vision and prophecy. The end of that vision would be the fall of Jerusalem. Jesus said none of the Old Law could pass until heaven and earth

103

passed at the fulfillment of every jot and tittle of the Law. And, in the Olivet Discourse, Jesus said that, "all things that are written" would be fulfilled at the destruction of the Temple and Jerusalem, Israel's "heaven and earth."

It is significant to note that the Jerusalem temple was known as the "heaven and earth" by the Jews of Jesus' day. Josephus, (Ant. 3:6:4 and 3:7:7) says the temple, with its Holy and Most Holy Place, was a "heaven and earth." Thus, as Jesus predicted the destruction of the temple, it was perfectly natural for him to say "heaven and earth will pass away" (Matthew 24:35). He was not speaking of the material cosmos. He was speaking of the Jewish "heaven and earth."[114]

Jesus said not one jot or tittle of the Law would pass until it was all fulfilled. *Resurrection was part of "the law"* (Acts 24:14-15). Therefore if the resurrection has not occurred, not one jot or tittle has passed from the Law.

Daniel said "vision and prophecy," *the entire prophetic corpus*, would be fulfilled by the end of the seventy weeks. The end of the seventy weeks was no later than AD 70.[115] Therefore, the resurrection was fulfilled no later than AD 70.

Finally, we must once again take note of the argument that the fate of the city lies outside the seventy weeks. The fact that Daniel was told that the seventy weeks were determined to seal vision and prophecy precludes the idea that the destruction of Jerusalem lies outside the seventy weeks.

Our argument is simple:

Seventy weeks were determined to seal vision and prophecy.

To seal vision and prophecy involved the total fulfillment of all prophecy.

But, all prophecy would be fulfilled in the destruction of Jerusalem (Luke 21:22).

Therefore, the sealing of vision and prophecy would be accomplished in the destruction of Jerusalem.

To follow up on that:

The sealing of vision and prophecy would be accomplished in the destruction of Jerusalem.

But, the sealing of vision and prophecy belongs within the confines of the seventy weeks of Daniel 9.

Therefore, the destruction of Jerusalem, to seal vision and prophecy, was within the confines of the seventy weeks of Daniel 9. (We prefer to think that it lay at the completion of the seventy weeks).

It would be *possible (though we certainly do not do so)* to argue that seal vision and prophecy entailed only the fulfillment of Daniel's prophecy of the seventy weeks. This *still would not help those who posit the fate of the city outside the seventy weeks.* To reiterate, Daniel was told that "seventy weeks are determined *on your holy city* to seal vision and prophecy."

So, seventy weeks were determined on the city, to seal vision and prophecy.[116]

To seal vision and prophecy means to fulfill the prophecy of Daniel 9. (Gentry and others)

But, the prophecy of Daniel 9 foretold the destruction of Jerusalem.

Therefore, 70 weeks were determined to fulfill the prophecy of the destruction of Jerusalem found in Daniel 9.

Summary of this Section

We have shown that the term seal vision and prophecy is referent to the fulfillment of the comprehensive prophetic corpus, i.e. all prophecy.

We have shown that to limit "seal up vision and prophecy" to the fulfillment of the specific prophecy of Daniel 9 violates Daniel, but since the prophecy of Daniel 9 is a prophecy of the resurrection it does not really matter. To admit that the seventy week prophecy is fulfilled, as argued by both the amillennial and postmillennial schools, is to argue that the resurrection is fulfilled.

We have shown that the idea of the comprehensive fulfillment of all prophecy at the time of the fall of Jerusalem, i.e. at the end of the Old Covenant age of Israel, is consonant with other emphatic passages of scripture. Jesus said all things written would be fulfilled in the fall of Jerusalem, and the fall of Jerusalem is the climax of Daniel 9.

Since Daniel was told that seventy weeks were determined to seal vision and prophecy, then the fulfillment of all prophecy lies within the parameters of the seventy weeks. Thus, the seventy weeks were not fulfilled prior to AD 70 and the seventy weeks were not postponed.

SUMMARY STATEMENT
IN REGARD TO DANIEL 9 AND HEBREWS 9

I hope that by now you have noted how directly Daniel 9 and Hebrews 9 are related. We have waited until after our discussion of the putting away of sin, the atonement and the sealing of vision and prophecy to offer this summary, in order that the reader can catch the full force of the relationship of Daniel and Hebrews.

It can justifiably be argued that five of the six elements foretold by Daniel 9:24 are to be found in Hebrews 9:

1.) The putting away of sin.

2.) The making of atonement.

3.) The sealing of vision and prophecy. This is true because Hebrews 9 anticipated the consummation of the typological / prophetic nature of Israel's cultus and that would be when the new order of Messiah arrived, i.e. the time of reformation (*diorthosis*). Thus, to "seal vision and prophecy" anticipated the fulfillment of Israel's hopes and Hebrews 9 anticipated the fulfillment of Israel's hopes.

4.) The bringing in of everlasting righteousness. Would not the putting away of sin and the making of the atonement in Hebrews 9 result in the bringing in of everlasting righteousness?

5.) The anointing of the Most Holy. This can be viewed as Christ's parousia to dedicate the new Most Holy, i.e. the presence of God in the new Jerusalem.

So, in one text, Hebrews 9 brings together virtually all of the eschatological and soteriological hopes of Israel and posits them at the time of Christ's fulfillment of the high priestly atonement praxis.[117]

What should not be missed is that, as we have continually noted, *not one* of these elements can be divorced from or extrapolated beyond the seventy week countdown. Everyone of them belongs within the confines of that divinely appointed countdown. In addition, let me re-emphasize the fact that *virtually everyone* acknowledges that Daniel 9 is focused on the consummation of God's dealings with Old Covenant Israel, and not the end of the Christian age, or the end of time. So what does that mean when we come to Hebrews 9?

Hebrews 9 was anticipating the future, to him, parousia of Christ out of the Most Holy place to perfect the putting away of sin, to complete the atonement through the fulfillment of Israel's prophecies and thus bring in everlasting righteousness in the new "Most Holy." Since those things were still future when the author of Hebrews wrote, it cannot be argued that the seventy weeks had already been fulfilled, as postmillennialists claim.

Notice something else here. If the blessings of Daniel 9 are the blessings of Hebrews 9, then we have a *prima facie* demonstration that the seventy weeks are *now* fulfilled. Let me express it logically:

The putting away of sin and the making of the atonement of Daniel 9:24, is the same putting away of sin and the same making of atonement in Hebrews 9.

But, the putting away of sin and the making of the atonement of Daniel 9:24, would be accomplished within the confines of, but by the end of the seventy weeks of Daniel 9.

Therefore, the putting away of sin and the making of the atonement of Hebrews 9 would be accomplished within, but by the end of the seventy weeks of Daniel 9.

Notice also what this means, when we turn it around and look at it from the perspective of Hebrews 9.

The putting away of sin and the making of the atonement of Daniel 9:24, is the same putting away of sin and the same making of atonement in Hebrews 9.

But, the putting away of sin and the making of the atonement of Hebrews 9 would be perfected when the prophetic elements of the Mosaic cultus were fulfilled and the Mosaic cultus was terminated (Hebrews 9:9-10).

Therefore, the seventy weeks of Daniel 9 would be consummated when the prophetic elements of the Mosaic cultus were fulfilled and the Mosaic cultus was terminated.

What this means, stated simply, is that *the end of the Mosaic Law, the end of the Mosaic age would be the end of the seventy weeks of Daniel 9*. It means that the Mosaic Law would remain valid and "standing" until the end of the seventy weeks.

Let me return to a point. Daniel 9 is not concerned with the end of time, of human history, or the end of the Christian age. *It is about the end of God's dealings with Old Covenant Israel.* Consider what this means since Daniel 9 and Hebrews 9 are essentially parallel texts.

Daniel 9 and Hebrews 9 both anticipated the same time and events, the consummation of God's covenant dealings with Israel. The Hebrew writer says the Old Covenant system would remain valid "until the time of reformation." The time of reformation is undeniably the goal of Israel's typological, prophetic cultus.

The consummation of Israel's typological, prophetic cultus would be the "second coming" of Christ for salvation. However, if the "second coming" of Christ is the consummation of Israel's typological and prophetic cultus, then that means that Christ's "Second Coming" would bring to an end that typological and prophetic Old Covenant age. Simply put, the second coming of Christ would be at the end of the Mosaic age, not the end of the Christian age.

Since the Hebrews author said that the Old Covenant was "nigh unto passing" when he wrote (Hebrews 8:13) and anticipated the coming of Christ "in a very, very little while" to bring the heavenly reward (Hebrews 10:32-37) it means that the consummation of the seventy weeks was "very, very near."

What Hebrews 9 anticipated was the fulfillment of the hope of Israel *as found in Daniel 9*. However, since the Hebrews writer affirmed the very soon fulfillment of those hopes at the end of the Old Covenant world, it therefore follows that the Hebrews writer knew nothing of a postponed kingdom or failure of Christ to fulfill his mission. The fact that the writer posits the still valid cultus and its abiding status until the fulfillment of all that it foreshadowed, proves that the writer did not see a postponed kingdom. The fact that he anticipated the very, very soon fulfillment of those promises falsifies the millennial view of Daniel 9. And, the fact that he still anticipated the perfecting of the atonement proves that the seventy weeks were not already fulfilled.

109

Hebrews 9 wraps up every blessing promised in Daniel 9 in one text, and says those blessings would come at the end of the Mosaic cultus. That would come in "a very, very little while." The consummation of the seventy weeks was not therefore, delayed, but to be fulfilled in a very short time!

The correlation between Daniel 9 and Hebrews 9 is incredibly important. Jesus came to confirm the promises made to the Old Covenant fathers (Romans 15:8). In his death he *initiated* the process of putting away of sin and the atonement foretold by the fathers. The writer of Hebrews knew that Israel's covenant would stand until it was fulfilled, when her salvation arrived. That soteriological climax of her history would come when the old cultus was swept away and the New Covenant world of the Messiah stood triumphant. And, unless Hebrews 9 anticipated a totally different putting away of sin, a totally different atonement, a different fulfillment of prophecy and a salvation different from that foretold by Daniel 9, this means that the writer of Hebrews understood very well, and with eagerness, that the consummation of the seventy weeks was very, very near.

RESURRECTION: THE HOPE OF *ISRAEL*!

One of the greatest failures of most futurist eschatologies is the failure to see that Biblically, eschatology is related to the promises to Israel,[118] and not the end of time or the Christian age. Mathison, Gentry, Pratt, Kistemaker and all the contributors to *When*, whether postmillennial or amillennial, believe that eschatology is linked to the end of the Christian age and the termination of "human history." Boettner expresses what many believe,[119] but this position is the root cause of much of the eschatological confusion in the world today: "For information concerning the first coming of Christ, we go to the Old Testament. He came exactly as predicted, and all those prophecies were fulfilled or were forfeited through disobedience. But for information concerning his Second Coming and what future developments will be, we go only to the New Testament."[120] The error of this theology must be exposed.

In reality, *Biblical eschatology has nothing to do with the end of the Christian age*. It has nothing to do with the end of time, or the end of human history. Biblical eschatology is *Covenant Eschatology*, not Historical Eschatology. And, more importantly, *all New Testament eschatology is nothing but the reiteration and explanation of Old Testament eschatology!* To sever our eschatology from the Old Testament is to doom ourselves to a misunderstanding of the Scheme of Redemption.

As Paul was on trial, he said his doctrine of the resurrection was nothing but that spoken by "Moses and the prophets" (Acts 24:14f). Before Agrippa, he said he was on trial, "for the hope of the promise made to our fathers." That hope was resurrection, for which, "our twelve tribes, earnestly serving God night and day, hope to attain." (Acts 26:6f). He preached that hope *as the gospel* and, it was, again, from Moses and the prophets (26:22f). If Paul said his gospel, his eschatology, his hope of the Second Coming in other words, was taken directly from Moses and the prophets, is it not egregiously wrong to say that we today "go only to the New Testament" for "what future developments will be"?

In Romans 8, the apostle wrote some of his more eloquent words in anticipation of, "the adoption, to wit, the redemption of the body" (Romans 8:23). This is, of course, resurrection. What is so often overlooked is that the promise of the adoption belonged to

Israel "after the flesh" (Romans 9:4-5) and was not a promise given to the church divorced from Israel. Likewise, in 1 Corinthians 15, Paul was looking for the fulfillment of God's OT resurrection promises to Israel (1 Corinthians 15:54) for he says that the resurrection would be when Isaiah 25 and Hosea 13 would be fulfilled.

It is an egregious distortion of the text to make Isaiah 25 and Hosea 13 refer to the raising of physical bodies out of the ground. Both texts, and virtually all OT resurrection prophecies, predicted the salvation of Israel from "sin-death," i.e. alienation from God caused by sin.

The point is that when the NT writers foretold the resurrection, they were Jews *anticipating the fulfillment of God's promises to Israel*, by the power of Messiah Jesus (cf. Acts 3:19f). They were not preaching a replacement theology that said Israel was not going to be given her promises, as a result of her sin. They were saying that what was happening (and what was to happen) was the fulfillment of what was actually foretold.[121] God was faithful, and would be faithful to His promises (Romans 11:29f). Thus, the resurrection promises made to Israel had not been taken from her and transferred to the church, to be fulfilled at the end of the church age. Israel's promises were to be fulfilled in *her last days*, at the climax of *her history*, at the Day of the Lord.

Daniel 9:24-27 is the prediction of the consummation of Israel's soteriological and eschatological hope. The removal of Israel's sin is inextricably linked with the parousia of Jesus in fulfillment of "all that the prophets have spoken" (Acts 3:21f): "repent so that your sins may be blotted out...and that he may send Jesus."

Note what the New Testament has to say about the promises to Israel. The *promise of the resurrection belonged to Israel* "after the flesh" (Romans 8:18f-9:5). When Paul wrote his definitive work on resurrection, he said it would be the fulfillment of God's Old Covenant promises to Israel (1 Corinthians 15:54f).

God's covenant with Israel would be fulfilled, "when I take away their sins," *at the parousia of Jesus* (Romans 11:26-27). One does not have to wonder where Paul got the idea of the removal of Israel's sin! Daniel 9 is the definitive promise of Israel's salvation: "Seventy weeks are determined...to put away sin...to make atonement for iniquity."[122]

112

The promise of the New Heavens and Earth, the world of everlasting righteousness, was promised to Israel. It was not promised to the church at the end of the church age (2 Peter 3:1-2; Revelation 21-22:6).

When we read 1 Thessalonians 4:13f we are reading about God's promise to Israel.[123] When we read 2 Thessalonians 1, we are reading about the fulfillment of God's promises to Israel.[124] When we read Acts, Romans, or 2 Peter 3, or Revelation, *we are reading about God's faithfulness to His promises to Israel.* To remove New Testament eschatological promises outside the framework, and the time, of God's judgment of Israel is to do a grave disservice to Biblical exegesis and hermeneutic.

We conclude our argument in this section:

The resurrection, the parousia of Christ and the New Creation promises were the salvation hopes of Israel.

But, the salvation hopes of Israel would be fulfilled by the end of the seventy weeks of Daniel 9.

Therefore, the resurrection, the parousia of Christ and the New Creation promises to Israel would be fulfilled by the end of the seventy weeks of Daniel 9.

This leads us to this:
The resurrection, the parousia of Christ and the New Creation promises to Israel would be fulfilled by the end of the seventy weeks of Daniel 9.

But, the seventy weeks of Daniel 9 were fulfilled no later than AD 70.

Therefore, the resurrection, the parousia of Christ and the New Creation promises to Israel were fulfilled no later than AD 70.[125]

DANIEL 9 AND DANIEL 12

Semi-preterists have no problem teaching that Daniel 9 extends no further than AD 70. However, they normally deny that Daniel 9 is a promise of the resurrection. While they deny that Daniel 9 predicts the resurrection, they affirm that Daniel 12 does predict the "final" resurrection. Thus, to demonstrate that Daniel 9 and Daniel 12 are parallel passages is to demonstrate the fulfillment of the resurrection by AD 70. The following chart will prove that the passages are parallel.

DANIEL 9	DANIEL 12
Concerning Israel (V. 24	Concerning Israel (V. 1-7)
Time of the end (V. 27)	Time of the end (V. 4)
Abomination of Desolation (V. 27)	Abomination of Desolation (V. 9F— cf. Matthew 24:15)
Resurrection (atonement)	Resurrection (V. 2)
Fulfilled by AD 70– The end shall be with a flood (v. 27)	"When power of the holy people is shattered." (V. 7)

Patently, Daniel 9 and Daniel 12 are parallel passages. This is significant because Strimple, Hill and Mathison all cite Daniel 12 as predictive of the "final resurrection" at the end of human history. This presents a dilemma for the authors of *When Shall These Things Be?*

Daniel 9 and 12 are prophecies about the consummation of God's Covenant dealings with Israel. These passages are not about the end of time. They are not about the end of the Christian age. Mathison and most other semi-preterists would concur with the true preterists that at least Daniel 9 has nothing to do with the end of the Christian age. But if Daniel 9 has nothing to do with the Church age or the end of time, *then neither does Daniel 12.*

114

Daniel 12 is the prediction of the "final resurrection" at the end of human history. (Mathison, Hill, Strimple and most semi-preterists).

But, Daniel 12 is parallel with, speaks of the same time and same events, as Daniel 9:24-27.

Therefore, Daniel 9 is the prediction of the "final resurrection" at the end of human history.

Do partial preterists believe that Daniel 9 speaks of the end of human history? No. Do semi-preterists believe that Daniel 9 even speaks of the "final resurrection?" No. Yet, it is abundantly clear that Daniel 9 and Daniel 12 do predict the same time and events.

Daniel 9 and Daniel 12 are parallel passages, speaking of the same time and same events. But, the events of Daniel 9 were all confined to the seventy weeks period that ended no later than the time of the fall of Jerusalem in AD 70. Therefore, the events of Daniel 12 were all confined to a period of time no later than the fall of Jerusalem in AD 70. But, if the events of Daniel 12 were confined to a period of time no later than AD 70, this means that the resurrection of the dead was confined to a period of time no later than AD 70. Daniel was told this exact thing.

Notice that Daniel 12:2 predicted the resurrection. Verse 3 is the prediction of the time of the end when the righteous would shine as the sun. Jesus said this text would be fulfilled at the time of his coming at the end of the age (Matthew 13:43). As a rule, semi-preterists apply Matthew 13 to the end of the church age.[126]

Daniel 12:4 instructed Daniel to seal up his book "until the time of the end" (*heos kairou sunteleias*).[127] It was far removed from his day, reserved for the "end."

Thus, in Daniel 12:2-4 we have two major eschatological passages. The prediction of the resurrection and the prediction of the time of the end, that Jesus applied to the end of the age, the time of the harvest.

In verses 5-7, Daniel overheard one angel ask another: "How long shall the fulfillment of these wonders be?" Undeniably, the question involves the time of the end and the resurrection. Heaven's answer is given as one angel raised his hands to heaven and swore by the name of Jehovah: "when the power of the holy people has been completely shattered, all these things shall be finished."

Mathison says Daniel 12:5-7 is one of several passages giving "nonspecific time frames" for its eschatological predictions. (*When*, 164). Now, while Daniel 12:7 does not give "the day or the hour" for the time of the resurrection and time of the end, the marker it does give is unmistakable: "when the power of the holy people is completely shattered, all these things will be finished."

Can there be any doubt as to when the power of the holy people was completely shattered? The holy people here *cannot* be the church being destroyed at the end of the Christian age. The kingdom will never be destroyed (Daniel 2:44; 7:13f). Further, there is no place in the postmillennial or amillennial paradigm for a total destruction of Israel at the end of the Christian age. Both views believe that Israel was finally destroyed in AD 70. This being true, this demands that the resurrection of Daniel 12 was fulfilled in AD 70.

Of course this agrees perfectly with Daniel 9. The time of the resurrection is the time of the putting away of sin and the making of the atonement, as we have seen. So, the time of the making of the atonement of Daniel 9 is the time of the resurrection of Daniel 12. But, the making of the atonement of Daniel 9 is confined to, and would be fulfilled no later than AD 70. Therefore, the time of the resurrection of Daniel 12:2 is confined to, and would be fulfilled no later than AD 70.

It cannot be argued that Daniel 12 foretold some kind of spiritual resurrection that occurred in AD 70 that foreshadowed the "real" resurrection at the end of time. If Daniel 12:2 is a prediction of the "final resurrection" as Hill, Mathison, Strimple and Gentry[128] affirm, then it is not a prophecy of AD 70 per their paradigm. To my knowledge, none of these men have affirmed this in *When Shall These Things Be*. They offer Daniel 12 as a straightforward prediction of the end, not a shadow, or type, but of the "real" resurrection. So again, if Daniel 12:2 is predictive of the "final resurrection" as the partial preterists affirm, there can be no doubt about when the resurrection was to occur. It was, "when the power of the holy people" was completely shattered. And that was at the end of the Old Covenant world of Israel in AD 70.

ROMANS 11 AND THE END OF ISRAEL'S HISTORY

Many partial preterists affirm that: "The destruction of Jerusalem and the temple was the final redemptive act in the entire complex of events which inaugurated the present age." (*Hope*, 154). Sproul has stated: "No matter what view of eschatology we embrace, we must take seriously the redemptive-historical importance of Jerusalem's destruction in AD 70."[129] Boettner describes AD 70 as "tremendously important," and "a landmark in history" (*Millennium*, 203). On the flip side, Pratt says the fall of Jerusalem was "relatively inconsequential." (*When*, 154)

One would initially think, from reading the material, that partial preterists believe that AD 70 was the end of God's covenant dealings with Israel. After all, that was the "break-up and abolition of the Old Testament economy." (*Millennium*, 203) However, partial preterists do not believe that God is through with Israel. (*Hope*, 121+) Romans 11 serves as almost the sole source of authority for this idea.

We do not have space to fully discuss Romans 11 here.[130] However, we can demonstrate that it cannot be removed from its first century context. There are several things that prevent a yet future fulfillment of Romans 11.

1.) Israel's salvation would come "when the fulness of the Gentiles is come in." (11:25). However, the fulness of the Gentiles is not a numeric fulness, but the completion of bringing the Gentiles into full equality with the Jews, in Christ. This process was the distinctive and personal responsibility of the apostle Paul (Romans 15:16f; Colossians 1:24-27. See our comments in our chapter on the time issue.

2.) The salvation of "all Israel" would be the consummation of the process of saving the remnant. That process was already underway as Paul wrote (Romans 9:24f; 11:5f). Further, Paul said that the salvation of the remnant would be consummated shortly (Romans 9:28).[131]

3.) It is widely recognized that Romans 11:25f anticipated the fulfillment of Isaiah 27 and 59 and Jeremiah 31. Thus, if these prophecies have not been fulfilled then most assuredly, the Old Covenant remains valid and Israel remains as God's chosen people! Jesus said that not one jot, not one tittle of the Old Law would pass. That means God's relationship with Israel would remain valid until it was all fulfilled. Thus, if the Covenant promises remain valid, then the sacrificial mandates that are expressions of that Covenant relationship, remain valid as well. You cannot maintain a future for Israel without at the same time asserting that Israel remains as God's covenant people. Yet, the partial preterists deny that Israel is still God's covenant people. This is a logical fallacy of major proportions.

4.) The prophecy of Isaiah 59 foretold the salvation of Israel at the coming of the Lord in judgment of Israel for shedding innocent blood (Isaiah 59:5-12). Jesus made it abundantly clear in Matthew 23 that the judgment of Israel for shedding innocent blood, "all the blood of all the righteous shed on the earth" (Matthew 23:33f) would occur in his coming in AD 70.[132] Thus, Romans 11:26f foretold the fulfillment of Isaiah 59. But Isaiah 59 foretold the coming of Christ in judgment of Israel for shedding innocent blood. Christ came in judgment of Israel for shedding innocent blood in AD 70. Therefore, Romans 11:26f was fulfilled at the coming of Christ in AD 70.

Notice the following parallels as well:

Daniel 9:26f foretold the destruction of Jerusalem for shedding the innocent blood of Messiah (and of course, all the martyrs).

Daniel 9:26f foretold not only the destruction of Jerusalem for shedding the blood of Messiah, but the salvation of Israel at the end of the seventy weeks.

Isaiah 59 foretold the coming of the Lord in judgment of Israel for shedding innocent blood.

Isaiah 59 also foretold the salvation of Israel at the time of the Lord's coming in judgment of Israel for shedding innocent blood.

Do Daniel 9 and Isaiah 59 predict different times and events? Does Daniel predict a different vindication of the martyrs than does Isaiah? Not unless the martyrs in Isaiah and Daniel are to be delineated. Does Daniel foretell a salvation for Israel totally different from that foretold by Isaiah 59?

Isaiah and Daniel predicted the same consummation. Our dispensational friends tell us that Romans 11, anticipating the fulfillment of Isaiah 59, belongs to the seventieth week of Daniel 9. However, if Daniel 9 and Isaiah foretold the same consummation, and I fully concur that they did, then how does one divorce those passages from Jesus' promise that the blood of all of the innocent, all the way back to Creation, would be avenged at his coming in his generation in the judgment of Jerusalem?

The problem is equally acute for the postmillennialists. If Romans 11:25-27 anticipated the fulfillment of Isaiah 59, and it unequivocally did, then since Isaiah and Daniel predicted the same events and same time, this proves beyond doubt that Romans 11 was fulfilled in Christ's parousia in AD 70. Unless the prediction of the Lord's coming in vindication of the suffering martyrs and judgment of their persecutors in Isaiah is totally different from that predicted in Matthew 23, then Romans 11 was fulfilled in AD 70. This proves that Israel's salvation came in AD 70. It falsifies postmillennialism.

5.) If Romans 11 has not been fulfilled, then Jeremiah 31:29f has not been fulfilled and *the New Covenant has not been established*! Jeremiah 31 foretold the time when God would take away the sin of Israel by establishing the New Covenant with them.[133] The Old Covenant could never take away sin, but the New Covenant could. But if Jeremiah has not been fulfilled, then the New covenant has not been made, because it was the New covenant whereby Israel's sins would be removed! And, if the New Covenant has not been established to take away Israel's sin that means the Old Covenant is still binding.

Hebrews said that God was in the process of establishing the covenant promised in Jeremiah (Hebrews 8:6f) The Old Covenant was "old and nigh unto vanishing away" (Hebrews 8:13). Since the promised New Covenant was being made and the Old was in the process of passing away, this demands that the "salvation of Israel" was near. The parousia of Christ would finally sweep away that Old Law, the "ministry of death written and engraven in stones" (2 Corinthians 3:5f) and fully establish the New Covenant.

RESURRECTION, MATTHEW 8
AND THE END OF ISRAEL'S HISTORY

We want now to show the correlation between Isaiah 24-27, Daniel 9, the resurrection and the end of Israel's history. And we want to do this by comparing these texts with Matthew 8:11f.

Daniel 9 is predictive of the kingdom. This is admitted by virtually every conservative scholar. Since the kingdom and the resurrection are inextricably connected, this means that Daniel 9 predicted the resurrection.

We have shown that Isaiah 24-25 and Daniel 9 foretold the same time and the same event, the consummation of Israel's soteriological and eschatological hopes.

Notice again that in Isaiah 24-25 we have four key constituent elements of Israel's hope, the judgment of the nation (24:1-20) the Messianic Banquet (Isaiah 25:6) the kingdom (Isaiah 24:19f–Jehovah ruling on Mt. Zion) the resurrection (Isaiah 25:8). Interestingly, we find these identical elements in Matthew 8:10f in the famous story of the healing of the centurion's servant:

"When Jesus heard it, He marveled, and said to those who followed, 'Assuredly, I say to you, I have not found such great faith, not even in Israel! And I say to you that many will come from east and west, and sit down with Abraham, Isaac, and Jacob in the kingdom of heaven. But the sons of the kingdom will be cast out into outer darkness. There will be weeping and gnashing of teeth.'"

Notice the parallels between Isaiah 24-25 and Matthew 8.

Isaiah 24-25	Matthew 8:10-12
Establishment of the Messianic Banquet (25:6)	The Messianic Table (8:11)
The Table in the *Kingdom* (24:5-6) "On this Mount the Lord shall prepare a banquet," i.e Mt. Zion	The Kingdom (v. 11)
The resurrection (25:8)	Resurrection (Abraham, Isaac, Jacob at the table)
Judgment of Israel for violating "the everlasting covenant" (24:5-6)	Sons of the kingdom cast out for rejecting Jesus ("I have not found such faith in Israel")
The destruction of Jerusalem (24:7-16)	The sons of the kingdom cast out (v. 11–cf. Matthew 21:40-43; Matthew 22:7)

The Messianic Banquet, sometimes called the Marriage Banquet (cf. Matthew 22:1f) was, in the words of France, "a prominent theme in Jewish eschatological expectation, derived from Isaiah 25."[134] Davies and Allison take note that in Jewish writings the dominant view was that the Messianic Banquet belonged to the time of the resurrection: "In Matthew 8:11 and par. the resurrection and the messianic banquet are in view."[135] Likewise, Hagner says concerning the Banquet and the kingdom: "The allusion is to the eschatological banquet, a great festival of rejoicing and feasting in celebration of the victory of God, anticipated in both the OT and the NT (see e.g. Isaiah 25:6; Matthew 22:1-14; 25:10; Revelation 19:9; Luke 14:15-16)."[136]

So, the Banquet, the kingdom and the resurrection are undeniably linked. But *the time of the judgment of the Old Covenant world belongs to the identical matrix of motifs.*

Notice that in Isaiah 65 the prophet foretold the time of the Banquet: "Behold my servants will eat, but you shall be hungry. My servants shall drink, but you shall be thirsty."(Isaiah 65:13)

When would this be? It would be when, "you shall leave your name for a curse to my chosen, for the Lord God shall slay you, and call His servants by a new name." (Isaiah 65:15). It would be when the Lord brought in the new heavens and earth, and the new Jerusalem. (Isaiah 65:17f) Clearly, the Banquet is set in the context of God's judgment of Old Covenant Israel.

The first century application of this prophecy, and the implications for the interpretation of Daniel 9 are important. In Romans 10 Paul laments the fact that Israel had rejected the gospel although it had been proclaimed to them throughout the world (Romans 10:16-18). The important thing is that Paul not only laments Israel's failure to respond positively, but he quotes Isaiah 65:1-2 as the prophetic justification for his ministry to the Gentiles and the implied, impending judgment on recalcitrant Israel (Romans 10:20-21). This means that for Paul, Isaiah 65, with its blessings and promised judgment was being and was to be fulfilled in his generation.

Israel's *first century rejection of the gospel* would bring the judgment forecast in Isaiah 65. But, the judgment of Isaiah 65 would result in the new heavens and earth, the new creation world in which God's new people, wearing the new name, would eat at the Banquet table. This is Isaiah 24-25 expanded and explained even further. These are not prophecies to be delineated, dichotomized and divorced from one another. They foretold the same time and same events, the full establishment of the everlasting kingdom of Messiah.

The new creation world is the New Covenant world, which was the goal of the seventy weeks prophecy of Daniel 9. The new heaven and earth and the new Jerusalem constitute and symbolize the world of "everlasting righteousness" promised in Daniel. The new Jerusalem would be the city in which sin had been removed for those blessed to sit at the table in the kingdom. And the table is for those for whom death had been swallowed up in victory.

Notice however, that in all three texts before us, Isaiah 24-25, Isaiah 65, and Daniel 9, that judgment of Old Covenant Israel is to the fore and precedes the arrival of the promised blessings. In Isaiah 24-25 judgment falls on the city of confusion, the city set in the midst of the land, and then the Banquet is set for the resurrected ones. In Isaiah 65 Jehovah judges and destroys those to whom He had stretched out His arms in vain and then the new creation arrives.

It is worth noting here that, to my knowledge, *no one has ever taught that literal creation will one day be destroyed as a result of Old Covenant Israel's disobedience.* Yet, if one is going to interpret these scriptures literally, as our millennial friends insist, then this is *precisely* what Isaiah 24-25 and Isaiah 65 predicted. Now, if *no one* teaches that literal creation will ever be destroyed as a result of Old Covenant Israel's disobedience, then patently, we must understand the prophecies of Isaiah to speak of creation in metaphoric, and we suggest, *covenantal*, terms.

Stated simply what we are saying is this:

The blessings of Isaiah 24-25 and Isaiah 65 are the same blessings promised in Daniel 9:24-27.

The blessings of Daniel 9:24-27 are confined to, and would come at the consummation of, the seventy week countdown (Daniel 9:24).

Therefore, the blessings of Isaiah 24-25 and Isaiah 65 are confined to and would come at the consummation of the seventy week countdown.

However, we need to emphasize the following as well.

The blessings of Isaiah 24-25 and Isaiah 65 are confined to, and would come at the consummation of, the seventy week countdown of Daniel 9.

But, the blessings of Isaiah 24-25 and Isaiah 65 would only come as a result of (or at the time of) the destruction of the Old Covenant world of Israel.

Therefore, the destruction of the Old Covenant world of Israel is confined to, and would come at the consummation of, the seventy week countdown of Daniel 9:24-27.

123

There is therefore, perfect harmony between these three key eschatological texts. The Messianic Banquet would be in the kingdom. The Banquet would be for those for whom death had been swallowed up in victory. But, the Banquet would only come when the city of confusion was destroyed. The new creation would come when rebellious Israel was destroyed and a new people created. The kingdom (and therefore the *Banquet*) would only come at the end of the seventy weeks.

Jesus brings all of these motifs and key eschatological elements together in Matthew 8. He promised the kingdom, the Banquet, the resurrection and all of these blessings would be realized when "the sons of the kingdom are cast out."

The casting out of the sons of the kingdom equates directly to the overwhelming flood of destruction of the city and people of Daniel 9:24-27. What cannot be missed is that the casting out of the sons of the kingdom results in, or occurs at the very time of the arrival of the Banquet and the resurrection. However, keep in mind that we must equate the Banquet and the kingdom with the world of everlasting righteousness and the time and world in which sin has been removed and the atonement made and enjoyed. This *entails the seventy week countdown.* (Would anyone deny that the privilege at the Banquet table is for those enjoying the blessings of sin being removed through the completed atonement?)

It follows from the above that not only do the blessings of Isaiah 24-25, and Isaiah 65 belong to the seventy week countdown of Daniel 9, but that the destruction of the city and holy people belong to the countdown every bit as much. If the blessings belong to, and are confined to the seventy week countdown, then since in the Isaiah passages those blessings are posited as resulting from the judgment of Old Covenant Israel, this demands that the judgment lies within the seventy week countdown as well. The destruction/judgment is the climax of the prophecies that results directly in the fulfillment of the blessing portion of the prophecies. This amounts to virtually *prima facie* proof that the seventy week countdown was not fulfilled in AD 35 and it was not postponed to some yet future period. The seventy weeks were consummated in the fall of Jerusalem in AD 70 when, "the sons of the kingdom" were cast out. Here is a summary of what we are saying.

Abraham would sit at the table in the *kingdom*.

The *kingdom* would fully arrive *at the end of the seventy weeks* of Daniel 9.

But, Abraham would sit at the table at the time of the *resurrection*.

Therefore, the resurrection would be at the end of the seventy weeks of Daniel 9.

Initially, the millennialist would concur in this assessment. Even the amillennialist and postmillennialist would agree to a certain extent. That is, the postmillennialist would argue that Old Covenant Judah was, in fulfillment of Matthew 8, cast out of the kingdom in the first century.[137] However, the relationship between that rejection, the establishment of the kingdom, the Messianic Banquet *and the resurrection* is virtually ignored.

However, since Jesus said that the gathering to the Banquet would be when "the sons of the kingdom would be cast out" and that gathering to the kingdom Banquet is the time of the *resurrection*, this is a serious exegetical oversight. One thing is certain. In Isaiah 25 there is no disjunction, no temporal gap between the establishment of the kingdom, the establishment of the Banquet and the resurrection. In fact, *the Banquet is for those for whom death has been swallowed up!*

For the millennialist this has profound implications as well, for the dispensational doctrine has no place in it for a yet future casting out of the sons of the kingdom. There is only place for the future restoration of the nation, not the casting out! It is little wonder therefore, that Robert Van Kampen in his tome, *The Sign*,[138] does not even list or discuss Matthew 8. Likewise, Pentecost, in his encyclopedic *Things To Come*, gives Matthew 8 no exegetical consideration at all.[139] Walvoord also totally ignores Matthew 8 in his discussion of *Major Bible Prophecies*.[140]

So, Matthew 8 predicted the establishment of the kingdom, i.e. the end of the seventy weeks. That consummation would come however, when "the sons of the kingdom are cast out." Of course, the sons of the kingdom were not cast out at the Cross, nor at

Pentecost. They were to be cast out for persecuting "the children of the promise" (Galatians 4:22f) and that most assuredly had not occurred at the Cross or Pentecost.

McKnight draws a correct parallel between Matthew 8 and the Wedding Feast of Matthew 22, noting that,

"the man who came to the wedding in inappropriate dress "symbolizes the 'sons of the kingdom' of Matthew 8:11-12, that is, those among Israel who have not repented, who have not seen in Jesus the kingdom being realized, and who have not aligned themselves with the new community of the restored Israel that Jesus has created around the Twelve. Tragically, they will be expelled from the kingdom (destroyed along with Jerusalem) and will not survive the judgment to enter the kingdom of joy and feasting." (*Vision*, 153)

The consummation of the seventy weeks was to be the establishment of the kingdom, the Banquet and the resurrection. The end of that seventy week period was also to be "the end" in "an overwhelming flood" of total destruction and desolation (Daniel 9:27). Likewise, Abraham, Isaac and Jacob were to sit down at the Messianic Banquet, in the resurrection kingdom, when "the sons of the kingdom are cast out." This demands that the seventy weeks were not completed until the sons of the kingdom were cast out and that is no other time than in the destruction of Jerusalem in AD 70. The seventy weeks were not fulfilled in AD 35 and they were not postponed. They were fulfilled and terminated in the cataclysmic abolition of the Old Covenant world and the arrival of the resurrection world of Messiah.

ROMANS 11, DANIEL 9
AND THE END OF ISRAEL'S HISTORY

To extrapolate Romans 11 beyond the first century framework is unjustified and violates the text. As we have just seen, Romans 11 gives no justification for a future salvation of Israel. Romans 11 was fulfilled at the end of the seventy weeks of Daniel 9.

Romans 11:25-26 would be fulfilled when God's covenant dealings with Israel were consummated. The time of the salvation of Israel is posited as the time "when I take away their sins" (v. 27).[141] When does Daniel say that Israel's sin would be removed? *Within the seventy weeks!* There is no delineation between the taking away of Israel's sin in Romans, and the putting away of sin in Daniel. Is the prophecy of Daniel different from the prophecies underlying Romans 11, i.e. Isaiah 27 and Isaiah 59? If the promise of Romans 11 is the same promise of Isaiah and Daniel then since the promise of Daniel is confined to the seventy weeks, this means that the parousia of Christ promised in Romans 11 is confined to the seventy weeks and this destroys the semi-preterist construct. Logically stated the argument would be:

The putting away of Israel's sin is confined to the seventy weeks of Daniel 9.

But, Romans 11:26-27 predicted the putting away of Israel's sin.

Therefore, the putting away of Israel's sin in Romans 11:26-27 is confined to the seventy weeks of Daniel 9.

This point can hardly be over-emphasized. Most postmillennialists, Gentry, DeMar, Mathison, et. al., believe the seventy weeks were fulfilled circa 34-35. Yet, most postmillennialists believe that Romans 11:25f refers to a yet future conversion of Israel.[142] This will not work.

If Daniel 9 foretold the same putting away of sin that Paul anticipated in Romans 11, it is inescapably true that Romans 11 is confined to the seventy weeks of Daniel 9. However, since Paul was still anticipating the fulfillment of that prophecy, the putting away of Israel's sin of Daniel 9, when he wrote, circa AD 57, then

127

the seventy weeks of Daniel 9 were not fulfilled and terminated circa AD 34-35.

This has devastating consequences for the postmillennial view, for it is held that the conversion of the Jews comes near or at *the end of the millennium*, i.e. just before the "final" coming of the Lord. So, if Paul was anticipating the fulfillment of Daniel's prophecy, and if, as the postmillennialists affirm, the conversion of Israel occurs near the end of the millennium, it therefore follows that Paul believed the end of the millennium was near when he wrote.

By positing the removal of Israel's sin into the future, at the end of the millennium, the postmillennialist creates a gap between the 69th and 70th week of Daniel 9 that is as large as the millennial gap that postmillennialists so vehemently reject!

Unless the postmillennialists are willing to extrapolate the 70th Week of Daniel 9 into the still distant future–thus allowing for a still future fulfillment of the putting away of sin,[143] then we must confine the fulfillment of that final consummative week to the first century context.

By extending Romans 11 into the future the postmillennialists unwittingly create the exact same "gap" between the 69th and the 70th Week of Daniel 9 that they so decry in the millennial construct. If the putting away of sin of Daniel 9 and the putting away of sin in Romans 11 are the same then if the fulfillment of Romans 11 is yet future, the fulfillment of the 70th Week is still future. This means that 70th Week was postponed just as the millennialists say!

There is no justification for delineating between the putting away of sin in these two texts. Therefore, unless the postmillennialists are indeed willing now to join the millennialists in positing a gap between the 69th and the 70th Week they must cede Romans 11 to the first century, AD 70 parousia of Christ, *thus stripping their eschatology of one of their most fundamental arguments for futurism.*

Consider the following arguments based on Daniel 9 and Romans 11 as they relate to the consummation of Israel's history. Some of the arguments may *seem* repetitious but pay close attention to how the arguments flow.

The consummation of Old Covenant Israel's history would be the resurrection of the dead (Acts 24:14f; 26:6f/ Romans 8:23; 9:3-5/ 1 Corinthians 15).

But, the consummation of Israel's history is confined to the seventy weeks of Daniel 9:24-27.

Therefore, the resurrection is confined to the seventy weeks of Daniel 9:24-27.

Next:

The consummation of Israel's history would occur at the time of the parousia of Romans 11.

But, the parousia of Romans 11:25f occurred at the time of the judgment of Israel in AD 70 in the judgment of the blood of the martyrs (Mt. 23:29f).

Therefore, the consummation of Israel's history, the resurrection, occurred at the time of the judgment of Israel in AD 70.

Next

The consummation of Israel's history-when God's promises to her would be fulfilled- would be when sin was "put away" (Daniel 9:24).

But the time when God fulfilled His promises to Israel by putting away sin would be at the parousia of Romans 11:25-27.

Therefore, the parousia of Romans 11:25-27 would be the consummation of Israel's history.

Next

129

The parousia of Romans 11:25-27 would be the consummation of Israel's history.

But, the consummation of Israel's history would be the resurrection of the dead (Acts 24:14f; 26:6f/ Romans 8:23; 9:3f/ 1 Corinthians 15).

Therefore, the parousia of Romans 11:25-27 would be the resurrection of the dead.

Next

The parousia of Romans 11:25-27 would be the resurrection of the dead.

But, the parousia of Romans 11:25-27 was in AD 70.

Therefore, the resurrection of the dead was in AD 70.

Next

The consummation of Israel's history occurred at the time of the judgment of Israel in AD 70 (Daniel 9:24-27).

But the consummation of Israel's history would be the resurrection.

Therefore, the resurrection, at the consummation of Israel's history, occurred at the time of the judgment of Israel in AD 70.

Next

The consummation of Israel's history would be the resurrection (Acts 24-28/ Romans 8:23/ 1 Cor. 15).

The consummation of Israel's history is confined to the seventy weeks of Daniel 9.

The seventy weeks of Daniel 9 ended in AD 70.

Therefore, the consummation of Israel's history, the resurrection, is confined to the seventy weeks of Daniel 9, that ended in AD 70.

If Romans 11:25-27 is confined to the seventy weeks of Daniel 9, this means that the parousia of Romans 11 is confined to the seventy weeks. This also means that if one posits the salvation of Israel for the last days of the millennium,[144] as do the postmillennialists, then the end of the millennium was at the parousia of AD 70.

The only way to avoid this devastating impact on the postmillennial paradigm[145] is:

A.) To prove that the putting away of sin in Daniel 9 and that in Romans are different events at different times. As we have seen, DeMar attempts to do this, suggesting that the seventy weeks ended in AD 33-35, but that Romans 11 was fulfilled in the deliverance of the remnant from the destruction of Jerusalem. This is a false dichotomy however, and as we have seen, defines the deliverance from physical death as the removal of the sin of Israel. This is untenable.

B.) Prove that Israel had, or has, two consummative, soteriological events. Yet, at least some of the leading postmillennialists acknowledge that AD 70 was a redemptive-historical event of unparalleled importance.

C.) To prove that perhaps the seventieth week of Daniel 9 has not yet been fulfilled. Of course to do this, one has to abandon the normal postmillennial view that the seventieth week was fulfilled in AD 34-35.

Furthermore, to posit the seventieth week as yet future inserts a 2000 year gap between the sixty-ninth and the seventieth week, something that postmillennialists are normally loathe to do.

Daniel 9 and Romans 11 contain the same theme, the same time, the same event, the salvation of Israel. That being so, Romans 11 cannot be used to justify a yet future conversion of the Jews at the end of the current Christian age. Romans 11 anticipated the consummation of Israel's soteriological and eschatological history in AD 70.

Why is the question of the consummation of Israel's history so important? It is because *the resurrection is the consummation of*

131

Israel's history! Contra the normal belief that the resurrection is to be the fulfilment of eschatological promises made to the church, for the end of the Christian age, Paul said, repeatedly, that his gospel was the "hope of Israel," and that the core of his message was the resurrection (Acts 24:14f; 26; 6f; 26:23f; 28:20f). When the apostle wrote his greatest discourse on the resurrection he stated that the resurrection would be when the Old Covenant promises to Israel were fulfilled (1 Corinthians 15:54f). Thus, to repeat, the question about the consummation of Israel's history is *the* fundamental question of the resurrection.

If in fact Daniel 9 and Romans 11 anticipated the consummation of Israel's history therefore (and that is undeniably true) then it follows that since Daniel 9 posited the consummation of Israel's history at the destruction of Jerusalem in AD 70, that this is the time of the resurrection.

DANIEL 12 AND 1 CORINTHIANS 15

Finally, we must take note of the direct parallels between Daniel 12 and 1 Corinthians 15. We have already shown that Daniel 9 and chapter 12 are directly parallel. Therefore, to demonstrate the inseparable connection between Daniel 12 and 1 Corinthians 15 unavoidably ties the fulfillment of Paul's greatest discourse on resurrection to the end of Israel's history.

Of course, this can be done by noting that in 1 Corinthians 15, Paul was anticipating the fulfillment of Isaiah 25 and Hosea 13. What is so significant about these texts is that they are, just like the Danielic texts, concerned, not with human history *per se*, but with the perfection of Israel's salvation.

Note that in Isaiah 25, Jehovah promised to make a great feast, *the Messianic Banquet,* on Zion.[146] That banquet would be for those for whom death was destroyed forever (Isaiah 25:6f).[147] What cannot be missed is this: "And it will be said in that day, Behold, this is our God; We have waited for Him, and He will save us. This is the Lord; we have waited for Him; We will be glad and rejoice in His salvation" (Isaiah 25:9). In other words, the day of the Messianic Banquet, *the day of the resurrection*, would be the day of *Israel's salvation!*

Is Isaiah's day of salvation in Zion different from the time of Israel's salvation at the parousia in Romans 11:26? Both texts posit salvation in direct connection with *Zion*.[148] And if Romans 11 and 1 Corinthians 15 both foretold the fulfillment of Israel's eschatological promises, what are the implications for those paradigms that ignore these connections, claiming that the fulfillment of Corinthians is "Christian Eschatology" *unrelated* to the fulfillment of Israel's eschatological hope? This is a serious issue indeed.

We reiterate that Paul proclaimed nothing but the hope of Israel. So, Isaiah foretold the time of Israel's salvation and said it would be when Jehovah made a glorious banquet on Zion, for those for whom death had been destroyed. And in Romans, Paul anticipated the time of Israel's salvation at the parousia. He even said that Israel's salvation would be "life from the dead" (Romans 11:15f)!

Our point of course, is that Isaiah foretold the resurrection and Daniel foretold the resurrection. Both prophecies dealt with the time of Israel's salvation. But unless Isaiah and Daniel foretold two different resurrections, both related to the consummation of Israel's hopes, at two different times, then since Paul's doctrine of the resurrection is based on Isaiah 25 that means his resurrection hope is tied directly to Daniel 12.

Stated simply, here is what that means:

The resurrection prophecy of Isaiah 25:6-8 predicted the same resurrection as Daniel 12.

But, the resurrection prophecy of Isaiah 25 is the source of Paul's resurrection hope and doctrine in 1 Corinthians 15.

Therefore, Daniel 12, being the same resurrection prophecy as Isaiah 25, is also the source of Paul's resurrection hope and doctrine in 1 Corinthians 15.

This connects Daniel 12 with 1 Corinthians 15, and the implications for this are profound. So, let us look directly at Daniel 12 and 1 Corinthians 15. For ease of study, notice the parallels between Daniel 12 and 1 Corinthians 15.

133

Daniel 12	1 Corinthians 15
Promise made to and concerning Israel (v. 1)	Resurrection promises made to Israel (v. 54f)
Promise of the resurrection (v. 2)	Promise of the resurrection
Resurrection to everlasting life (v. 2)	Resurrection to immortality (v. 54)
Time of the end (v. 4, 9f)	Time of the end (v. 19f)
Time of the kingdom (v. 3)	Time of the kingdom (v. 50-51)
Fulfilled "when the power of the holy people is completely shattered" (v. 6-7)	Fulfilled when "the law that is the strength of sin" i.e. the Mosaic Law,** removed.

** See our earlier comments on the identity of the law that was the strength of sin.

There is a direct and precise parallel between Daniel 12 and 1 Corinthians 15. And this being true, it follows that the resurrection was to occur at the end of the Old Covenant age of Israel, "when the power of the holy people" was completely shattered.

What is clear from Paul is that he was anticipating the consummation of God's promises to *Israel*. Daniel 12 was concerned with the consummation of *Israel's* Messianic and soteriological hopes. So, if Daniel 12 and 1 Corinthians 15 speak of the same time and same events, then since Daniel 12 was to be fulfilled when Israel would be finally destroyed, it therefore follows inexorably that 1 Corinthians 15 would be fulfilled at that time.

A STUDY OF DANIEL 2, 7, 9 AND 12
HARMONIZING FOUR MAJOR
ESCHATOLOGICAL PROPHECIES

While there is so much more that could be said, I want to take note, ever so briefly, of a few final thoughts.

In Daniel 2 we find the vision of Nebuchadnezzar concerning the four kingdoms. The last of the four kingdoms is the Roman Empire.[149] It would be in, "in the days of these kings that the God of heaven shall set up a kingdom that shall never be destroyed" (Daniel 2:44).

In Daniel 7 one like the Son of Man came before the Ancient of Days and, "to him was given dominion and glory and a kingdom, that all peoples, nations and languages should serve Him. His dominion is an everlasting dominion, which shall not pass away, and His kingdom the one which shall not be destroyed" (Daniel 7:13-14). The persecutorial "little horn" that had persecuted the saints would be destroyed, and the God of heaven would vindicate His suffering saints. At that time, "the kingdom and dominion, and the greatness of the kingdoms under the whole heaven shall be given to the people, the saints of the Most High" (Daniel 7:27).

So, Daniel 2 and Daniel 7 both foretold the establishment of the kingdom of Messiah. And this cannot be over-emphasized, the kingdom would be established in the days of the Roman Empire. There is not one shred of textual evidence to suggest a "revived Roman Empire" as postulated by the millennialists. We cannot state strongly enough that the idea of a revived Roman empire is a theological fabrication.

> **There is not one shred of textual evidence to suggest a "revived Roman Empire" as postulated by the millennialists.**

This doctrine came about, not through serious exegetical investigation, but as a result of the same kind of preconceived ideas about the kingdom exhibited by the two disciples on the Emmaeus road (Luke 24:25f). They believed that the Cross had, at the very least, *postponed the kingdom*. At the worst they believed the Cross had *destroyed* their kingdom hope. Likewise, dispensationalism says that due to the Jewish rejection of Jesus the kingdom was postponed. Yet, because Daniel predicted that the kingdom would be established in the days of the Romans empire, then since the kingdom was postponed, that means the Roman empire must be revived.

It seems never to have dawned on the millennialists that not once in the entire prophetic corpus does the Bible ever use the words, revived, restored, raised again, or any other restorative word to speak of the Roman empire. *Never.* And while millennialists allude to Daniel 2 for the basis of that doctrine, it is allusion alone, and not exegesis. There is a dramatic disjunction between what Daniel actually says and what the millennialists say about Daniel.

The fact that Jesus said "the time is fulfilled, the kingdom of heaven has drawn near" dispels any possibility of a revived Roman empire theology.

The fact that the NT writers never so much as hint at the idea of a postponed kingdom falsifies the idea of a revived Roman empire.

The fact that the NT writers affirm, repeatedly, that they were living in the days foretold by the OT prophets destroys the idea of a revived Roman empire.

The fact that the NT writers affirm that the time and events anticipated by the OT prophets had arrived ("the end of the ages has come upon us" (1 Corinthians 10:11)[150] is *prima facie* proof that the theory of the revived Roman empire is wrong.

The fact that the NT writers all affirm, repeatedly and emphatically, that the end of the age, the parousia and the judgment were very near in the first century, denies the idea of a revived Roman empire.

The fact that the dispensationalists cannot point to one single text that clearly affirms the revival of the Roman empire strongly suggests that the doctrine is contrived and specious. Furthermore, dispensationalists actually have their kingdom count all wrong!

Mark Hitchcock, author of several books on dispensationalism, comments on the seven kings of Revelation 17, and identifies them as seven kingdoms. His count is 1.) Egypt, 2.) Assyria, 3.)

Babylon, 4.) Persia, 5.) Greece, 6.) Rome, 7.) Revived Rome, and 8.) "the final form of gentile world rule."[151]

The problem for Hitchcock and the millennialists is that in this count the seventh king (kingdom) is the revived Roman empire, but in Revelation the seventh king (kingdom per Hitchcock) *is of virtually no consequence at all.* It is not the persecuting power. It lasts "only a little while," and is most definitely not, "the final form of gentile world rule." In Revelation it is the *eighth king* that is the villain! In order to make the eighth king to be the revived Roman empire Hitchcock and the millennialists must make the eighth king do be a *revived, revived Roman empire!* Unless the eighth is indeed a revived, revived Roman empire, then for the millennial scheme to work the kingdom has to be established in the days of the seventh king.

If the kingdom is established in the days of the eighth king, when the beast would be destroyed and the kingdom delivered to the saints, then if Hitchcock's count is right this means that Daniel's prophecy is wrong! Remember, Daniel said the kingdom would be established in the days of *the fourth empire.* Yet, per Hitchcock's calculation we would have Rome, the revived Roman empire (the seventh king of Revelation 17) and then, the eighth.

However, again, in Revelation the seventh is inconsequential and thus, not the time of the establishing of the kingdom. So, the millennial count is wrong. But, if the eighth is the pivotal one, then, as noted this means that the eighth must be the revived, *revived* Roman empire, or, if it is not the revived, revived Roman empire *it is not the Roman empire at all.* In this case however, the eighth cannot be of the fourth kingdom of Daniel, and consequently cannot be the time of the fulfillment of Daniel 2. This is untenable.

There is something else here in regard to the revived Roman empire, something that receives scant attention, yet, is very important. When one pays attention, it becomes apparent that the millennial scheme absolutely demands the restoration of *many* ancient kingdoms. Since the kingdom was to be restored in the days of the Roman Empire, but of course wasn't per the millennial view, then, naturally they claim that the future will see the revived Roman empire. But this likewise means that Philistia (Jeremiah 47), Moab (Jeremiah 48), Edom (Obadiah), Ammon (Jeremiah 49), and a host of other historical nations, that are the focus of Day of the Lord predictions in the OT, must be revived if the literalism of millennialism stands true.

For instance, in Jeremiah 50-51 in the prediction of the destruction of Babylon, we are told that this is actually a prediction of the end times destruction of *literal* Babylon. Well, then that means that literal Babylon will be restored.[152] However, if literal Babylon is restored, then her destroyer, *the Medes*, must be restored as well. In Jeremiah 51:11 it declares that it would be the Medes that would destroy Babylon.

Furthermore, not only would the Medes destroy Babylon in Jeremiah's prophecy, but they would do it with ancient weapons such as bows and arrows, the lance, etc. and they would ride on horses (Jeremiah 50:14, 42)! Historically of course, that is exactly what happened, but that seems not to phase the millennialists. Their literalism suddenly sees in these allusions references to missiles and bullets, armored personnel carriers, etc.!

Mark Hitchcock plays word games in regard to the restoration of the various nations of the end times. Commenting on Ezekiel 38-39 he lists the ancient names of the text, and then subtly gives the name of the "modern nation" that is the equivalent of the ancient nation![153] He fails to tell the reader that the "modern nations" bear *no resemblance* to the ancient nations. The ancient nations / kingdoms do not exist anymore, in many instances! Yet, the millennial paradigm simply ignores this inconvenient fact of history, and either tacitly posits the restoration of these ancient kingdoms, or, like Hitchcock, holds that the modern nations will somehow "fill the bill."

One has the right to wonder where the literalistic hermeneutic so essential to millennialism, has gone? They insist that the Bible must be taken literally, and to "spiritualize" does violence to the text. However, when it comes to the actual text of prophecy we are now told that it is not actually the kingdoms that existed in the time of the prophets and that are named in Isaiah, Jeremiah, Ezekiel, etc, but in reality it is the *modern nations*, bearing totally different names, cultures and identities from those in the text that are the focus of the prophecies.[154] This is disingenuous to say the least.

These critical facts are seemingly lost on the millennial world. Exactly how Hitchcock can make the seventh king (kingdom) to be

138

the critical revived Roman empire, yet totally ignore what Revelation says about the seventh king we do not know, for he does not tell us. He simply asserts his position and does not exegete.

While Daniel's prophecy, and Revelation 17 are somewhat difficult, the millennial count of the kings and kingdoms will not work. We must keep the predicted events within the confines of the original, historical Roman empire, and not make wild, speculative claims that remove the prophecy to times far removed from their original, textual parameters. Enough of this for now.

For brevity, what we want to do now is to establish, as if it were truly necessary, that Daniel 2, 7, 9, and 12 are all predictive of the same time and events. They all foretold, with different nuances and emphasis, the time of the end, establishment of the kingdom and the triumph of the people of God. This much is admitted by virtually all conservative scholars.

Daniel 2 foretold the last days, (v. 28) and the establishment of the everlasting kingdom, in the days of the fourth kingdom, i.e. the days of Rome.

Daniel 7 predicted the establishment of the everlasting kingdom, in the days of the fourth beast, i.e. the Roman empire. During the days of Rome, the saints would be persecuted "for a time, times, and a half time," until the coming of the Messiah in judgment of the persecutor of his people.

Daniel 9 anticipated the establishment of the world of "everlasting righteousness" in the days when "the people of the prince that is to come will destroy the city and the sanctuary" (Daniel 9:26).[155] This destruction would surely be as a result of the slaying of the Messiah. This is the prediction of the establishment of the kingdom in the days of the Roman empire.

Daniel 12 predicted the time of the end, the time when the righteous would shine in the kingdom (cf. Matthew 13:43) and the vision would be ultimately fulfilled after a period of time described as "at time, times and a half of a time" (Daniel 12:7). This critical time period, along with the reference to the end and deliverance of the people (v. 1) undeniably conflates this text with Daniel 7. And since Daniel 9 foretold the Abomination of Desolation that links Daniel 9 with chapter 12 as well.

Perhaps a couple of charts demonstrating the parallelisms would be helpful.

Daniel 7	Daniel 9
Days of Rome (fourth beast, cf. Daniel 2)	Days of Rome
The little horn	Abomination of Desolation
Persecution of the saints (v. 25-27)	Killing of Messiah (v. 26)
Coming of the Son of Man	Arrival of the kingdom at the end of the seventy weeks
Vindication of the saints (v. 23f- Destruction of persecutor)	Vindication of saints (v. 27, (Destruction of persecutor)
Arrival of the Kingdom (v. 25)	Arrival of the kingdom (everlasting righteousness)

It should be clear from these comparisons that Daniel 7 and chapter 9 truly are parallel. With this being true, the suggestion is that since Daniel 9 sees no further than the destruction of Jerusalem as the time for the vindication of the martyrs, that this is also the terminus for Daniel 7. This is confirmed by a comparison with Daniel 7 and chapter 12.

Daniel 7	Daniel 12
Time of tribulation (v. 23f)	Time of tribulation (v. 1)
Time of the end	Time of the end (v. 4)
Time, times, half time (v. 25)	Time, times, half time (v. 7)
Little Horn (v. 24-25)	Abomination of Desolation (v. 9f)

140

Kingdom given (v. 25-27)	Time of the kingdom (v. 3, cf. Matthew 13:43)
Vindication of the saints (v. 27)	Vindication of the saints (v. 1, 3, 13)
Coming and enthronement of the Son of Man (v. 13-14, 26-27)	End of the age, resurrection (v. 2, 4)

Notice the parallel nature of chapter 9 and 12 as well.

Daniel 9	Daniel 12
Time of the end foretold	Time of the end foretold
Kingdom foretold	Kingdom foretold (v. 2-3)
Time of martyrdom (v. 26)	Time of martyrdom (v. 1)
Abomination of desolation (v. 27)	Abomination of desolation (v. 9f)
Time of the resurrection (see earlier discussion)	Time of the resurrection (v. 2)
All fulfilled by end of seventy weeks and destruction of the "holy city" (v. 24, 27)	All fulfilled when "the power of the holy people is completely shattered" (v. 7)

Daniel 9 and chapter 12 posit the vindication of the blood of the saints, the reception of the kingdom, and the destruction of the persecutor, at the time of the judgment of Old Covenant Judah. This all but forces us to see that this is also the terminus of Daniel 7. With these parallels before us, certain things become apparent. **1.)** The events of all of the chapters were to be fulfilled in the days of the Roman empire that existed in the first century. As we have seen, there is not a shred of evidence to support the idea of a revived Roman empire.

2.) This means that the seventy weeks of Daniel 9 are confined to that time period as well.

3.) Not only were the events confined to the days of the Roman empire, but more specifically, to *the last days of the Old Covenant age of Israel* that occurred within the framework of the Roman empire. This is true since the vision of Daniel 9 climaxes in the fall of Jerusalem. Daniel 12 likewise climaxes with the destruction of Old Covenant Judah (12:7) and as we shall see, *even Daniel 7 finds its consummation in the judgment of Israel.*

To establish this later point, please note that there are *three harmonious constituent elements,* often overlooked by commentators, in three of the four Danielic prophecies.[156] The elements are:

1.) The persecution of the saints, and their vindication at the coming of the Son of Man in judgment, in Daniel 7.

2.) The destruction of Jerusalem–for killing Messiah–in Daniel 9.

3.) The time of the end, and the resurrection, "when the power of the holy people is completely shattered" (Daniel 12:2-7).

These three key constituent elements allow us to not only identify the time of the completion of the last days, but the consummation of the seventy weeks and the interpretation of several other key eschatological texts.

It will be noticed that the three constituent elements can actually be summarized under two thematic elements; the avenging of the blood of the saints, and the judgment of Old Covenant Israel, the slayer of the saints. As we have developed the theme of the vindication of the blood of the saints from Deuteronomy 32 on page 9f, we will only summarize those thoughts here.

Jehovah said that in the last days of Old Covenant Israel He would "avenge the blood of His saints" (Deuteronomy 32:43). Other key OT texts (e. g. Isaiah 2-4) agree in placing the time of the avenging of the saints in the last days, at the judgment of Israel.

Jesus taught this as clearly as possible when he affirmed that all of the blood of all the righteous shed on the earth would be judged and avenged in his generation, in the judgment of Jerusalem (Matthew 23:29-39).

As we have seen, Jesus' teaching in Matthew 23 is a powerful commentary on Daniel 9 since the judgment on Jerusalem foretold there is patently a result of the killing of Messiah. This means that the judgment of Jerusalem would be the climax of the seventy weeks! However, Deuteronomy 32, along with Jesus' temple discourse in Matthew 23, also gives us insight into Daniel 7.

Daniel 7 predicted the arrival of the "little horn" that would exalt himself, "he shall persecute the saints of the Most High"(Daniel 7:25). It is normally argued that this little horn must be one of the Roman rulers, and there is no doubt that he would exist in the days of Rome. However, I think it worthy of note that it is distinctly possible that Daniel is casting Old Covenant Israel as the persecutorial enemy of the true saints, i.e the remnant!

There is a concept found in the scriptures, and that is the idea that through her rebellion and disobedience, *Israel became the enemy of God.* See my extended discussion of this concept in my *Like Father Like Son,* book.[157] *She came to stand in the same role as a pagan nation!* This concept is found in several OT as well as NT passages.

In Isaiah 63:10 Jehovah rehearsed Israel's history, and how He had guided and protected them. In spite of His guidance, "they rebelled and grieved His Holy Spirit; so He turned Himself against them as an enemy." Psalms 106:39f laments Israel's sin that caused Jehovah's wrath to burn against them "the wrath of the Lord was kindled against His people, so that He abhorred His own inheritance, and He gave them into the hand of the Gentiles."[158] At a time later than Isaiah, Jeremiah lamented the fall of Jerusalem, "Standing like an enemy He has bent His bow; with His right hand, like an adversary, He has slain all who were pleasing to His eye; On the tent of the daughter of Zion He has poured out His fury like fire. The Lord was like an enemy. He has swallowed up Israel. He has swallowed up all her palaces, He has destroyed her strongholds" (Lamentations 2:4).

The New Testament prophets also testify that Old Covenant Judah was becoming the enemy of God, and would suffer that fate.

In Acts 3 after healing the crippled man at the entrance of the temple, Peter calls on that crowd to repent "so that times of refreshing may come from the presence of the Lord, and that he may send Jesus" (Acts 3:21f). Peter then does something remarkable. He recalls the prophecy made to and through Moses, that God would raise up another prophet, like Moses, "Him you shall hear in all things, whatever He says to you. And it shall be that every soul who will not hear that Prophet shall be utterly destroyed from among the people" (ἐκ τοῦ λαοῦ– literally, out from among, Acts 3:22-23). Notice what Peter is doing.

Peter says that according to Moses, the last days prophet would be like him. God called on Israel to obey the voice of this Second Moses, and here is what is critical, failure to obey him would result in utter destruction *"from among the people."* Do you catch that? For Peter "the people" would be those in Israel that followed this second Moses. Those in Israel who rejected him would be "utterly destroyed out from among the people."

For Peter then, the true Israel, the true "the people" would be, as defined by Jehovah through Moses, those who followed this Second Moses! To reject this last days Moses would be to identify oneself as *not* "the people." This naturally means that since the old Jerusalem had rejected him, then the old Jerusalem was no longer "the city of God," *but the apostate enemy of Jehovah*! See Philippians 3:16-18 also, where Paul calls the unbelieving Jews of his day "the enemy of the Cross."

In Matthew 24:30, Jesus predicted his judgment coming against Jerusalem, and cites Daniel 7:13-14 about the Son of Man coming on the clouds of heaven. Thus, *Jesus applied the time of judgment of the little horn to the judgment of Israel.* This is remarkable, but not unnoticed by the scholars. France says, "Whereas in Daniel 7 the Son of Man represented the triumph of Israel over other nations, the triumph of Jesus is, in the first instance, over the Jews."[159] France explains this by saying, "The suggestion is that Jesus' teaching that He himself, and through him His disciples, now constituted the true people of God was deliberately carried to the extent of applying to the unbelieving Jews the Danielic visions of the crushing of the pagan opposition. In rejecting Jesus, the Jews, no less than the pagan empires were the opponents of the kingdom of God." (France, 147).

Likewise, Wright says Jesus, "Made the book of Daniel thematic for his whole vocation. He understood it to be referring to the great climax in which YHWH would defeat the fourth world empire and vindicate his suffering people. He projected the notion of the evil empire on the present Jerusalem regime, and identified himself and his movement with the people who were to be vindicated." (*Victory*, 598). Interestingly enough, even the dispensational writer Tim LaHaye, speaking of Jerusalem just prior to the BC 586 captivity and the reason for that destruction said, "If ever a nation deserved the judging hand of God it was the children of Israel. *Their leaders and many of the people had become pagans right there in the Holy City of God, Jerusalem.*"[160] The question that is fair to ask in regard to LaHaye's comment is, if Judah had become "a pagan nation" in the sixth century BC through her idolatry and rebellion, then how much more was this true in Jesus' generation when they were not only guilty of "idolatry" but of killing the Son of God?

So, our point is that in Daniel 7, when we find the reference to the "little horn," although it is assuredly set within the time of the Roman empire, this does not demand that the little horn is a Roman emperor, or a long line of Roman emperors, as posited by Calvin.[161] Nor is there justification for identifying the little horn with the Roman Catholic church, as do amillennialists.[162]

The one thing that is, in my mind at least, definitive for the identity of the little horn, is the theme of the persecution and vindication of the martyrs that stands at the heart of Daniel 7:23f.

> **From Genesis to Revelation the blood of the martyrs flows and their prayers ascend, crying, "How long, O Lord?" Heaven's answer to their prayer, found in both the OT and the New, is that the time of vindication would occur in Israel's last days, in the destruction of Jerusalem, in the first century! Exegetes and commentators that ignore this motif and divine statements are doing themselves and their readers a grave disservice.**

I have commented often, in sermons and other venues, that the theme of the suffering and vindication of the saints is an eschatological theme and motif that is seldom given its proper due, even among preterist writers and speakers. Yet, from Genesis to Revelation there is a stream flowing with the blood of the righteous, their prayer for vindication, and the promise that their blood will be vindicated in the Day of the Lord. Furthermore, in the N. T., the promised vindication is invariably said to be near.

We have just noticed that Deuteronomy 32, Isaiah 2-4, and a host of other passages posit two central truths, 1.) The culpability of Old Covenant Israel for shedding the blood of the martyrs, 2.) That it would be in Israel's last days, and in the first century destruction of Jerusalem, at the Day of the Lord, that the martyrs would be vindicated.

What should never be overlooked in discussions of the shedding of the blood of the saints is that there is only one people, one city, one nation that is *consistently* blamed for shedding the blood of the saints. That is Old Covenant Israel. Stephen's words in the temple were not only true when he spoke them, but they chronicled the long and bloody history of Israel, "Which of the prophets did your fathers not persecute? And they killed those who foretold the coming of the Just One, of whom you have now become the betrayers and murderers" (Acts 7:52; Compare 2 Chronicles 36:15f)

What is even more amazing is that in Matthew 23, a text we have already examined above, Jesus said, "all of the righteous blood shed on the earth, from righteous Abel to Zecharias, son of Berechias" would be avenged, their killers judged, in his generation. It should be noted, yet seldom is, that this judgment is far more comprehensive than a localized, "Jewish" judgment. There were no Jews in the days of Abel! Yet, his righteous blood, that cried to Jehovah from the ground (Genesis 4:10) would be avenged in the judgment of Judah in AD 70!

The comprehensive nature of the judgment foretold in Deuteronomy 32 and in Matthew 23 should guide our understanding of Daniel 7, not to mention chapters 9 and 12. Unless the promise in Deuteronomy 32 of the avenging of the blood of the saints, is different from the avenging of the blood of the saints in Daniel 7, then the two prophecies are synchronous. That means that Daniel 7 would be fulfilled, not in the last days of human history, not in the last days of Rome, not in the last days of the Christian age, but *in the last days of Old Covenant Israel.*

Furthermore, since the seventy weeks would terminate and consummate in the destruction of the city *for killing the Messiah*

(Daniel 9:26-27) this posits the Daniel 7 coming of the Son of Man in vindication of the saints, at that time as well.

It is widely admitted that the judgment of Jerusalem would be the result of killing Jesus (cf. Matthew 21:33f).[163] So, unless the Daniel 7 coming of the Son of Man in vindication of the suffering martyrs is totally unrelated to the judgment of Jerusalem in AD 70–which of course was the comprehensive vindication of all the blood shed on the earth–then we must view the parousia in Daniel 7 as the consummation of the seventy weeks. There is no such disjunction however, since the coming of the master of the vineyard (Matthew 21) to vindicate the death of His son was also in vindication of the servants sent earlier.

There is thus, an indissoluble unity between the martyrdom / vindication of Christ and the rest of the saints. Since this unity is undeniable, meaning that the saints and Christ would be vindicated in the fall of Jerusalem in AD 70, then there is no way to extend the fulfillment of Daniel 7 to the time of the fall of Rome, and that vindication certainly cannot be extrapolated to a yet future destruction of the Roman Catholic church. The parameters for the vindication of the martyrs, including Jesus, are simply too clear-cut. That vindication was to occur in the last days of Old Covenant Israel, in the destruction of Jerusalem in AD 70.

Simply stated, our argument is this:

The vindication of the blood of all the martyrs, (all the martyr's blood shed on the earth) would occur in the last days of Israel, and in the fall of Jerusalem in AD 70 (Deuteronomy 32; Daniel 9:26-27; Matthew 23:33-39).

Daniel 7:23f foretold the vindication of the blood of the martyrs.

Therefore, the vindication of the martyrs foretold in Daniel 7:23f would occur in the last days of Israel, in the fall of Jerusalem in AD 70.

Stated another way, the parallels between Daniel 7 and Daniel 9 teach the following:

147

Daniel 7:13-25 and Daniel 9:24-27 foretold the same time and the same events, i.e. the avenging of the blood of the saints and the full establishment of the kingdom.

But, Daniel 9 posits the time of the avenging of the blood of the saints no later than the fall of Jerusalem in AD 70.

Therefore, the avenging of the blood of the saints in Daniel 7 must be posited no later than the fall of Jerusalem in AD 70.

Now, unless the avenging of the blood of the saints in Daniel 7 is totally unrelated to the avenging of the blood of the Messiah –who of course stands as the corporate symbol of the body of the martyrs-- in Daniel 9, there is no way to extend the fulfillment of Daniel 7 beyond the judgment of Jerusalem in AD 70.

We know who it was in the first century whose cup of sin, for persecuting the saints, was full. It was none other than Old Covenant Judah (Matthew 23; 1 Thessalonians 2:15f).

The implications of the foregoing for our understanding of NT eschatology are profound. We will only take the time to chart out the relationship between the prophecies of Daniel and a few key NT texts, but when these connections are seen their significance will be apparent. We will keep our comments brief and present our argument by means of charts.

Daniel 7:13-27	Matthew 24:29f
Coming of the Son of Man on the clouds	Coming of the Son of Man on the clouds
Time of tribulation	Immediately after the tribulation
Little Horn	Abomination of Desolation
Vindication of the martyrs	Vindication of the martyrs
Time of the kingdom	Time of the kingdom (Luke 21:31)

Deuteronomy 32 and the various other passages cited, including the definitive statements of Matthew 23, posit the vindication of the martyrs in the last days of Israel consummating in AD 70. This means Daniel 7 must be interpreted in this light. However, since Daniel 7 is indubitably parallel with Matthew 24 that means that Matthew 24:29f must also be acknowledged to be a prediction of the vindication of the martyrs in AD 70.

But, let's take a look at another text from the Olivet Discourse.

Daniel 7	Matthew 25:31f
Coming of the Son of Man	Coming of the Son of Man
Kingdom given (v. 13-14)	Then shall he sit on the throne of his glory (v. 31-32)
Time of the judgment (books were opened, v. 11ff)	Time of the judgment (books opened, cf. Revelation 20:1f)
Saints given the kingdom	Saints given the kingdom
Destruction of the enemies of the Son	Destruction of the enemies of the Son

Our argument would be framed like this:
Daniel 7 and Matthew 25:31f predicted the same time and the same events.

Daniel 7 predicted the time of the avenging of the martyrs and saints (Daniel 7:25-27)

But, the time of the avenging of the martyrs and saints would be in the last days of Israel, at the destruction of Jerusalem in AD 70 (Deuteronomy 32; Matthew 23).

Therefore, Matthew 25:31f would occur in the last days of Israel at the destruction of Jerusalem in AD 70.

It is widely held that Daniel 7:13-14 is referent to Jesus' ascension in Acts 1 and the reception of the kingdom. While that is an attractive view, and one I held for many years, I must now demur. Acts 1 simply does not meet the textual criteria of Daniel 7, either in the visionary verses, or in the interpretative verses.

Notice the entire preceding context of Daniel 7:13-14:

V. 8. "I was considering the horns, and there was another horn, a little one, coming up among them, before whom three of the first horns were plucked out by the roots. And there, in this horn, were eyes like the eyes of a man, and a mouth speaking pompous words. I watched till thrones were put in place, And the Ancient of Days was seated; His garment was white as snow, And the hair of His head was like pure wool. His throne was a fiery flame, Its wheels a burning fire; A fiery stream issued And came forth from before Him. A thousand thousands ministered to Him; Ten thousand times ten thousand stood before Him. The court was seated, And the books were opened. I watched then because of the sound of the pompous words which the horn was speaking; I watched till the beast was slain, and its body destroyed and given to the burning flame. As for the rest of the beasts, they had their dominion taken away, yet their lives were prolonged for a season and a time. I was watching in the night visions, And behold, One like the Son of Man, Coming with the clouds of heaven! He came to the Ancient of Days, And they brought Him near before Him. Then to Him was given dominion and glory and a kingdom, That all peoples, nations, and languages should serve Him. His dominion is an everlasting dominion, Which shall not pass away, And His kingdom the one Which shall not be destroyed."

We have given the entire context to show that verses 13-14 are the climax of the vision. *Before the bestowing of the kingdom* of verses 13-14 however, there is *first* the appearance of the Little Horn, which of course corresponds to the persecution of the saints (v. 23f) the sitting of thrones, the opening of the books, the judgment of the Horn, and then, *and not until then*, the bestowal of the kingdom on the one like the Son of Man.

Thus, if we take the vision of verses 8f in any kind of chronological order, the coming of the Son of Man occurs only *after* the appearance of the Little Horn, *after* the work of the Horn, at the destruction of the other kingdoms, in the judgment when the books would be opened. It is of course, *impossible* to correlate this scenario or time line to fit Acts 1 and Christ's ascension. The only way to say that the persecutorial Little Horn had persecuted the saints prior to the ascension is to identify the Horn as someone other than any Roman emperor. Yet, many, if not most, commentators see the Little Horn as either Titus, or Nero, or some other Roman emperor. And to say the least, if you identify the Roman Catholic church as the Little Horn, this presents all sorts of exegetical– not to mention historical– problems with the flow of the text in Daniel 7:8f.

Most significantly, Daniel 7:15f gives the inspired *interpretation of verses 8-14,* "So he told me and made known to me the interpretation of those things." This interpretation, while following the flow of verses 8f *precludes* any application of the earlier verses to the ascension of Christ.

Again, here is the flow of verses 8-14: ☞ The days of the fourth empire (Rome) ☞ the appearance of the Little Horn ☞ his evil work ☞ the sitting of judgment ☞ the opening of the books ☞ the coming of the Son of Man ☞ the reception of the kingdom.

Here is the flow of the *interpretation* of those verses: The days of the fourth empire (v. 17f) ☞ the appearance of the Little Horn (v. 20) ☞ the work of the Little Horn is revealed as the persecution of the saints (v. 25) ☞ the sitting of judgment (v. 26) ☞ the judgment of the Little Horn (v. 26) ☞ the bestowal of the kingdom on the saints (v. 27).

Based on the interpretation of verses 8-14, Daniel 7:13-14 cannot refer to the ascension of Christ. The Little Horn had not yet appeared. The saints had not yet been persecuted (unless you want to identify the saints as OT saints– but that eliminates Rome altogether!). There was no judgment of any kind that took place at the ascension!

Jesus' use of Daniel 7 in Matthew 24:30 and 25:31 should therefore be definitive for our understanding of Daniel 7:13-14, in spite of any difficulties of the terminology of Jesus coming *to* the Ancient of Days. Regardless of that difficulty, and it is admittedly difficult, unless Daniel 7:13-14 is some kind of parenthetical interjection into the vision, or unless the interpretation of the earlier verses breaks the chronological flow, or unless verses 26-27 do not interpret verses 13-14, then it is established that Daniel

7:13-14 is predictive of Christ's coming in judgment of the persecutorial Little Horn. And that had nothing to do with Pentecost.

This interpretation is also confirmed by a comparison of Daniel's vision with Revelation.

Daniel 7	Revelation 17-22
In the days of the fourth beast (Rome)	John was writing during the days of Rome and said his vision was to be fulfilled shortly.
Little Horn	Babylon the Persecutor
Persecution of the saints	Babylon had a cup full of the blood of the saints (17:6f)
Opening of the books	Opening of the books (Revelation 20:10f)
Judgment of the persecutor	Babylon is Fallen! (18)
Coming of the Son of Man	Coming of Christ (19)
Giving of the kingdom	"The kingdoms of this world have become the kingdoms of our God and of His Christ, and they shall rule forever (11:16f); The New Creation (Revelation 21)

Based on these comparisons, I find it difficult to see Daniel 7:13-14 as predictive of the ascension of Christ. Revelation, in its depiction of the coming of the Son of Man and the reception of the kingdom, does not look backward to the ascension, but to his coming in judgment of Babylon, the persecutor of the saints.

For brevity, we will confine ourselves to one more comparison, of several that could be given.

Daniel 7	Revelation 11-22
Persecution of the saints (v. 25f)	Persecution of the saints (including of course, Jesus 11:8; 17; 18)
Persecution by the Little Horn	The city "where the Lord was slain" (11:8)
Time of the resurrection*	Time of the resurrection (11:16f)
Destruction of the persecuting power	Destruction of the city that had slain the prophets, Jesus and his apostles (18)
Vindication of the martyrs	"Rejoice over her, apostles and prophets, for God has avenged you on her" (18:20f, 24; 19:2f–cf Deuteronomy 32:43)
Coming of the Son of Man	Coming of Christ (Revelation 19-22)

*Since we have established that Daniel 7, 9, 12 are parallel and synchronous, then since Daniel 12 predicted the resurrection, this means that Daniel 7 predicted the resurrection. This is confirmed by the scriptural fact that the full arrival of the *kingdom*, i.e. Daniel 7, is the time of the *resurrection* (Matthew 25:31f; 2 Corinthians 4-5; 1 Corinthians 15:50f; etc.).

These parallelisms should definitively identify for us the time and framework for the fulfillment of Daniel 7 and Revelation. Fulfillment was to be in Israel's last days, in the destruction of Jerusalem, in AD 70.

The trouble with most eschatologies is the abject failure to correlate the theme and motif of the avenging of the martyrs with the words of Jesus. As a result, most eschatological prophecies, although they may emphatically promise imminent vindication of the first century suffering martyrs, are, for all practical purposes, ignored, or applied to times and events that do violence to the promise of soon coming vindication. This can be seen most powerfully in a quick listing of (some of) the NT prophecies of the soon coming vindication of the martyrs and suffering saints. The chart will outline the issue well.

Suffering Experienced in / by the First Century Saints	Promise of Vindication, and judgment on their persecutors at the time of the end
Matthew 10:22-23– When they chase you from city to city...	"You will not have gone through the cities of Israel until the Son of Man is come"
Matthew 23– We have commented sufficiently on this. See above	"All of these things shall come upon this generation" (v. 36)
Luke 18- "Will not the Lord avenge His elect who cry out to him?"	"Verily I say unto you, He will avenge them speedily" (v. 8)
Romans 8:18- "I reckon that the suffering of this present time..."	"Are not worthy to be compared with the glory that is about to be revealed in us"
1 Corinthians 7: 28f– the present distress	The time has been shortened
2 Corinthians 4:16f– "For our light affliction"	"Which is but for a moment"
Galatians 4:22f– "As it was then, even so it is now, children of the flesh persecuted the children of promise..."	"Cast out the bondwoman and her children!"

1 Thessalonians 2:15ff– "You suffered at the hands of your countrymen..."	The Jews killed the prophets, Jesus, and now persecute us...the wrath of God has come upon them to the uttermost."
2 Thessalonians 1:4-10– To you who are being troubled (*thlipsis*)...	"rest (relief, *anesis*) with us, when the Lord Jesus is revealed from him"
Hebrews 10:32f– "You took joyfully the spoiling of your goods..."	"In a very, very little while, the one who is coming will come, and will not tarry" (v. 37).
James 5:1-10– "You have condemned, you have killed the just..."	"Be patient therefore, brethren until the coming of the Lord...the coming of the Lord has drawn nigh...the Judge is standing right at the door" (v. 6-9)
1 Peter 1:3f– "you are in heaviness through manifold trials" (cf. 4:13)	"for a little while" "the salvation *ready to be revealed* in the last times"
Revelation 6:9f– "those who had been slain... How Long, O Lord, do you not avenge..."	"Rest for a little while, until their fellow brethren who should be slain as they were, should be fulfilled"

The passages listed are not all of the texts that speak of the first century reality of the suffering and martyrdom of the saints. What should not be missed in all of these texts is the Jewish source of the suffering, and the emphatic promises that the Lord was coming very soon to vindicate their suffering and judge their oppressors.

What these parallels also should prove for us is that the fulfillment of Daniel 7 was very near in the first century, and was to be fulfilled in the judgment of Judah. Unless the suffering motif in all of these texts is unrelated to Daniel then we must see them as the fulfillment. However, if that *suffering of the saints* in the first century generation was in fact the fulfillment of Daniel's prophecy, this means that the coming of the Lord to vindicate the suffering saints foretold by Daniel was to occur in the first century.

DANIEL, TRIBULATION AND THE RESURRECTION

There is a final thought in regard to the chapters in Daniel that we are considering. Daniel foretold what is normally known as the Great Tribulation. This is an unchallenged fact. What is not noticed by so many commentators is that Daniel posits the Great Tribulation just before, or *in the same temporal context as the resurrection*. Pitre has developed this concept perhaps better than most modern scholars in his work cited herein. Other scholars have seen the idea, however. Daube for instance noted, "It was indeed a common expectation that a time of severe testing would necessarily precede the dawning of the messianic age."[164]

In fact, it might be said that *the resurrection would come as the time of deliverance from the Great Tribulation*. And if this is granted, then not only do we have definitive proof that the seventy weeks was fulfilled in the first century, but the traditional futurist views of eschatology are called into question as well.

Daniel 7 presents a time of tribulation and persecution against the saints. However, "the saints" are *delivered out of that tribulation* and receive the kingdom. I am convinced that "the saints" are to be identified as the righteous remnant, the elect if you will, the followers of Jesus. Old Covenant Israel was not delivered out of that tribulation, but was *destroyed* during the days of the fourth beast. The saints here cannot refer to Israel as a whole since Israel as a whole, "has not obtained that for which she sought, but the elect has obtained it, and the rest were blinded" (Romans 11:7).

The thing to see is, as noted already, the time of the kingdom is the time of the resurrection. This is clear in Matthew 25:31f when the Son of Man –*the personage of Daniel 7:13-14*– comes in power and glory, to sit on the throne of his kingdom. At that time, his followers are also given the kingdom. This all occurs at the Great White Throne Judgment, which of course is the time of the resurrection (Revelation 20:11-12).

So, what we have in Daniel 7 is a very clear-cut prediction of the Tribulation and the resurrection occurring at the end of that period. This has tremendous implications for the amillennial and postmillennial construct, because both of those paradigms see the full establishment of the kingdom as occurring in the first century.

One thing is for certain, you cannot extend the fulfillment of Daniel 7 beyond the days of the Roman empire, the fourth beast of Daniel 7. The view that the little horn represents the Roman Catholic church violates the parameters of the text, creating a modified form of the revived Roman empire theory of dispensationalism. If the dispensationalist is wrong to posit a revived Roman empire in Daniel 2, where is the justification for seeing a modified form of that doctrine in Daniel 7?

So, the vision of Daniel 7 does not extend beyond the days of the Roman empire. Since Daniel foretold the time of tribulation, vindication, and of course resurrection, this demands that the resurrection occurred in the days of the Roman empire.

Of course, as we have already seen, Daniel 9 and chapter 12 further define the time of the resurrection as the end of the Old Covenant age of Israel. Our point here however, is simply this:

The time of the kingdom / resurrection is **tied** *to the time of the tribulation.*

The time of the tribulation is confined to the days of the Roman empire (Daniel 7).

Therefore, any schema that posits the resurrection beyond the days of the Roman empire is falsified by Daniel 7.

Not only does Daniel 7 place the time of the kingdom and resurrection strictly within the context of *the tribulation*, but Daniel 9 does as well.

Daniel 9 posits the cutting off of the Messiah, after the sixty-ninth week of the seventy week countdown. Not only so, but Daniel 9:27 foretold the coming Abomination of Desolation, and of course, when Jesus discussed the end times he said that the setting up of the Abomination of Desolation would lead directly to the Great Tribulation (Matthew 24:15-22). So, Daniel 9 presents to us the following scenario: death of Messiah ☛ Abomination of Desolation ☛ Tribulation ☛ end of the seventy weeks ☛ the time of the kingdom and resurrection.

If it is the case therefore, that the resurrection belongs to the end of the seventy weeks, and we have established that this is true, then the link between the Great Tribulation (not to mention the Abomination of Desolation!) and the resurrection is firmly established. Here is what we are saying:

The kingdom / resurrection would occur at the end of the seventy weeks.

But, the Great Tribulation (and the Abomination of Desolation) also belongs to the time of the climax of the seventy weeks (Daniel 9:26-27).

Therefore, the Great Tribulation (and the Abomination of Desolation) would constitute signs of the imminence of the resurrection / kingdom.

This is of course, confirmed by Jesus in Matthew 24. When asked by his disciples for a sign of his parousia and the end of the age (Matthew 24:2-3) Jesus appealed directly to Daniel 9:27: "When you see the abomination of desolation, spoken of by Daniel the prophet standing in the holy place, (let him who reads understand), then let those who are in Judea flee....for then shall be great tribulation" (Matthew 24:15-22). Jesus also stated that all of these things would occur in his generation (Matthew 24:34). We thus have an undeniable prediction that the resurrection was to occur in the first century at the time of the fall of the Old Covenant world.

There is no clearer demonstration of the link between the tribulation and the resurrection than in Daniel 12:1-2

"At that time Michael shall stand up, The great prince who stands watch over the sons of your people; And there shall be a time of trouble, Such as never was since there was a nation, Even to that time. And at that time your people shall be delivered, Every one who is found written in the book. And many of those who sleep in the dust of the earth shall awake, Some to everlasting life, Some to shame and everlasting contempt."

As Pitre says, "The most explicit OT reference to the resurrection of the dead is also preceded by the most explicit OT reference to the tribulation of the last days." (*Tribulation*, 187) The significance of this connection can hardly be over emphasized.

It is virtually unanimously agreed among amillennial and postmillennial commentators that the Great Tribulation occurred in the first century, during the Jewish War of AD 66-70.[165] Gentry even calls postmillennialists "orthodox preterists," and notes their belief that "the great tribulation occurred in the first century." (*When*, 50) It seems not to have dawned on these good men of the respective schools that *the Tribulation was the immediate precursor of the resurrection!* Patently, according to Daniel, if the Tribulation was a first century reality, then one must place the resurrection at that time as well. To suggest that Daniel 12:1 is referent to first century events, but that verse 2 is referent to *end of time* events inserts an unwarranted temporal gap between the verses. How, therefore, can the amillennialists or postmillennialists condemn the dispensationalists for their insertion of gaps into the Biblical text, when in fact, they insert equally long gaps into texts where there is no justification whatsoever?

Let me state my argument succinctly.

The Great Tribulation would occur immediately before–and as a sign of-- the resurrection (Daniel 12:1-2).

But, the Great Tribulation of Daniel 12:1 occurred in the first century in the context of the destruction of Jerusalem in AD 70 (amillennial and postmillennial commentators agreeing).

Therefore, the resurrection occurred in the first century in the context of the destruction of Jerusalem in AD 70.

The fact that the Tribulation was a first century event is confirmed for us in the book of Revelation. Consider the following from my *Babylon* book.

In Revelation 7 and 14 John saw the 144,000 out of the twelve tribes of Israel. Notice what is said of the 144,000 in Revelation 14:4, "These are the ones who were not defiled with women, for they are virgins. These are the ones who follow the Lamb wherever He goes. These were redeemed from among men, being first fruits to God and to the Lamb."

160

Did you catch the power of what is said? *The 144,000 were the first fruits of those redeemed by Jesus Christ!* The text does not say that the 144,000 were the first fruit of the nations. That was said of Old Covenant Israel in Jeremiah 3:2. The text emphasizes that the 144,000 were *followers of the Lamb.* These were Christians!

But these are not just Christians. They are Christian "Jews."[166] They are out of the 12 tribes of Israel and they are followers of the Messiah. Further, these are not just Jewish Christians, they are *the first generation of Jewish Christians!* As Stuart says, "The writer doubtless refers to the 144,000 as being among the earliest Christians."[167] Russell concurs, "They are the first fruits unto God and the Lamb; the first converts to the faith in Christ in the land of Judea."(*Parousia*, 470) Notice that they "were redeemed from among men, being first fruits (*aparche*) to God and to the Lamb." The significance of the first fruits must not be missed, or dismissed, for it places the book of Revelation, the Great Tribulation, and thus, *the resurrection*, in an early context.

You and I are living 50 generations beyond the first fruit of Christians. Furthermore, the longer time marches on, the farther removed we are from the first fruit generation.

> **The 144,000 were the first fruit of "Jewish" Christians. You and I live 50 generations removed from the generation of the 144,000. You cannot posit the 144,000 anywhere except the first century generation, the generation of the first fruit!**

James wrote early in the first century generation and said, "To the twelve tribes scattered abroad" (James 1:1). What did he have to say about the first fruit concept? Hear him, "Of his own will he brought us forth by the word of His mouth, that we might be a kind of first fruit (*aparche*) of His creatures" (James 1:18). Likewise, the writer of Hebrews said, "You have come to Mount Zion and to the city of the Living God, the heavenly Jerusalem, to an unnumerable company of angels, to the general assembly and church of the firstborn who are registered in heaven" (Hebrews 12:22). Chilton is certainly correct to note, "The New Testament uses the term first fruits to describe the church of the Last Days, the 'first generation' Church." (*Vengeance*, 357)

There can be no doubt as to the meaning of "first fruits." When Paul wrote to the saints in Rome, he gave greetings to Epaenetus, "who was the first (*aparche*) convert to Christ in the province of Asia" (Romans 16:5 NIV). Likewise, in 1 Corinthians 16:15, the same apostle sent greetings to the household of Stephanas that was "the first (*aparche*) converts in Achaia." Paul was referring to the very first converts.

John did not say that the 144,000 were the first fruit of some far distant time. He did not say that they were to be the first fruit of a different preaching of a different gospel message. Nor did he, as Beale seems to suggest, say that the 144,000 were representative of the entirety of all the redeemed, of all the ages, being referred to as the first fruit. (*Revelation*, 741f). The term "first fruit" has a temporal significance that cannot be mitigated. The 144,000 were simply the very first generation of Christians, and this has profound implications for the time of the resurrection.

John saw that the 144,000 were to come out of the Great Tribulation (7:14). If the 144,000 were the first Christians, and if they were to endure the Great Tribulation, then if follows undeniably, that the Great Tribulation was to occur in the first century generation. Of course, this is precisely what Jesus

> The 144,000 were to endure the Great Tribulation. But the 144,000 were the *first generation of Jewish Christians*. Therefore, the Great Tribulation had to occur in the first century generation.

predicted in the Olivet Discourse (Matthew 24:15-34) in spite of the dispensational objections. You cannot divorce the 144,000 from the Great Tribulation. No other generation than the first can ever be "the first fruits unto God and to the Lamb" (Revelation 14:4). Patently, the Great Tribulation was in the first century.

James and Hebrews, writing to the first generation of Jewish Christians, called them the first fruits and the first born. There is no justification for positing the Great Tribulation outside of that first century context. Further, both James and Hebrews were written in the context of persecution. Both were written before the fall of Jerusalem. This means that the resurrection had to have occurred in the first century according to Daniel 12.

Remember that Daniel foretold the Great Tribulation, followed immediately by the resurrection. John, writing to his first century contemporaries, says that the first generation of Christian Jews would come out of the Great Tribulation. This undeniably posits the Great Tribulation in the first century. But if the Great Tribulation was in the first century, then, again, according to Daniel, the resurrection had to occur at that time as well. Here is what we are saying.

The 144,000 of Revelation 7, 14 were *the first generation of Christians* (Revelation 14:1-4).

The 144,000 of Revelation 7, 14 would come out of the Great Tribulation (Revelation 7:14).

Therefore, the Great Tribulation occurred in the first century generation.

We follow that up with this,

The Great Tribulation occurred in the first century generation.

But, the resurrection was to occur immediately following the Great Tribulation (Daniel2:1-2).

Therefore, the resurrection occurred in the first century generation.

This conclusion is confirmed, again, in Matthew 24:15-31. As we have already noted, the Abomination of Desolation would bring about the Tribulation, followed by the parousia. This is precisely the pattern of Daniel 7 and 9. It is also the pattern in the Olivet Discourse.

Jesus foretold the arrival of the Abomination (v. 15). Notice Jesus' use of the term "those days," and its reference to the days of the Tribulation. In verse 19, he spoke of the need and hope that they would not be pregnant or nursing children "in those days" i.e. the days of the Abomination. It would be "then" in the days of the Abomination, that the Tribulation would occur (v. 21). Jesus said that unless "those days" the days of the Abomination and subsequent Tribulation, were shortened, "no flesh would be saved."

Then, in Matthew 24:29, Jesus said, "Immediately after the tribulation of those days" the Son of Man would come in power and great glory, and, "he will send His angels with a great sound of a trumpet, and they will gather His elect from the four winds, from one end of heaven to another" (Matthew 24:31). Simply stated, this gathering at the sound of the trump is nothing less than the resurrection! (Cf. 1 Thessalonians 4:13-18).

Notice the complex of events, the Abomination, the Tribulation, parousia, the gathering of the elect. It should be noted that the parousia and gathering of the elect (the resurrection) would come "immediately after" the Tribulation. Many commentators try to say there is a disjunction here and that all Jesus was saying is that at some point in the future the parousia would occur. Or, it is claimed that the "immediately after" simply means, "the next thing on the prophetic agenda, regardless of when it occurs."

This rather desperate attempt at exegesis fails on grammatical grounds as well as contextual. The word translated as immediately, is *eutheos* (Εὐθέως). This is the word that is used the most often to describe the effect of Jesus' healing miracles. The healing always took place "immediately," and that does not mean that the person *eventually* got better! They were healed, *instantly*. The only reason that anyone suggested that "immediately" in Matthew 24:29 does not have temporal significance is because of what they perceive as a failed prediction. In other words, *their literalistic concept* of what Jesus predicted did not happen immediately, therefore, rather than honor the normal, consistent definition and use of the word they completely redefine the word.[168] This is unjustified and should be rejected.

The parallels between Daniel and the Olivet Discourse are direct and precise. Daniel 9 foretold the death of Messiah, the Abomination of Desolation, which of course would lead to the Tribulation and the destruction of Jerusalem, and the consummation of the seventy weeks. The consummation of the seventy weeks would be kingdom and resurrection, the salvation of Israel.

Although the death of Jesus is not specifically mentioned in Matthew 24, it lies behind the text nonetheless. We then find the Abomination, the Tribulation, the parousia and the gathering of the elect. Jesus emphatically posited all of those things for his generation (v. 34).

Daniel 7 and the Discourse are also parallel. Daniel's prediction is focused on the days of the fourth kingdom, i.e. Rome. The Little Horn persecutes the saints. The Son of Man comes in judgment of the persecutor, vindicating the saints, and delivering the kingdom to them.

In the Olivet Discourse, which Jesus said would be fulfilled in his generation (during the days of the Roman empire!) Jesus predicted the persecution of the saints (Matthew 24:9f). The persecutor however, is identified as *the nation of Israel*. Jesus foretold the Abomination of Desolation, the Tribulation, followed by his coming on the clouds of heaven in vindication of the saints. This would be the time of the kingdom (Luke 21:28-31).

Daniel 12 contains the identical motifs. We find the Abomination of Desolation (12:11), the time of tribulation (12:1), the deliverance of the saints (12:1), the time of the end (12:4) and the time of the kingdom (12:3). Significantly, Daniel was told that the final fulfillment of his vision would be when Israel was completely destroyed (matching Daniel 9:27 perfectly) and Jesus said that his prediction would be fulfilled in the destruction of Jerusalem in his generation. The dove-tailing of these details is no mere coincidence and should not be ignored. Daniel posits the Tribulation in the context of Israel's judgment and last days. Jesus does as well.

Our study of Daniel, the Tribulation, the resurrection, and thus, of course, the Day of the Lord has demonstrated that not only does the Tribulation belong to Israel and her last days, but the Tribulation was to be an immediate precursor and sign of the resurrection and kingdom.[169] The fact that not only Daniel, but Jesus and the NT said that the Tribulation was to occur in the first century generation is *prima facie* proof that the parousia and the resurrection was to occur in that same generation.

It is interesting to note that in scholarly circles, there is a growing awareness of the first century fulfillment of eschatology, although there is a reluctance to "go all the way." Wright, commenting on the Day of the Lord foretold by Paul says,

"For Paul, 'the Day of the Lord' by no means denoted the end of the world. Just as in Amos and Jeremiah the really appalling thing about the Day of YHWH' was that there would be another day after it–had it been the actual end of the world it would have been a shame, but there would not have been anybody around to worry about it after it had happened–so in Paul the 'Day of the Lord' is clearly something which might well happen during the continuing lifetimes of himself and his readers. It is something you might read about by letter. Nevertheless, it is a great moment of judgment as a result of which everything will be different, and the world will be changed. ...I have no hesitation in saying that, had Paul been alive in the year we call AD 70, when the convulsions in Rome during the Year of the Four Emperors were quickly followed by the destruction of Jerusalem, he would have said, 'That's it. That's the Day of the Lord.'"[170]

Make no mistake, Wright affirms that he still maintains a futurist eschatology. Yet, this kind of statement, especially in light of the link between the Tribulation and the resurrection gives us every right to challenge any concept of a futurist eschatology. If the Day of the Lord was in the first century, then the resurrection, so inextricably bound to the Day of the Lord, occurred then as well.

166

SUMMARY AND CONCLUSION

We fully understand that this work will leave the reader with questions about the nature of the resurrection, "the body," the resurrection of Christ as it relates to the resurrection of the dead and many other questions. And those are valid questions. However, as we stated at the outset, our focus here has been on the framework and timing of the resurrection. For good discussions of these relevant questions, I suggest reading Sam Frost's *Exegetical Essays on the Resurrection of the Dead,*[171] and my work "Resurrection Now" on my website.

We have demonstrated that the partial preterist agrees that Daniel 9 cannot extend beyond the first century, and that Daniel 9 is not concerned with the church, or the church age, *per se*, but with the consummation of the hopes of Israel.

We have shown that the seventy weeks of Daniel 9 did not end before AD 70.

We have shown that the semi-preterists stop short of the correct application of the promises of Daniel 9. The putting away of sin, the atonement, and the bringing in of everlasting righteousness were *initiated by the Cross*, but not consummated at the Cross.

We have shown that the putting away of sin, the atonement, the bringing in of everlasting righteousness, and the sealing up of vision and prophecy are all related to the "final resurrection."

We have shown that the seventy weeks could not have been completed in AD 32-35 because the NT writers were still anticipating, well after that time, the putting away of Israel's sin, the completion of the atonement, the sealing of vision and prophecy and the bringing in of everlasting righteousness. All of these elements are restricted to *within the seventy weeks*, not beyond them.

We have shown that each of Daniel's constituent elements is related to the resurrection of the dead. Thus, since the seventy weeks of Daniel cannot be extended further than the destruction of Jerusalem in AD 70, the "final resurrection" must have occurred at the time of the fall of Jerusalem in AD 70.

We have shown that the promise of the resurrection was the hope of Israel, belonging to the end of her age, not the end of human history. We have demonstrated how two of the major futurist paradigms, amillennialism and postmillennialism, ignore this Biblical fact, divorcing eschatology from its proper framework, and posit the resurrection as Christian Eschatology, to be fulfilled at the end of the Christian age. But to ignore the roots and proper framework of the resurrection is to be doomed to wrongly understand Biblical eschatology.

We have proven that Daniel 9 and Daniel 12 are parallel passages that were fulfilled at the end of the Old Covenant age in AD 70. And since Daniel 12:2 predicted the resurrection this means that the resurrection of Daniel 12:2 was fulfilled, "when the power of the holy people" was "completely shattered."

We have proven that all attempts to posit a future for ethnic Israel at a future parousia of Christ violates the text of Romans 11. Romans 11 had to be fulfilled within the same parameters as Daniel 9, the seventy weeks.

We have proven that Romans 11 and Daniel 9 predicted the same time and same event, the consummation of the history/hope of Israel. We have shown that the consummation of Israel's hope was the resurrection. Since therefore, the consummation of Daniel 9 was to be in AD 70, and Daniel 9 and Romans 11 are prophetically synchronous events in regard to fulfillment, it follows that the resurrection in fulfillment of Israel's history and hope was in AD 70.

We have shown that Daniel 12 and 1 Corinthians 15 are also parallel and are concerned with the fulfillment of God's promises to Israel, "when the power of the holy people is completely shattered." This unequivocally posits the resurrection of 1 Corinthians 15 at the climax of the seventy weeks of Daniel 9.

Daniel 9 therefore, is normative in defining the framework and the time for the resurrection of the dead. Daniel 9 demands that the resurrection of the dead occurred by the time of the catastrophic destruction of Jerusalem in AD 70. The *spiritual implications* of that reality are profound, reassuring and exciting!

For more works by Don K. Preston, go to:

www.eschatology.org
www.bibleprophecy.com

END NOTES

1. I was raised as a fifth generation amillennialist in the church of Christ denomination. The amillennial view says that the resurrection is *at the end of the church age*, at the end of time. It was a total shock to me to discover that the Bible is emphatic in teaching that the Christian age has no end.

2. See my article "Resurrection Now!" At our website: www.eschatology.org, or, www.bibleprophecy.com.

3. See my *Can God Tell Time?* for a full discussion of the time issue, and an examination of some of the proposed solutions to the thorny issue of Christ's predictions. The problem is very acute, and there is only one solution, and that is to believe Jesus kept his word.

4. See my *Like Father, Like Son, On Clouds of Glory*. This major work, 350+ pages, demonstrates that Christ never promised to come back literally, bodily and in an optically visible manner. Available at: www.eschatology.org, or www.bibleprophecy.com.

5. Milton Terry, *Biblical Hermeneutics*, (Grand Rapids, Zondervan,1983)594.

6. Keith Mathison, general editor, *When Shall These Things Be?: A Reformed Response to Hyper-Preterism*, (Phillipsburg, New Jersey, P and R Publishing, 2004).

7. The true preterist view of prophecy is the view that all prophecy, including the Second Coming, Judgment and Resurrection, was fulfilled in the events of the fall of Jerusalem in AD 70. This was the end of the Old Covenant world of Israel. Preterism, otherwise known as Covenant Eschatology, holds that the Bible does not predict the end of time and human history (Historical Eschatology) but the end of the Old Covenant of Israel (thus, *Covenant* Eschatology). Preterism is the fastest growing view of eschatology in the world and is the only answer to the ages old problem of the question of Jesus' prediction that he was to come in the first century. All futurist eschatologies posit a failed eschatology in one form or another. Only Covenant Eschatology can truly defend and maintain the integrity of God, the Deity of Jesus and the inspiration of scriptures.

8. I presented some of the material in this book in public debate with Thomas Thrasher, March 13, 2004, in Indianapolis, Indiana. I gave a PowerPoint presentation on Daniel 9 and the resurrection. The impact of that presentation was so devastating that Thrasher got up and admitted that he had no answers for Daniel 9. Videos of that debate, including the PowerPoint charts, are available at www.eschatology.org

9. John Goldingay, Word Biblical Commentary, Vol. 30, *Daniel*, (Dallas, Word, 1989)258.

10. Meredith Cline "The Covenant of the Seventieth Week." The article can be found on-line at:
http://www.covopc.org/Kline/Covenant_70th_Week.html

11. Kenneth Gentry, *He Shall Have Dominion*, (Tyler, TX, Institute for Christian Economics, 1992)329+.

12. Keith Mathison, *Postmillennialism: And Eschatology of Hope*, (New Jersey, P and R Publishing, 1999)220, "Traditionally, the church has interpreted this prophecy in Daniel as a prophecy of the first advent of Christ and the destruction of Jerusalem by the Roman armies."

13. See Gary DeMar, *Last Days Madness*, (Atlanta, American Vision1994)231f; Lorraine Boettner, *The Millennium*, (Philadelphia, Presbyterian and Reformed Press, 1957) 224+; Gentry, *Dominion*, 329f.

14. To affirm the past accomplishment of resurrection normally elicits the charge of the Hymenaean Heresy. Opponents of Covenant Eschatology, i.e. preterism, are, however, guilty of anachronistic hermeneutic in leveling that charge against preterists. Hymenaeus claimed that the resurrection was past, *prior to the time when it was supposed to happen*. We today live *beyond* the time divinely appointed for the resurrection, i.e. the time when "the power of the holy people is completely shattered" (Daniel 12:2). Thus, in reality, those today who deny the accomplishment of the resurrection are the ones that are in denial of the divine truth, not the preterists! I have produced a 6 CD presentation, *The Hymenaean Heresy: Reverse the Charges*, that is the most in-depth analysis of the Hymenaean heresy available today, to my knowledge. It is available from my website, www.eschatology.org.

15. Just one caveat here. *Technically speaking*, the appropriation and application of atonement are synchronous events Biblically. When the High Priest came out of the Most Holy Place is when the blessings of the atonement were "applied" (Leviticus 9:22). Thus, there was no huge gap of time between appropriation and application. Yet, that is precisely what the millennial view does. Furthermore, all futurist views imply that identical gap.

16. We might note here that millennialists generally do not understand "finish the transgression" as referent to filling the measure of sin. Ice, *End Times Controversy*, Eugene, Ore, 2003)312, says that the term applies to a yet future repentance on the part of national Israel. Even if one were to grant the millennial definition of "to finish transgression" (and I do *not* accept their interpretation) it does not help. Daniel 9 still speaks of the vindication of the death of Jesus and this is inseparably bound *with Israel's last days* (Deuteronomy 32). So, one could grant that "finish the transgression" is not referent to filling up the measure of sin, but still argue, irrefutably, that the end of the seventy weeks must be confined to the time of AD 70 and the out pouring of Covenant Wrath on Israel for shedding innocent blood.

17. Eusebius, *Demonstration of the Gospel*, Bk. VIII, chapt. 2, (Grand Rapids, Baker, 1981)119

18. Peter O'Brien, *Word Biblical Commentary*, Colossians and Philemon (Waco, Word Publishers, 1982)80.

19. N. T. Wright, *Jesus and the Victory of God*, (Minneapolis, Fortress, 1996)511.

20. Cf. Joseph Fitzmeyer, *The Acts of the Apostles*, Anchor Bible (New York, DoubleDay, 1998)267. Fitzmeyer says Peter draws from Deuteronomy 32. Likewise, Bruce and other scholars take note that Peter was citing Deuteronomy 32. cf. F. F. Bruce, *Acts of the Apostles, Greek Text with Introduction*, (Grand Rapids, Eerdmans, 1984)99.

21. Thomas Ice and Kenneth Gentry, *The Great Tribulation, Past or Future*, (Grand Rapids, Kregel, 1999)115.

22. It is interesting that Thomas Ice admits, of course, *inadvertently*, to the significance of the AD 70 judgment, when he says, "The use of 'this generation' in all other contexts is *historical*, but 24:34 is *prophetic*. In fact, when one compares the historical use of 'this generation' at the beginning of the Olivet Discourse in Matthew 23:36 (which is an undisputed reference to AD 70) with the prophetic usage in 24:34, a contrast is obvious." (*Tribulation*, 103).

23. The NT writers identify the righteous remnant as the body of Christ in the first century. The NT writers know nothing of the dispensational theory of deliverance of the nation from the Great Tribulation.

24. Thomas Ice and Timothy Demy, *Fast Facts on Bible Prophecy*, (Eugene, Ore., Harvest House, 1997)135.

25. Of course, the suffering of the Jews in WWII also raises the identical question. What covenant had they broken in such an egregious manner to cause Jehovah to bring such awful punishment on them? The fact is that Israel was *not* in violation of the Mosaic Covenant. WWII was not a divine judgment on them and there is no coming Great Tribulation.

26. I am available to hold seminars on Covenant Eschatology. I also welcome honorable public debates, panel discussions, special guest lectures on Revelation, radio interviews, etc., on eschatology. I can be contacted through my website: www.eschatology.org.

27. See my book *Blast From the Past, the Truth About Armageddon*, for a discussion of "the war" mentioned in Daniel 9:27. I show that "the war" is the Great Day of the Lord in Revelation 6 and 16, when the Lord would avenge the blood of His saints, i.e. in fulfillment of Deuteronomy 32:43. This demands a fulfillment in AD 70. The book is available at: www.eschatology.org, or, www.bibleprophecy.com.

28. Notice the perfect correspondence between Daniel's prediction that seventy weeks were determined to seal vision and prophecy, i.e. to fulfill all prophecy and Peter's declaration that at the parousia, all prophecy would be fulfilled. This is perfect correspondence and without doubt confines the fulfillment of all prophecy to Israel's last days.

29. The efforts to make "Israel" in Romans 11:25f to be the church, completely divorced from OT Israel are a dismal and contextual failure. The Israel of v. 26-27 was the Israel that at the time Paul wrote, was *the enemy of the gospel* (v. 28f)! Was

the church the enemy of the church, awaiting conversion, when Paul wrote?

30. Most semi-preterists have the seventy weeks ending with the stoning of Stephen, or the conversion of the Gentiles. See my *Seal Up Vision and Prophecy* for a full discussion of why these proposals are untenable. Simply stated, whereever one posits the termination of the seventy weeks it is at that point that resurrection, i.e. *the putting away of sin*, occurs. Thus, if one places the putting away of sin at the Cross, per Gentry, Mathison, etc, you must place resurrection there as well.

31. In debates with both amillennialists and postmillennialists, I have asked the question, "What was the law that Paul defined as 'the strength of sin' in 1 Corinthians 15:54f?" *Almost invariably* the answer has been that it was the Mosaic Covenant. It seems not to have dawned on the good men that gave these answers that if the Law that was the strength of sin was the Mosaic Law, then that means that the resurrection is inextricably tied to the end of the Mosaic Law. If therefore, the resurrection has not occurred, the Mosaic Law remains as the strength of sin!

32. It is fascinating that Athanasius (296-373 A.D.) wrote the following words, "Have no fears then. Now that the common Savior of all has died on our behalf, *we who believe in Christ no longer die, as men died afore time, in fulfillment of the threat of the law*. That condemnation has come to an end; and now that, by the grace of the resurrection, corruption has been banished and done away." (*Incarnation*, ch. 4, my emphasis, DKP)). It is questionable whether Athanasius fully grasped what he was saying, but the fact that he expressed as a *reality*, what Paul was *predicting* in 1 Corinthians 15 is very clear and worthy of more research. Paul said that the death brought through the Law would be overcome when the Law came to an end. Athanasius said that the death that came through the Law was abolished and that life and immortality are a reality.

33. It will be noted that Hymenaeus and Philetus argued that "the resurrection is past already," (2 Timothy 2:18). Others argued that the Day of the Lord had already come (2 Thessalonians 2:1-2). If the resurrection and Day of the Lord is an earth burning, time ending, cosmic catastrophe, as traditionally posited, how in the name of reason could anyone be convinced those things had already happened? No thoughtful person could be convinced that the universe had passed away, and yet they were reading about it in an epistle! The fact is that Paul did not argue with the concept of the nature of the eschatological events. He simply said that they were not past, and said certain things, that were already at work, had to occur first. This demands that we see the Day of the Lord and resurrection in a totally different light than tradition suggests. I have prepared a six CD presentation on *The Hymenaean Heresy: Reverse the Charges!* in which I show that neither Paul nor Hymenaeus were teaching or expecting the raising of physical corpses out of the ground. To my knowledge, this presentation is the most comprehensive examination of the Hymenaean issue available. It is available from: www.eschatology.org.

34. It simply will not to do say that the child of God is truly forgiven today, but that they await the resurrection to get the body back. If forgiveness is genuinely given at the moment of conversion and imputed through faith as the child of God lives in Christ, then why is it that their biological body is not "forgiven and redeemed" as well? If forgiveness and redemption is real and instantaneous then resurrection life is real and instantaneous. You cannot dichotomize these issues.

35. Leon Morris, *1 Corinthians, an Introduction and Commentary*, (London, Tyndale, 1969)235.

36. The reason that Paul could affirm the continuing validity of Torah as the strength of sin in 1 Corinthians 15, and yet affirm that the law of the Spirit of life in Christ set one free from the law of sin and death, is because Paul stood between the two worlds. He was the minister of the New Covenant (2 Corinthians 3:1-4; 4:1-2) and well understood that the world of Torah was still standing, although it was "nigh unto passing away" (Hebrews 8:13). He, through the Spirit, was bringing about the transformation from that Old Covenant to the New. Thus, he could still speak of the Torah as present and working its death bringing power, while also affirming that Christ's life giving power was already at work, but awaiting perfection.

37. We cannot go into detail, but it is admitted by virtually everyone that Jesus and the New Testament writers do link forgiveness and resurrection, *at least on some level*. See John 5:24f; Romans 6:1-10; Ephesians 2:1-5; Colossians 2:11-13; 3:1-2; 2 Timothy 2:10f). Unfortunately, most commentators

174

then claim that this *spiritual resurrection* occurs now, in conversion, but that we are still awaiting the physical resurrection at Christ's parousia. What this overlooks is that this violates the fact that God has always operated from the natural to the spiritual, not vice versa (1 Corinthians 15:46) it ignores the fact that the resurrection that was future in the New Testament was imminent, and it ignores the fact that the resurrection that was future in the New Testament was to be of the same nature as the "death" that the Christians had experienced "in Christ." See Colossians 3:1-2; 2 Timothy 2:10f). See my lengthy article "Resurrection Now!" on my website: www.eschatology.org, for an extensive study of this issue.

38. The millennialists of course, argue that the New Covenant has not yet been established, although the church is currently experiencing the blessings of that non-existent covenant. Exactly how the church can reap the benefits of a covenant that had to be established with Israel first, before its blessings could then flow to the nations (Isaiah 56) but that has not yet been established is a great mystery! To suggest that anyone can benefit from *something that does not exist* is a theological fabrication of the worst sort.

39. See my *Into All the World, Then Comes the End*, for a fuller discussion of this distinctive Greek term. It is only used six times in scripture and invariably refers to the end of the Old Covenant world of Israel. The book is available from my website: www.eschatology.org

40. Our millennial friends will of course insist that this motif demands a literal, future restoration of Israel to the literal land. However, *this is not true*. See my *Israel and the Land Promises* DVDs that demonstrates that the Messianic prophecies of the return to the land were interpreted by the inspired New Testament writers as the restoration of Israel "in Christ" *the true dwelling place*. Available from my websites.

41. John Watts, *Word Biblical Commentary, Isaiah*, Vol 24, (Waco, Word, 1985)344.

42. Brant Petrie, Jesus, *The Tribulation, and the End of the Exile*, (Mohr Siebeck • Tubingen, Baker Academic, Grand Rapids, 2005)403.

43. Wright, *Victory* 268; Scott McKnight, *A New Vision for Israel*, (Grand Rapids, Eerdmans, 1999)224-227.

44. N. T Wright, *Jesus and the Victory of God*, 126f.

45. N. T. Wright, *The Resurrection of the Son of God*, (Minneapolis, Fortress, 2003)114+.

46. Wright (*Victory*, 433) also notes the "controversy" created when Jesus and his disciples did not fast on the given dates. At the time of Jesus, Israel observed four fasts to commemorate the destruction of Jerusalem in the sixth century, i.e. *the entrance into exile.* However, in the prophecies of her restoration, Zechariah 8:19 promised Israel that those fasts would be turned into a time of joy! Thus, Jesus' refusal to fast sent a powerful message that the time of Jerusalem's exile, *the time of resurrection*, had arrived! The fact that the people were already in the land, however, demands that we see the prophecies of her restoration in a different manner than the promise of a geographical gathering. These living lessons, all but lost on the modern reader, were shocking to Jesus' audience.

47. A *Todah* prayer was a specific kind of prayer within the praxis of the ancient world: "The *Todah-prayer* was a response by the condemned vassal-people to the indictment of the Lord, admitting the justice of the sentence." (Cline, 457). All of these elements are found in Daniel 9, confirming the fact that Daniel 9 is all about God's dealings with Israel, and not the Christian age.

48. For instance, McKnight sees that Jesus believed that in his ministry the hopes of Israel were to be fulfilled in his generation. While McKnight acknowledges that in his eschatology, "Jesus saw no further than AD 70,"and, "in seeing the future in this way, Jesus was not mistaken" (*Vision*, 139) he nonetheless says, "For Jesus, the final kingdom would be the consummation of history, the goal toward which God had been directing his energies since the days of Abraham." (*Vision*, 155). Now, if by "the consummation of history" McKnight meant the redemptive goal of history would be reached in AD 70, we would agree (cf. 1 Cor. 10:11). If, however, he means that Jesus expected the end of *human history* in AD 70, then plainly, human history did not come to an end and Jesus was in fact wrong.

49. I am personally convinced that Hosea, the entire book, serves as Paul's working outline for his resurrection doctrine in 1 Corinthians 15. This little noticed fact is a crucial hermeneutic key for understanding 1 Corinthians 15. Yet, I have yet to read a commentary that develops the parallels between Hosea and 1 Corinthians 15. I develop a series of parallels between the two texts in a class, "Hosea in Thirty Lessons." Available from my websites.

50. R. C. Sproul Jr., says, "I am a postmillennialist. That means I believe that we-that is, the church of Christ-will experience a thousand-year golden age before Jesus returns to make all things right. Despite that strong conviction, I pray regularly *Maranatha, Lord Jesus*, imploring the King to come now. I'm pretty sure, however, that that prayer will not be answered, not because of my eschatology, but because of the promises of God. He tells the children of Israel in Exodus 20 that if they will refrain from idolatrous worship, He will bless them to a thousand generations. The pious, literalist dispensationalists, of course, do not think that thousand means thousand. It is a symbolic number. And they may be right. But it symbolizes a large number, not a small one. He may return after more than a thousand generations. It could even be a round number, and return after only 951 generations. Either way, if a generation is roughly forty years, that means He'll be back somewhere around 39,000 AD; two down, thirty-seven to go. If, on the other hand, He comes tomorrow, 1000 symbolizes roughly 75." R. C. Sproul Jr. article, "To A Thousand Generations," on the website: http://www.gospelcom.net/hsc/ETC/Volume_Five/Issue_Two/FamilyCircle.php.

51. It is interesting to say the least, that Pratt's discussion of Daniel 9 is prefaced with the heading: "Daniel's Eschatological Delay." Pratt's thesis is identical to the millennial concept of the postponed kingdom. How Pratt would seek to refute the idea of the millennial posit of a postponed kingdom we are not told. Perhaps he would agree with the millennialist.

52. F. F. Bruce, *The Time is Fulfilled*, (Exeter, UK, Paternoster, 1978) 20f.

53. It is significant that Jeremiah foretold the rebuilding of Jerusalem and gave the dimensions of that project (Jeremiah

31:38f). In Nehemiah 3:1, 27f, we find those very parameters given in the reconstruction of the city. So, what Jeremiah foretold, Nehemiah records as fulfilled.

54. See my refutation of the gap theory in my book *Seal Up Vision and Prophecy*. Also, in a two day formal debate with Ice and his partner Mark Hitchcock, October of 2003, I presented my material on the gap theory. The material left Ice and Hitchcock visibly stunned and they made no effort to respond to it. Furthermore, both men now adamantly refuse to debate me again! My book on Daniel 9 and the DVDs of that debate are available from our websites www.eschatology.org, or, www.bibleprophecy.com.

55. Kenneth Gentry and Thomas Ice, *The Great Tribulation: Past or Future?* (Grand Rapids, Kregel, 1999)115

56. Tim LaHaye and Thomas Ice, *End Times Controversy,* (Eugene, Ore, Harvest House, 2003) 85

57. Keith Mathison, *Dispensationalism: Rightly Dividing the People of God?,* (Phillipsburg, New Jersey, 1995)110

58. Kenneth Gentry, "Daniel's Seventy Weeks," (1991)13. I ordered the 13 page paper from Gentry at 46 Conestee, South Carolina, 29636. I am assuming that one can order it from him from his website now. We cite Gentry in this discussion because Mathison recommends Gentry's work contra dispensationalism. Gentry would vehemently reject Pratt's view that man's rebellion can postpone God's prophetic intent.

59. Lorraine Boettner, *The Millennium*, (Philadelphia, Presbyterian and Reformed Press, 1957)225.

60. Cf. Psalms 89:34.

61. See my *The Elements Shall Melt With Fervent Heat,* for a full discussion of the claim that Peter was coping with the Christian community's disappointment of a failed or postponed parousia. Peter was not, in fact, arguing for a delayed or postponed parousia. He reminded them of what he had said in his first epistle, and that was that the Day was very near (2 Peter 3:1-2). He argued, very effectively, that God is faithful, that the scoffers who said the parousia was not going to happen were wrong, and that the day was in fact "hastening" upon them.

62. See Mark Nanos, *The Mystery of Romans*, (Minneapolis, Fortress, 1996) for a good discussion.

63. In Leviticus 9:22-23, the blessings of the Atonement were not bestowed until the completion of the sacrifices, when the priest came out of the MHP.

64. In no less than three formal debates with amillennialists, my opponents have held the view that upon death the faithful Christian goes to the Hadean realm, *not heaven*, to await judgment. You can read two of those formal written debates on my website: www.eschatology.org., or www.bibleprophecy.com.

65. The force of the Greek text in Hebrews 9:6f is that as long as the Old Covenant System had *validity*, i.e. "standing," man could not enter the Most Holy Place, i.e. the presence of God. It is not a statement that as long as the physical edifice of the temple stood no one could enter heaven, although the symbolism of the standing temple and the validity of its cultus is *somewhat* inter-related. However, the fall of the temple in 586 BC did not prove that the Old Covenant had been removed. It did prove that Judah was in violation of the covenant, but not that the covenant itself was removed. For the writer of Hebrews however, his point is that the Old System would stand, *covenantally binding*, until all that it foreshadowed and typified was fulfilled. It would be then, upon fulfillment and man's access to the Most Holy Place that the cultus itself would be removed by God Himself.

66. See my extended discussion of "the time of reformation" in my *Like Father Like Son, On Clouds of Glory*, (Ardmore, Ok., JaDon Management Inc, 2006)198f. Available at www.eschatology.org. The time of reformation was the anticipated time of the arrival of Israel's hope when Messiah would come in judgment and salvation.

67. See my revised and expanded *Who Is This Babylon* for an extensive demonstration that Babylon was indeed Old Covenant Jerusalem. Also, see Kenneth Gentry's *Dominion*, David Chilton, *Days of Vengeance* (Ft. Worth, Dominion Press,1987) and other works. My *Babylon* is available at: www.eschatology.org.

68. Eusebius, *The Proof of the Gospel*, BK. VIII (383), (Grand Rapids, Baker, 1981)118.

69. John Walvoord, *Daniel, The Key to Prophetic Revelation*, (Moody Press, Chicago, 1971)221.

70. Thomas Ice argues that there is a gap in the actual text of Daniel 9, between the 69th and 70th week. His articles on Daniel 9 can be found at:
http://www.according2prophecy.org/seventy-weeks-pt1.html

71. Don K. Preston, *Seal Up Vision and Prophecy*, (Ardmore, Ok. JaDon Management Inc, 2003). Available at www.eschatology.org. In that book, I show that if there was a gap between the 69th and 70th week of Daniel, then John the Immerser and Jesus were patently wrong to say the kingdom was near in the first century. They could not have been telling the truth to say the kingdom was near, if, in fact the kingdom was still over two millennia removed.

72. It is highly suggestive that Israel was said to become the people of God only at the giving of the Law, even after the Passover had been instituted. No less than three times, God declared that on the day of the giving of the Law Israel had become His distinctive people (Deuteronomy 26:17f; 27:9f). The parallels with the New Covenant are striking. Jesus instituted the New Passover. The people began their journey to the Promised land, and the writer of Hebrews exclaims, "You have not come to the mount that might not be touched (Sinai, DKP) but, you have come to Mt. Zion" (Hebrews 12:18f). In prophecy, Zion was to be the source of the New Covenant (Isaiah 2) so the imagery is all there. The New Israel, given the New Passover, nonetheless became, *officially*, the New Covenant people of God at Zion. Here is "the manifestation of the Sons of God" (Romans 8).

73. Joseph Stallings, *Rediscovering Passover*, (San Jose, Resource Publications, 1988)251+.

74. Petrie (*Exile*, 443) and Wright, *(Victory*, 557) both make the provocative suggestion that Jesus scheduled the Passover in such a way that the traditional, and mandated lamb was not actually slain and eaten. They suggest that Jesus purposely omitted the lamb so that when he said "this is my body," that he was saying to the disciples, "I am the true Passover, and our

180

New Exodus, as the True Israel, begins now!"

75. Peter's emphatic declaration that the events of Pentecost were the initiation of the fulfillment of Joel cannot be ignored or waved away. Peter's "this is that" cannot be construed to mean "this is like it will be" or even, "this is not that." Further, in Romans 10:13 Paul's proclamation that now, through faith "whosoever calls on the name of the Lord shall be saved," is also a direct quote from Joel 2. This demands that as a result of the outpouring of the Spirit and the promised restoration of Israel, that now, all men, any men, can be brought into the blessings of Israel's salvation. Had the kingdom been postponed in Matthew 12 as millennialists claim, then both Peter and Paul were wrong.

76. Notice that the definite article is used for "*the* New Covenant." Jesus was not simply establishing "a New Covenant" but *the* New Covenant anticipated by his Jewish disciples in fulfillment of their Messianic hope.

77. Jesus' language in Luke 22, brings not only Daniel 9 to mind, but Daniel 7 and the promise of Christ on the throne, the suffering of the Messiah and his saints, the kingdom being given to the saints, the image of glory and other motifs. See Petrie, (*Exile*, 390f) for a good discussion of this connection. Petrie is one of the few scholars to see the connection between Daniel 7, 9 and the institution of the Supper.

78. If I am right in these things, then for the modern church to take of the Supper "in anticipation" of a yet future parousia, tacitly says that God has not yet been faithful to His promises to Israel. Israel's promises would be ultimately fulfilled at the parousia, i.e. at the end of the seventy week countdown. That would occur when the New Covenant would be fully in place. Thus, to posit a futuristic element to the Supper as the great majority of evangelical churches do, tacitly denies the reality of the New Covenant as well. I am currently working on an article demonstrating that 1 Corinthians 11:26, often cited to prove that the church must take the Supper only until the parousia, does in fact contain a "temporary" element for the Supper, but also contains a permanent element. It is, lamentably, the permanent element—Christ taking the Supper "new," *fulfilled in his kingdom* that is being ignored.

79. See my *Feasting or Fasting* MP3 study. In this three part study, I show the relationship between the Messianic Banquet and the Lord's Supper. I show that the phrase "shew forth his death until he comes" is not a statement of the discontinuance of the Supper after the parousia, but spoke directly to the question of the early church's participation with Christ in the eschatological suffering, as his body. Luke 22 addresses the question of the continuance of the Supper and teaches that the Supper is taken today, in "newness," fulfillment and the kingdom. The three part MP3 study is available on my website: www.eschatololgy.org.

80. Jesus made it abundantly clear that the eschatological sufferings would be filled up in his generation, and vindication and judgment would occur in the judgment of the Old Covenant world of Judah (Matthew 23:29f; see also 1 Thessalonians 2:15f; Revelation 6:9f). See my discussion of "Paul: Last Days Martyr" in my *Who Is This Babylon* (234f) book.

81. Charles BoutFlower, *In And Around the Book of Daniel*, (Grand Rapids, Kregel, 1977)183.

82. It is significant that in several formal debates, I have asked my opponents to specifically identify the law that was "the strength of sin" in 1 Corinthians 15:54-56. Virtually everyone of my opponents has (correctly) identified that law as the Mosaic Law, without seeing the incredible dilemma for their futurist eschatology. Stated simply, here is the problem: The resurrection would occur when "the law" that was the strength of sin was removed (1 Corinthians 15:54f).
But, the law that was the strength of sin was the Mosaic Law. Therefore, the resurrection would be when the Mosaic Law was removed.
If the Mosaic Law was the Law that was the strength of sin, *and it patently was*, and if the resurrection was to be when the Law that was the strength of sin was removed, then if the resurrection has not occurred, *the Mosaic Law remains valid as the strength of sin*. Yet, no one today believes that the Mosaic Law remains as the strength of sin. The dilemma is acute, but all futurist views seem blind to the problem.

83. This is destructive to the millennial posit that insists that the Mosaic Law has been completely fulfilled and removed. Yet, they claim that the resurrection (when the Law that was the strength of sin would be removed) does not occur until the parousia of Christ, seven years after the end of the church age! If the Torah was the strength of sin, and we have shown that it is, then for the millennialists to posit the removal of the Law of Moses *during the sixty-nine week countdown*, and then place the resurrection at the end of the seventieth week is patently a false view.

84. It should be clear that one cannot get physical death and physical graves out of the context of Ezekiel 37. The "death" in view is alienation from God caused by violation of the covenant.

85. Interestingly, Wilken takes note that in Jewish thought, when they contemplated Ezekiel 37, "When the Scriptures speak about the 'resurrection of the body' (in Ezekiel) the Jews believe that there will be a 'restoration of Jewish polity.'" Robert Wilken, *The Land Called Holy*, (New Haven, Yale University Press, 1992)70.

86. N. T. Wright, *Paul*, Minneapolis, Fortress, 2005)54.

87. Bruce Longenecker, *The Triumph of Abraham's God*, (Edinburgh, T and T Clark, 1998)37.

88. The consummation of the New Creation would be at the revelation of the new Jerusalem from heaven, when the Old Jerusalem was cast out, with her children (Galatians 4:22f). Thus, the Old Covenant world that could never give life and righteousness, would give way to the new Jerusalem in which there is no sin (atonement is perfected!) and no death (Revelation 21). The object was not *physical death* but alienation from God, the kind of death that Paul said was experienced by himself and all those "under the Torah" (Romans 7:7f).

89. Johannes Munck, *Paul and the Salvation of Mankind,* (Richmond, John Knox, 1959)43.

90. See my article on 1 Corinthians 10:11 at http://www.eschatology.org/index.php?option=com_content&task=view&id=66&Itemid=61.
What Paul was saying was that the *goal* of all the previous ages had arrived! Now, as the proclaimer of the hope of Israel, for Paul to say that the goal of all previous ages had come, (in truth, of course, about to be consummated), could mean

nothing less than that *the end of the seventy weeks was right upon them!*

91. It *can* be proven that the *arrabon* was indeed the miraculous manifestation of the Spirit. See my *Into All the World, Then Comes the End*, for a discussion of the last days framework for the charismata. According to prophecy the miraculous gifts were to be poured out in Israel's last days, as a sign of the impending Day of the Lord to sweep away His enemies and glorify the Branch (Joel 2; Isaiah 28, Zechariah 13, etc). The book is available from my website, www.eschatololgy.org. I am also working on a larger MSS dedicated entirely to the issue of the charismata.

92. It is highly significant that in several formal debates, I have asked my opponents to specifically identify the law that was "the strength of sin" in 1 Corinthians 15:54-56. Virtually everyone of my opponents has (correctly) identified that law as the Mosaic Law, without seeing the incredible dilemma for their futurist eschatology. Stated simply, here is the problem: The resurrection would occur when "the law" that was the strength of sin was removed (1 Corinthians 15:54f).
But, the law that was the strength of sin was the Mosaic Law. Therefore, the resurrection would be when the Mosaic Law was removed.
If the Mosaic Law was the Law that was the strength of sin, *and it patently was*, and if the resurrection was to be when the Law that was the strength of sin was removed, then if the resurrection has not occurred, *the Mosaic Law remains valid as the strength of sin.* Yet, no one today believes that the Mosaic Law remains as the strength of sin. The dilemma is acute, but all futurist views seem blind to the problem.

93. It is interesting that scholars who see that Jesus anticipated the consummation of Israel's aeon do not see the connection with the end of the seventy weeks. Scot McKnight says, "Jesus prophesied of the destruction of Jerusalem as the climactic event in Israel's history that would end the privilege of Israel in God's plan. He also attached to this the final resolution of Israel through the images connected with remnant and redemption." (*Vision*, 138). While he makes these astute observations, his book does not even mention the prophecy of Daniel 9!

94. Tim LaHaye and Thomas Ice, *Charting The End Times,* (Eugene, Ore, Harvest House, 2001)26: "The prophets did not see the long church age separating the two comings." On page 48 they say, "The church was an unforeseen mystery in the Old Testament. The church began suddenly on Pentecost and will come to an abrupt end at the Rapture."

95. N. T. Wright, *Jesus and the Victory of God,* (Minneapolis, Fortress, 1996)577.

96. Let me be clear in what I am saying. I am not confining "the New Covenant of Christ" to the *revelation* of the New Covenant canon. While the revelation of the New Covenant word is integral to the thought, it is not the *totality*. It is the New Covenant *world*, the New Covenant *relationship* that was the determinative goal of Daniel 9.

97. The NT terminology of being "found" in Christ is thoroughly eschatological, and speaks normally of being found in Christ at the *parousia*. This means that Paul's desire to be found righteous was linked with the coming parousia and resurrection. In other words, Paul was still anticipating the world of righteousness, i.e. attaining to the resurrection of Christ, as future, although certainly *near*, to him.

98. The translation "eagerly await" is from the Greek word *apekdekomai*, a word of strong imminence. There is no doubt that Paul saw the fulfillment of his hope of righteousness as on the verge of fulfillment.

99. There is considerable debate as to the identity of the "Most Holy" to be anointed during the seventy weeks of Daniel 9:24. Many semi-preterists believe it is referent to the anointing of Christ at his baptism. (Mathison, *Hope*, 221) However, as Keil and Delitzsch note, the words used of this anointing are never used of persons, but of objects, and cultic objects of the temple at that. Keil and Delitzsch *Daniel,* (Grand Rapids, Eerdmans, 1975)349. Thus, while there is no doubt that Christ was "the anointed one," the idea seems to be that seventy weeks were determined to anoint the Most Holy of the New Temple. This conforms to the prediction of the destruction of the "city and sanctuary" of 9:26. At the end of the seventy weeks, Jehovah would remove the Old Most Holy, and anoint the New Temple of Messiah. The idea of the passing of the Old Temple, and the anticipation of the completion of the New Most Holy of Messiah permeates much of New Testament theology. I have a MSS prepared, *Leaving the Future Behind*, in which I examine the NT concept of the impending anointing of the New Temple at the coming of the Shechinah glory of Christ.

100. Keil and Delitzsch, vol. 9, (Grand Rapids, Eerdman's, *Daniel*,1975)343.

101. Although as we have seen, Gentry posits 2 Peter 3 as the end of human history and Revelation 21 as AD 70.

102. Philip Mauro, *The Seventy Weeks and the Great Tribulation,* (PA, Bible Truth Depot, I. C../ Herendeen, Swengel Union Co., 1944)50+.

103. Kenneth Gentry, *The Charismatic Gift of Prophecy,* (Memphis, Tn., Footstool Publications, 1989)54.

104. See my further development of this issue in my *Seal Up Vision And Prophecy*, (JaDon Management Inc, Ardmore, Ok. 2003) available from my website: www.eschatology.org.

105. See my formal written debate with Kurt Simmons for a full discussion of this. Kurt affirmed that the Atonement was finished at the cross. Scripture says the atonement would be consummated at Christ's parousia. If all goes well, that debate will be in book form in 2011.

106. In my public debate with Thomas Thrasher, March 13, 2004, I noted that there is no article in the Hebrew text. Incredibly, Thrasher claimed, contrary to all Hebrew scholars, that the article is present. He let the cat out of the bag however, when he admitted the article is "supplied." It showed Thrasher's desperation that he tried to cling to that argument although I demonstrated that even if the article were present, it means that Daniel's prediction i.e. *the* vision and *the* prophecy" *which is the prophecy of the resurrection*, would be fulfilled by the end of the seventy weeks.

107. Jerome's Commentary, *Daniel*, (Grand Rapids, Baker, 1958)108,

108. Gentry, Jordan, Mathison, DeMar and most semi-preterists agree that the "heaven and earth" of Old Covenant Israel passed away in the destruction of Jerusalem.

109. The Jerusalem temple was called "heaven and earth" by the Jews of Jesus' day. Josephus, Antiquities 3:6:4 and 3:7:7 says the Jews called the temple, with its Holy and Most Holy Place, "heaven and earth." Thus, as Jesus predicted the destruction of the temple, it was perfectly natural for him to say "heaven and earth will pass away" (Matthew 24:35). He was not speaking of the material cosmos. He was speaking of the Jewish "heaven and earth." See my *The Elements Shall Melt With Fervent Heat* book for a fuller discussion.

110. Contra the Theonomists, *the Old Law is not still binding, unless the sacrificial system is still binding.* The very passage that Theonomists appeal to for the continuing validity of the Law says not one jot or tittle would pass until it was all fulfilled. Yet, the Reconstructionists argue that the sacrificial laws have passed! Well, if *any* of the Law has passed, then heaven and earth have passed. More importantly, all of the Law has passed, resurrection has occurred and Theonomy has "passed" as well!

111. "The law" that was the strength of sin was none other than the Torah, the Mosaic Law, as we show elsewhere in this work. Thus, since resurrection would be when the Torah was removed, this means that the resurrection would be at the end of the Old Covenant age of Israel.

112. The inseparable connection between the seventy weeks, the mystery, Paul's ministry and the fulfillment of Revelation is a topic little explored in the literature. See my *Who Is This Babylon* for a solid examination of the significance of Paul's ministry and mission for understanding the Apocalypse.

113. Gentry, Jordan, Mathison, DeMar and most partial preterists agree that the "heaven and earth" of Old Covenant Israel passed away in the destruction of Jerusalem. However, interestingly enough, they hedge on the identity of the "heaven and earth" in Matthew 5:17-18.

114. See my book *The Elements Shall Melt With Fervent Heat*, for a full discussion of this important issue. I document from a wide array of sources that the Temple was indeed called "heaven and earth." The book is available from my website, www.eschatology.org.

115. If one says that "seal up vision and prophecy" was accomplished in AD 35, (as Gentry, Mathison, Bahnsen, et.al. do) then if "seal up vision and prophecy" is indeed referent to the entire prophetic corpus as the great majority of commentators agree, this means that all prophecy was fulfilled by AD 35. Patently, these commentators do not agree with this, so, in violation of the text of Daniel 9, they subtly *insert a definite article into the text* and say (e.g. Gentry) that Daniel 9 says, "seal up *the* vision and *the* prophecy."

116. Let me emphasize here what Daniel 9 does not say. It does not say, "Seventy weeks are determined to *determine* the fate of the city." Yet, this is precisely what it should have said if Gentry, DeMar and Noê are right. Notice that Daniel emphatically says the overwhelming flood of the final destruction would be what Daniel was predicting, I. e. *what Daniel was determining!* So, the destruction was determined in Daniel 9, and seventy weeks were determined to seal vision and prophecy through fulfillment.

117. While Hebrews 9 does not specifically mention the filling up of the measure of sin foretold by Daniel, as we have seen that process was on-going when Hebrews was written. It was being accomplished through the Jewish persecution of the church as recorded in Hebrews (10:32f). Furthermore, the vindication of the suffering saints is very much present and promised to come at the parousia (10:32-37). So, it can be effectively argued that Hebrews 9-10 contains every element of Daniel 9:24-27.

118. In two formal debates with amillennialist Thomas Thrasher, I affirmed that the resurrection belonged to Israel "after the flesh" (Romans 8-9). Thrasher mostly ignored the argument, hoping the audience would not notice his failure to deal with this most fundamental issue. Audio (of the first debate) and DVDs (second debate) of the two debates are available from me, $50.00 Postpaid. Send check of MO to Don K. Preston, 1405 4th Ave. N. W. #109, Ardmore, Ok. 73401. Likewise, in written debates with A. G. "Buster" Dobbs, editor of the Firm Foundation journal, and a formal written debate with Larry Bunch (amillennialist) both said that *their eschatological hopes are not based on the OT promises made to Israel. Dobbs went so far as to claim that the OT contains no prophecies of Christ's ultimate second coming*

and the resurrection of the dead! This kind of ignorance of the OT source of NT eschatology is appalling, but typical of many in the amillennial paradigm. The Dobbs-V-Preston exchange and Bunch-V-Preston debate are available for reading on my website: http://www.religiousdebates.com/

119. Boettner's eschatology is postmillennial, like Gentry, Mathison, et. al. However, his views concerning the Old Testament and the New are shared to a great extent by the amillennial world in which the current author was raised. I was once criticized, strongly, by an elder for even preaching from the Old Testament.

120. Lorraine Boettner, *Four Views of the Millennium*, (Downers Grove, InterVarsity, 1977)102

121. See Mark Nanos, *The Mystery of Romans*, (Minneapolis, Fortress, 1996). Nanos notes that Paul's message to Israel was one of *fulfillment*. Even his Gentile mission was in *fulfillment of God's promises to Israel*, not an indication of failure. While there are issues in Nanos we would reject, he nonetheless does a good job establishing this premise. The key thing to understand is that for Paul and the NT writers, *the Gentile mission was proof positive that God was faithful to Israel, and that Israel was being restored as promised.* Thus, the Gentile mission was not an unforeseen, interim measure that interrupted God's scheme with Israel. The Gentile mission is proof positive that Israel had been restored as actually foretold by the prophets. I am currently working on a MSS, entitled *The Restoration of the Land*, to show that the NT writers believed and taught in unequivocal terms, that all of God's promises to Israel were fulfilled in Christ and his spiritual body.

122. Romans 11:26f alludes to three OT prophecies, Jeremiah 31; Isaiah 27 and Isaiah 59. The common theme in the two Isaianic prophecies is that Israel would be saved through judgment. This is what Daniel foretold.

123. See my *We Shall Meet Him In The Air, The Wedding of the King of kings (*Ardmore, Ok. JaDon Management Inc. 2009)* for an extensive discussion. Available at www.bibleprophecy.com.

124. See my discussion of 2 Thessalonians 1 in my *Like Father Like Son, On Clouds of Glory*, and my smaller work, *In*

Flaming Fire. Paul quotes directly from Isaiah 2:10; 19-21 in his prediction of the Day of the Lord. Isaiah 2-4 is a prediction of the last days when Israel would be judged for her blood guilt (4:4; cf. Matthew 23) when her men would die by the edge of the sword (3:18-24). Jesus applied those identical verses from Isaiah to his judgment coming against Jerusalem. If Jesus applied Isaiah to Israel's judgment in AD 70, what right does anyone have to apply Paul's use of those verses to the end of church history?

125. It will not do to argue that there was "a resurrection, of sorts" for Israel in AD 70, but that event foreshadowed the "real" resurrection at the end of the Christian age. The Christian age has no end. Further, when the New Testament writers tell us that their hope of the resurrection was what was promised to Israel, and not a mere foreshadowing of something greater, we must take them at their word. There is no Biblical merit for saying that Israel was resurrected in some manner, in fulfillment of the Old Testament promises, but that there is to be another resurrection, the real one, in the future. Israel's hope was "the resurrection" not a shadow of a greater resurrection. Thus, if Israel's resurrection hope has been fulfilled. Biblical resurrection has been fulfilled.

126. See my discussion of Matthew 13 and Daniel 12 in my *Babylon* book

127. There is virtual unanimity among the scholars that the LXX Greek term "time of the end" from Daniel 12:4 is the source for the references to the time of the end in Matthew 13:39f and Matthew 24. Jesus and the disciples clearly had Daniel's prediction of the end in mind in their discussions of the end.

128. Since the writing of the first edition of this book, Gentry has changed his position on Daniel 12. He now says Daniel 12:2 was, after all, fulfilled in AD 70. See my *We Shall Meet Him In The Air, The Wedding of the King of kings*, for documentation of Gentry's dramatic change.

129. R. C. Sproul Sr., *Last Days According to Jesus,* (Grand Rapids, Baker, 1998)26

130. I am currently working on a MSS entitled, *All Israel Shall Be Saved*. Paul's great prophecy has been, and continues to be the source of a great deal of confusion. Yet, there are arrows within the text, emphatic indicators, that should point us to a proper understanding of what he had in mind, and it was not national restoration, not universal conflagration, but the completion of the covenant history of Israel through the salvation of the remnant, of all twelve tribes, in the body of Christ.

131. Mathison seeks to negate this argument by delineating between the remnant and "all Israel." He says that the remnant were the believing of Israel, while "Israel" was the then currently hardened Israel. While this is undeniably true, it overlooks the fact that even the remnant were unbelievers *until they turned to Christ in faith!* Thus, the salvation of "all Israel" most assuredly could have been the consummation of the salvation of the remnant by the process of "the rest of the remnant" turning to Christ in faith. Even Mathison does not posit the salvation of truly "all Israel." Why go outside of Paul's definition of those being saved and violate his temporal parameters to interpret Romans 11?

132. In April of 2002, Ed Stevens and I debated two amillennialists. I presented a major affirmative on Romans 11 and the resurrection. The material visibly stunned our opponents and they literally said not one word in response. That debate is available from my website: www.eschatology.org

133. How can God establish or even fulfill the promise of the New Covenant with "ethnic Israel" when no such entity exists today? All genealogical records verifying the identity of "ethnic Israel" perished in AD 70. Even Jewish authorities agree that there is no such thing as a "race" of Israel, descended from Abraham today. See my book *Israel, 1948: Countdown to No Where*, for a fuller discussion of this.

134. R. T. France, *Tyndale New Testament Commentaries, Matthew*, (Grand Rapids, Eerdmans, 1987)156.

135. W. D. Davies and Dale Allison, *International Critical Commentary, Matthew 8-18*, (London, T and T International, 2004)30

136. Donald Hagner, *Word Biblical Commentary, Matthew* (Vol. 33A), (Dallas, Word, 1993)205

137. Greg Bahnsen and Kenneth Gentry, *House Divided*, (Tyler, Institute For Christian Economics, 1989)165

138. Robert Van Kampen, *The Sign*, (Wheaton, CrossWay Books, 1992. Van Kampen is not strictly speaking a dispensationalist in the manner of Pentecost, Lindsay and others, but is a premillennialist nonetheless, and believes in the future restoration of Israel, not the future rejection.

139. Dwight Pentecost, *Things To Come*, (Grand Rapids, Zondervan, 1980)

140. John Walvoord, *Major Bible Prophecies*, (Grand Rapids, Zondervan, 1991)

141. Isaiah 2-4 also identifies the time and framework when Jehovah would remove the sin of Israel. We can only sketch it here briefly, but see my extended discussion in my *Who Is This Babylon*. Briefly, Isaiah 2-4 posits the time of the removal of Israel's sin as in the last days, (2:2-3) consummated by the Day of the Lord (2:19-21) which would be a time of great famine and warfare (3:1-3, 13-18). The "Branch of the Lord" would be revealed and glorified (4:1-2) and in that day the remnant would be delivered (4:3-4). Jehovah would remove the blood guilt from Jerusalem, by the spirit of fire and judgment (4:4) and establish His tabernacle of covering among the people.
Both Jesus and Paul quoted Isaiah's prophecy of the Day of the Lord when the bloodguilt of Israel would be judged, and Jesus emphatically posited fulfillment in his generation.

142. Interestingly, DeMar believes that Romans 11:26-27 was fulfilled in the salvation of the remnant prior to the destruction of Jerusalem in AD 70. He poses the question "Save them from what? Save them from the coming judgment upon Jerusalem that took place in AD 70." See his fuller comments at: http://www.americanvision.org/articlearchive/10-22-04.asp While DeMar's view relieves him of the dilemma of Gentry and Mathison, it also creates some serious problems. The salvation that Paul was anticipating in Romans 11, when God would remove the sin of Israel, is directly related to the time of the reception of the New Covenant as promised in the prophecy of Jeremiah 31, as cited by Paul. Also, it involved *the removal of sin*! Is the "simple" deliverance from physical death and destruction to be equated with the removal of the sin

of Israel, and the reception of the New Covenant? Romans 11 is patently soteriological, and cannot be limited to the mere deliverance from the Judean catastrophe.

143. To do this of course, the postmillennialists would be creating the exact same "gap" between the 69th and the 70th Week of Daniel 9 that they so decry in the millennial construct! If the putting away of sin of Daniel 9 and the putting away of sin in Romans 11 are the same, then patently, if the fulfillment of the 70th Week is still future, then the 70th Week was postponed just as the millennialists say! There is no justification for delineating between the putting away of sin in these two texts. Therefore, unless the postmillennialists are indeed willing now to join the millennialists in positing a gap between the 69th and the 70th Week, they must cede Romans 11 to the first century, AD 70 parousia of Christ, thus stripping their eschatology of one of their most fundamental arguments for futurism.

144. *The end of the millennium was near in the first century.* In my debate with Jim Jordan, October 2004, in Tampa, Florida, I gave a sampling of the evidence that can be produced in demonstration of this thesis. While all futurist eschatologies say that we are either now in the millennium, or that the millennium is yet future, the Bible shows, in no uncertain terms, that the millennium was in fact near its end in the first century, and ended in AD 70. Audio and video of the debate with Jordan are available at our website: www.eschatology.org.

145. Naturally, it is not just the postmillennial eschatology that is destroyed by the truth that the millennium ended in AD 70. If the millennium ended in AD 70, *all futurist eschatologies are falsified.* See my *Who Is This Babylon* for a full discussion and demonstration that the end of the millennium was near in the first century.

146. Space forbids development of the *Zion* motif, but consider this:
The Messianic Banquet, for those for whom death was destroyed, would be on "Zion."
But, the author of Hebrews affirmed, "You have come to Mt. Zion." (Hebrews 12:21)
Therefore, the time of the Messianic Banquet–and thus resurrection-- had arrived.

193

See my articles on Zion on my website: www.eschatology.org.

147. We will not take the time here to develop the fact that the Banquet was one of Jesus' favorite themes, except to note that he announced that the time for the banquet had come: "all things are ready, come to the feast!" That was, in the context and consideration of Isaiah, *an emphatic declaration that the time of the resurrection had arrived!*

148. Some make a great deal of the fact that in Isaiah 59 Jehovah would come "to Zion" whereas in Romans, He would come *"out* of Zion." Furthermore, in Isaiah 25 the Messianic Banquet would be "on this mount" i.e. in Zion. I am persuaded that we find in these respective passages the doctrine of the Two Jerusalems, or Two Zions. On the one hand, Jehovah would come *to* Zion, in judgment, but salvation would be *in* Zion, the Jerusalem that is above. It is from the heavenly Zion that he would come to the earthly Zion in judgment. One cannot make a hard fast decree on this, but it certainly has some degree of validity. See my discussion of the Two Jerusalems in my revised *Who Is This Babylon?*.

149. For an conservative defense of the Roman identification of the fourth kingdom, see John Evan's, *The Four Kingdoms of Daniel*, (Xulon Press, 2004). The book can be ordered from Evans. His email is jevans06@midsouth.rr.com.

150. As we have seen, Paul's statement in 1 Corinthians 10:11 actually says that the goal (*telos*) of all previous ages had arrived. This incredible statement denies the idea of a postponed kingdom, and falsifies the revived Roman empire theory.

151. Mark Hitchcock, in *End Times Controversy*, (145).

152. Of course, the millennialists do believe in the restoration of literal Babylon, and until the second gulf war, were seemingly convinced that the restoration of Babylon was fully underway. The carnage in Iraq has wreaked havoc with that view however, and that is why you hear nothing more about it at the present time.

153. Mark Hitchcock, *101 Answers to the Most Asked Questions About the End Times*, (Sisters, Ore, Multnommah Publishers, 2001)65.

154. The inherent contradictions of the millennialists are compounded by the fact that they insist that it is literal Babylon that will be restored. It is literal Israel that will be restored. Yet, it is not the literal nation of Put, or the Medes, or the Scythians, but rather, a modern nation bearing a totally different name! Well, if literal Babylon must be restored, then why must not literal Put or literal Persia, or literal Media, or literal Cush not be restored as well?

155. I am personally inclined to the view that "the people of the prince that is to come" is actually referent to the Jews themselves. Jesus blamed Israel herself for her impending destruction (Matthew 23:36f) and Josephus also blamed Judah for her own destruction. The grammar of the text in Daniel certainly allows, indeed points in that direction. This in no way mitigates the fact that the time period in view was the days of the Roman empire.

156. It is refreshing to see that more and more scholars are taking note of the Biblical emphasis on the vindication of the martyrs, and particularly how Jesus and even the OT prophets, posited that to occur in the AD 70 judgment of Jerusalem. See our quotes from Wright, McKnight, France, and other noted scholars to this effect.

157. Don K. Preston, *Like Father Like Son, On Clouds of Glory*, (JaDon Management Inc, Ardmore, Ok., 2006)174f.

158. It should be noted that for Israel to be given into the hand of the Gentiles meant that they were "swallowed up" by the Gentiles. See Hosea 8:8. In effect, this means that Israel, by sinning *like the Gentiles*, became like the Gentiles, and were consigned by Jehovah to be reckoned as them!

159. R. T. France, *Jesus and the Old Testament*, (Grand Rapids, Baker, 1971)146

160. Tim LaHaye, internet article. Link good as of 11-19-06: (http://www.timlahaye.com/about_ministry/pdf/lahaye.babylon.pdf) September, 2000,

161. See *Calvin's Commentaries*, Vol. XIII, (Grand Rapids, Baker, 2005).

162. Amillennialist Wayne Jackson argued that the little horn represents the Roman Catholic church, and that Daniel 7 is therefore a prophecy of the coming of the Lord at the end of time. See my refutation of this at www.eschatology.org/index.php?option=com_content&task=view&id=217&Itemid=61. Jackson's view supports a "gap theology," sets a date for the parousia, ignores and distorts history, and manipulates the text of Daniel 7.

163. It is almost unbelievable to read Kampen, (*Sign*, 200) deny any first century application of Matthew 21, and posit it in the future. This essentially denies that Israel was judged in AD 70 for killing the prophets or Jesus, in spite of Jesus' emphatic declaration to the contrary in Matthew 23.

164. David Daube, *The New Testament and Rabbinic Judaism*, (Peabody, Mass, Hendrickson)288

165. See for instance the written debate between dispensationalist Thomas Ice and postmillennialist Kenneth Gentry, cited herein. *The Great Tribulation Past of Future?* Gentry argues for a first century fulfillment of the Tribulation. The respected postmillennialist Boettner affirmed the first century fulfillment of the Tribulation. Likewise, amillennialists posit the Tribulation within the same context. See for instance William Kimball, *What the Bible Says About the Great Tribulation,* (Phillipsburg, N.J. Presbyterian and Reformed Publishing, 1983.

166. I am using the term "Jew" in its broadest possible meaning here. There is a distinction between Israel and the Jews, between Israel and Judah that needs to be honored. The Apocalypse is about the time when the scepter passed from Judah (Genesis 49:10) because the Lion of the tribe of Judah had come and was worthy to open the scroll (Revelation 5:5). Thus, Babylon, the seat of Judah's authority, the temple, was about to pass away and the *Lion* was about to rule in his kingdom.. We cannot develop this further here, but just wanted to take note of the generic use of the term Jew in our usage.

167. Moses Stuart, *A Commentary on the Apocalypse*, (Eugene, OR, Wipf and Stock, 2001)294

168. While it is difficult to tell for certain, this appears to be the position of Charles Hill in *When* (72). He cites the *Didache*, which, "anticipates the fulfillment of Matthew 24:30-31, a section of the prophecy which can easily be seen as speaking of the unmistakable last coming of the Son of Man."

If Hill applies Matthew 24:29-31 to a yet future parousia, then patently, he has to redefine *eutheos*, and ignore its consistent usage in scripture. Significantly, Hill's view directly contradicts that of Mathison, the editor of *When*. Mathison is certain that Matthew 24:29-31 refers to the AD 70 parousia of Christ (*Hope*, 114).

169. Many other OT passages contain the idea of last days tribulation, the suffering of the saints, and the judgment of Israel in vindication of the martyrs. Note Psalms 69:21-28 particularly, as well as Isaiah 26-27. Psalms 69, cited often in the N. T., contains a rich matrix of eschatological motifs, and virtually everyone of them is to be found in the Temple Discourse that led to the Olivet Discourse. This is no mere coincidence.

170. N. T. Wright, *Paul*, (Minneapolis, Fortress, 2005)141+

171. Frost's book can be ordered from me. Cost is $17.95 postpaid. Check or MO, to Don K. Preston,1405 4th Ave. N. W. #109, Ardmore, Ok. 73401. My work is on the website www.eschatology.org., or www.bibleprophecy.com.

Scripture Index

(Written and Compiled by Samuel G. Dawson)

Topic Index

(Written and Compiled by Samuel G. Dawson)